PETERSON'S

The Insider's Guide to
COLLEGE ADMISSIONS

Find out what you really need to know about getting into college

THOMAS C. HAYDEN, former Vice President, Admissions, Oberlin College and Director of College Counseling, Phillips Exeter Academy

PETERSON'S
Princeton, New Jersey

About Peterson's

Peterson's is the country's largest educational information/communications company, providing the academic, consumer, and professional communities with books, software, and online services in support of lifelong education access and career choice. Well-known references include Peterson's annual guides to private schools, summer programs, colleges and universities, graduate and professional programs, financial aid, international study, adult learning, and career guidance. Peterson's Web site at petersons.com is the only comprehensive—and most heavily traveled—education resource on the Internet. The site carries all of Peterson's fully searchable major databases and includes financial aid sources, test-prep help, job postings, direct inquiry and application features, and specially created Virtual Campuses for every accredited academic institution and summer program in the U.S. and Canada that offers in-depth narratives, announcements, and multimedia features.

Excerpts from "The Road Not Taken" from *The Poetry of Robert Frost* edited by Edward Connery Lathem, copyright 1916, © 1969 by Holt, Rinehart and Winston, copyright 1944 by Robert Frost, are reprinted by permission of Holt, Rinehart and Winston.

Material from *Behavioral Counseling: Cases and Techniques* edited by John D. Krumholtz and Carl E. Thoresen, copyright © 1969 by Holt, Rinehart and Winston, is reprinted by permission of Holt, Rinehart and Winston.

Visit Peterson's Education Center on the Internet (World Wide Web) at http://www.petersons.com

Copyright © 1999 by Peterson's

Previous editions © 1981, 1986, 1989, and 1995 as *Handbook for College Admissions*

All rights reserved. No part of this book may be reproduced, stored in a retrieval system, or transmitted, in any form or by any means—electronic, mechanical, photocopying, recording, or otherwise—without written permission from Peterson's.

Library of Congress Cataloging-in-Publication Data

Hayden, Thomas C.
    The insider's guide to college admissions : find out what you really need to know about getting into college / Thomas C. Hayden.
       p.   cm.
    Rev. ed. of: Peterson's handbook for college admissions. 4th ed. c1995.
    Includes index.
    ISBN 0-7689-0231-2
    1. Universities and colleges—United States—Admission. I. Hayden, Thomas C. Peterson's handbook for college admissions. II. Title. III. Title: College admissions.
LB2351.2.H38 1999
378.1'616'0973—dc21   99-29690
                                                                           CIP

Printed in Canada

10 9 8 7 6 5 4 3

BIOGRAPHY

A true college admissions insider, Thomas C. Hayden has more than 25 years of experience on both sides of the admissions process. In his sixteen years as Director of College Counseling at renowned Phillips Exeter Academy, Mr. Hayden counseled more than 5,000 elite secondary school students on how to win admission to the nation's top colleges. As Director of Admissions and later, Vice President for Admissions, Financial Aid and Research, at prestigious Oberlin College, he managed the admissions process from the other side of the table, deciding which of some 4,000 annual applicants would be admitted to the college. Mr. Hayden currently serves as Director of Communications for the Kiski School in historic Saltsburg, Pennsylvania, and still consults for colleges and schools on admissions matters, student recruitment and retention, institutional marketing, and other management operations.

dedication
To:
M. C. C. H.

CONTENTS

Introduction   ix

1 ■ Thinking About College   1
Assessing Yourself: Skills, Values, and Personality • The World of Work • The "Major" Question • The Other You: Extracurricular Life and Interests • Academic Assessment • Assessing the Family • Philosophical Considerations

2 ■ Choosing the Right College   19
Fundamental Factors to Consider • Software, Books, and Videos • Catalogs and Viewbooks • Getting Answers • College Costs • School Size • Admissions Difficulty • The Strategy of Selective Applications • Early Decision • Early Action • Rolling Admissions • Telling a School They Are Your First Choice • Be Wary of the Shotgun Approach • What Is a Quality Education?

3 ■ Visiting a College   43
The Virtual Tour • The Actual Visit: A Case Study • Guidelines for Your Interview • Tips for Being a Good Interviewee • Martha Prentice's Interview • How Interviews Really Work

4 ■ Talking, Testing, Planning   69
The Freshman Year—Talking and Awareness • The Sophomore Year • The Junior Year—Setting Strategy • The Senior Year—Active Engagement • Tests, Tests, Tests • Improving Your Scores on Your Own • Registration for SAT and ACT • Dealing with Test Anxiety • The Real Thing: Tips for Taking the Tests • Interpreting Your Scores

5 ■ The Application Makes All the Difference   99

How the Competitive Process Works • Developing an Edge • Electronic Applications • Answering Application Questions • Extracurricular Activities • Essays: How to Answer Those Perennial Questions • A List of Common Mistakes • Final Parts of the Application • Keeping Track

6 ■ Constructing a Powerful Candidacy   135

The Strategic Paragraph • Your High School Record • The Strong Transcript • The Weak Transcript • Academic Preparation • Course Content • Marketing Your Extracurricular Activities • Special Talents and Abilities: How Much to Say and Do • Help From Your Counselor • Your School Recommendation • Enlisting Help from Teachers • Enlisting Help From Coaches and Special Instructors • Lobbying for Admission • You Are the Concertmaster

7 ■ Financing Your College Education   161

Planning Ahead for College Costs • Saving Money While at College • Some Encouraging Signs • The Financial Aid System • Terms and Their Abbreviations • Loan Programs • Aid Application Forms • Evaluating Your Financial Aid Award • Questions Frequently Asked • A Word on Loans • Ways to Reduce College Expenses • For More Information

8 ■ For Parents Only—The Myths and the Magic of the College Search   195

How to Think for Yourself and Your Child about College • The Liberal Arts • Thinking Beneath the Surface • Some Practical Steps to Help Your Child • The Application • The Guidance Counselor • Independent Counselors • When to Intercede • Helping Out While Letting Go

9 ■ How Colleges Make Decisions   219

A Short History Lesson • The Selection System • Navigation Pointers

10 ■ Acceptance, Rejection, or Wait List: What to Do Now — 235

Acceptance • Which College to Choose • Revisiting the Original Selection Criteria • If You Are Put on a Waiting List • No Acceptances? • Applying to a New College • Reapplying to a College • Taking a Year Off

11 ■ Making the Most of the Freshman Year — 259

Charting the Academic Path • Drawing Up a Plan of Study • What Courses Should I Choose? • Where Will I Live and with Whom? • Deans, Counselors, and Resident Advisers • The Transition to College Life • Maintain Ties with Your Family • Dealing with Differences • Grade Frenzy • Parting Thought: Use Your Freedom Wisely

Index — 287

INTRODUCTION

This is a guidebook for high school students and their families, written from the perspective of a college guidance counselor, college admissions and financial aid dean, and parent. It is designed to help students and families plan the "college" journey: selecting a suitable list of schools, gaining admission to many of them, and being able to pay for, enroll in, and adjust successfully to one of them.

This book cannot guarantee to a family or student admission to a particular school, but it can and does pose the significant questions that parents and children ought to be asking themselves and college admissions officers as they go through the complex college search process. The book also provides a range of practical advice about "presenting" yourself to colleges, where to find needed information—from individuals and on the Internet—and what strategies can be employed to make the most of your talents and accomplishments. This book comes from three decades of observing and operating within the college admissions system, and its purpose is to make that "system" work for you.

Like all complex systems, the college admissions process is shrouded in myths, and the most prominent of these need to be exploded so that we can have a clear field of vision.

Myth #1: Selectivity Equals Quality. Not true. The difficulty of gaining admission to a school does not determine its quality or prestige. Difficult schools can be expensive, impersonal, far away, and self-centered, and they can have a number of other negative attributes that do not make them a good fit for you. The real challenge students and families face is finding a school where the student's talents will be appreciated, stretched, and formed into the person they want to become.

Myth #2: Prestige and Name Make the School. Another false belief. In recent years the rating game and the successful efforts of many colleges and universities to market themselves to the public have enabled some schools to rise to an undeserved level of prominence. Touting their high volume of applications or the football games won or the one or two graduates who have distinguished themselves, some schools have built up a national image that obscures the reality of the educational experience of their undergraduates.

Myth #3: College Is Karma. Many families and students become ensnared in the belief that college is the be all and end all of their lives and that they must gain admission to a particular school, otherwise their pride will be irrevocably damaged and their future shattered. This myth often grows from believing that a particular school will deliver the particular result that a family wants: social acceptance, graduate school admission, or a successful business career. The roots of such beliefs are often complex and inevitably bring hard feelings when the student is not admitted. The fact is that education at a particular school cannot ordain the future. A college education should open up possibilities for the future, not set them.

Myth #4: The Best Kids Get into the Best Schools. This myth is particularly pernicious. It suggests that somehow the purpose of the college selection process is to separate the weak from the strong, the best from the not as good. This is not the case. Colleges are trying to find the right match of students to their institution; they are trying to 'build a class,' to use a phrase from the trade. They are seeking all kinds of diversity of talent, interest, and personality in admitting students, so that their institutions can take full advantage of diverse students educating one another as well as being educated by the faculty.

Moreover, admissions officers are really not admitting people; they are admitting applications. They are reading folders, looking at SAT scores and grades and recommendations; they are trying to make an educated guess as to the kind of person you are. So, if you happen to be rejected, remember it was your "application" that was rejected, not "you."

Myth #5. The Higher the Price, The Better the School. The price of a college or university education is a most misleading factor. Families should focus on actual cost, not sticker price. They need to consider affordability and how financial aid can often reduce a high tuition price to an acceptable cost for attending the school. Furthermore, all students and families need to understand that all schools, public and private, are highly subsidized. Public institutions are subsidized by the taxpayers, and private schools often have large endowments that enable them to charge less than what their education actually costs.

If you find yourself succumbing to any of these myths, you will pay the costs of cynicism and sometimes frivolous or even devious behavior that they engender. This book was written in reaction to these five myths. It tries

INTRODUCTION

to illuminate the rational, orderly, and educational route toward college that has worked so well for so many for so long.

* * *

This book now enters its fifth edition as a guide to the intricacies of the college search and application process, but it is more than a guide. It is designed to help students assess themselves and find a new appreciation for their talents and for their potential as they try to figure out the college selection process. It is designed also to enhance their growth as independent individuals and give them a glimpse of the dynamic role they can play in our global society once their college education is complete.

For parents, the book suggests new ways for them to transmit their wisdom and values to their teenagers. It shows them how they can assist and support their children—without being intrusive—and then move on to their new roles as parents of young adults. It advises parents on sharing their expertise, their time, and their resources, while nurturing the emerging maturity and independence of their children.

For students *and* parents, this book will show that the process of applying to college affords a very practical form of education for every individual. Listening to one another, students to parents and parents to students and both to guidance counselors and admissions officers, reading closely what is said and unsaid in viewbooks, applications, brochures, and on the Web sites, and trusting one's instincts and judgment—all will bring students and their families to a higher level of understanding and mutual respect. Still, students and families have to allow this process of insight and trust to grow. They have to trust themselves, and then each other, and then the system this book describes.

As rational as we try to make the process, there is always room for creativity, calculated risk, and even humor. Part of your education and newfound confidence will come from dealing adroitly with the unexpected—the flat tire on the way to the interview, a new way to finance college costs, or the unexpected interview question. Be assured that there will be some surprises on the road to the college of your choice and some fun, too.

Make the most of them.

The advice in this book comes from the perspective of a teacher who was called upon to learn about the college admissions process with a particularly interesting group of students, parents, and college admissions officers. That learning experience went on for twenty years. The students—and their parents—were highly motivated and bright and came from around the country and abroad. The college admissions officers represented about one hundred of America's best-known colleges and universities. Observing the decision-making patterns of these colleges, visiting their campuses, and studying their evaluation processes have enhanced my experience.

The advice in this book is also enriched by nearly a decade as a college admissions dean and vice president for admissions and financial aid and the institutional perspective that the colleges bring to the student recruitment marketplace. The insider's knowledge of how applicants are evaluated, how financial aid is apportioned, and how statistics are used to enhance institutional reputation is a part of this experience.

In addition, this book draws on the candid and informative conversations I have had with countless college admissions deans, high school counselors, and the new purveyors of financial and electronic services to college-bound students and families. I have tried to distill these three streams of experience into a coherent and readable format that takes the candidate's side and attempts to help him or her navigate the complex shoals that lie between the junior year and admission to the college that will develop his or her potential to the fullest. This approach entails a few assumptions about the reader that are typically American: an interest in acquiring knowledge as a means to personal fulfillment, the reliance on hard work, and a commitment to using education to serve society as well as oneself.

In writing this book, I have sought to be fair to the institutions mentioned and to my readers. For any errors or misinterpretations that mortals make, I am responsible. I hope they are few. I hope that readers will find in this book a store of useful advice and that in the course of following it, they will realize during their college years and beyond, the best that is within them.

Thomas C. Hayden
Pittsburgh, Pennsylvania

ONE

Thinking About College

Inscribed above the entrance to the ancient temple at Delphi are two words: "Know Thyself."

This motto is classic, and its meaning today is just as valid as it was for the ancient Delphinians and the countless pilgrims who came to the temple where priests would prophesy the future. There was only one problem. The pilgrims were often confused by the prophecies of the priests, because they did not know themselves and know how to apply the knowledge the priests imparted.

So much for history. The motto "Know Thyself" applies powerfully to the college admissions process because the key to that process is making a *match* between yourself and your college. The *match* involves a voyage of self-analysis in which you discover yourself in all your various forms: as a person; as a student; as an athlete, musician, or techie; as a member of a team, club, or community; and as a member of your family.

All too often students become so fixated on gaining entrance to a particular school or focusing on one aspect of the admissions process, such as test preparation, that they miss the vital importance of knowing themselves. To begin this process of knowing oneself or self-assessment, try keeping a diary, beginning in your junior year. You don't have to confide your deepest thoughts in the diary; merely keeping track of what you do with your time and your reactions to national and local events will suffice. The diary exercise will help you see yourself in motion; it will help you identify valuable learning experiences that you have, whether in the classroom or quite by accident; and it will help you begin to think about your goals and routes toward them. A little spiral notebook, something inconspicuous and handy, will serve very well as a diary so you can write down an impression or an event and then stow it away in your backpack or under the front seat of the car.

THE INSIDER'S GUIDE TO COLLEGE ADMISSIONS

There are also formal ways in which you can begin to know yourself. They are called self-assessment tests. Ask your guidance counselor if one of the following personal inventory tests is available in your high school: Myers-Briggs, California Psychological Inventory, or the Minnesota Multiphasic Personality Inventory. Some self-assessment tests will soon become available on the Internet, but there will be fees involved.

ASSESSING YOURSELF: SKILLS, VALUES, AND PERSONALITY

Using your diary, make a list of your major activities in the past week, and beside each one indicate the skill it involved. Be sure to include skills that involve relationships with other people—managing them, negotiating with them, or caring for them. Don't neglect the simple things you do because they may not be so simple to someone else. When you are done with your list, draw a line and list other skills you possess from your summer camp or work experience. Then draw another line and develop a list of skills that you would like to acquire during your college years.

Activities	Skills
■ *This Week*	
Chemistry lab	Observation, titration, distillation, understanding molecular structure, and writing a report
Took out trash	No skill involved
Spanish homework	Memorization, writing and speaking another language
Ballet practice	Physical coordination, balance, and motion and integration of my movements with others
Web site maintenance	Set up and maintain own Web site and manage mother's catering orders on her site

Activities	Skills
■ **Last Summer**	
Camped in Maine woods	Reading maps, building fires, cooking simple meals, how to pack and walk with heavy load, observation of plants and animals; persuading my parents to let me go on my own
Set up mother's Web site	Installed modem and new memory board in computer, designed site and order fulfillment process for her business
Learned to sail	Elementary navigation, physics of wind and water, sharpened observation of weather changes and water patterns
■ **The Future—College Years**	
Work on team project	Produce plan to improve poor neighborhood, with other students with different skills than mine
Run a marathon	Physical conditioning, understanding role of diet and exercise, understanding the physics of running, setting up a training plan
Produce a multimedia paper	As a history major I would enjoy learning how to use a digital camera to produce slides and pictures for a paper on urban renewal and to blend my text with voice and music to produce a multimedia product
Study abroad	Perfect my language skills—writing, speaking, and understanding; understand the history, politics, and culture of a Spanish-speaking country

After the skills section of your self-assessment, consider next your own values. You may not be aware of how strongly you believe in some of your values and how uncertain you are of others. To clarify this crucial area of knowing yourself, conduct what psychologists call a values auction. Write down the following values and add any others that occur to you. Feel free to edit these to suit your culture and outlook.

Health	Religion, Faith	Security
Family	Power	Marriage
Justice	Personal Recognition	Honesty
Love	Independence	Friendship
Emotional Stability	Attractive Appearance	Knowledge, Wisdom
Pleasure	Charity	Achievement

Now assume you have a budget of $1,000 to spend on "purchasing" some or all of the values you have listed. Carry out the "spending" exercise by putting a price on your various values. Then look at yourself. Which values were the most important to you, and which were less so? Which ones did you omit and why? Rank your values in a new list, according to their "price." Keep that list in mind as you read about various colleges, encounter their graduates and students, and talk to their admissions and financial aid officers. In the end, make sure that your personal values align with those of the institution you decide to attend.

Another slant on the importance of your values to your college education is revealed in another fantasizing exercise—your obituary! What would you want to be written about you at life's end? Your achievements? What weaknesses would you like concealed? Jot these thoughts down in your diary, and as you do, think about the type of college that would best help you meet your career and life objectives and in the process help you to refine and act on the values you care about.

Personality forms the third piece of the assessment exercise. What type of person are you? What kind of working and learning environment suits you best, intellectually and socially? You need to understand this part of yourself so that you can match yourself with the "right" college.

Richard N. Bolles wrote a clever and helpful book called *What Color is Your Parachute?* His models for individual and group behavior ask us to imagine a party at which people with the same or similar interests have gathered. They have divided themselves into six groups in different areas of the room. As you stand at the door of the room, about to enter the party, Bolles offers you six choices of groups to join.

Group A: People with athletic or mechanical ability who prefer to work with objects, machines, tools, plants, or animals or who prefer to be outdoors

Group B: People who have clerical or quantitative ability who like to work with data and like to carry things out in detail or follow through on others' instructions

Group C: People who like to work with others, influencing, persuading, leading, or managing them as they seek organizational goals, particularly financial ones

Group D: People who like to work with others, to inform, enlighten, train, develop, or cure them, or who are skilled with words

Group E: People who have artistic, innovative, or intuitive abilities and like to work in unstructured situations using their imagination and creativity

Group F: People who like to observe, learn, investigate, analyze, evaluate, or solve problems

Make a note of the group you would most like to join. Then imagine that the group breaks up for some reason and its members go home. Which group would you join next? Which group would be your third choice? Having made these decisions and written them down, think about how your values relate to the group settings you have chosen. Next think about the skills you would be perfecting as a member of a chosen group. As you go through this process think about the degree of personal fulfillment your choices would bring, were this a real-life situation.

Now transform this into a real-life situation. Whom do you know and admire and how would they fit into the different groups you have chosen? Identify the projects from your skills assessment exercise that would be fun to revisit with one of these groups. Which projects fit which groups? How do you see your role in carrying out these projects? Now think about a possible career for yourself. How does your preference for a certain career relate to the groups you prefer to join? Remember, career goals may not just involve one group. In the field of medicine, people who like group D would obviously enjoy the role of a family doctor. However, those who like to function in a

Group A setting might be more suited to being a surgeon or radiologist. Students who like Group F clearly would find fulfillment as research doctors in a large university or pharmaceutical company.

THE WORLD OF WORK

The next task is to hook up your fantasy exercises with the reality of the world outside. This does not have to be an extensive exploration at this stage. The ideal first step would be to ask your guidance counselor to let you take the Jackson Interest Inventory Test or the Holland Self-Directed Search Test and then go over the results with you. The Armed Services Vocational Aptitude Battery (ASVAB) can also be taken through the Guidance Office. You can do this on line, too. At http://library.iacnet.com/lifecenter/ you will find a career-decision-making module that is very helpful. Note that there is a fee involved, unless you access the site from your local library.

Once you have two or three career goals that interest you, you can explore routes to reach these goals in the *Dictionary of Occupational Titles* or the *Occupational Outlook Handbook*. Help yourself to understand what is involved in meeting the requirements for a particular career and what the society's projected needs for workers are by exploring these two titles. Once you have a grasp of what skills, personality traits, and values a career involves, you should develop a set of questions that will help you focus on the reality of working in your chosen career(s). Plan to ask these questions of a person you identify who is working in a field in which you are interested. This person could be an uncle who is a businessman, your family doctor, or the computer programmer who lives next door. You might want to shadow someone for a day. This would involve following the person through the workday, and if possible asking him or her questions on the commute to and from the workplace. Whatever the location and circumstance, here are the questions you should seek answers to:

Working Conditions: What are the hours of work? Is the environment clean/dirty/dangerous/noisy/quiet/safe?
Duties: What are four typical duties you might be expected to carry out? (Would you like doing them?)
Education/Training: What special education and training and certification do you have to obtain in this particular career? To what extent did your education and your summer jobs and internships prepare you for your chosen field?

Benefits: What are the salary and benefits associated with your work, including travel? What about overall compensation, including retirement benefits, educational benefits for your children, health care, and opportunities for research or consulting?

Disadvantages: What do you dislike most about your work? Has your job challenged your value system in any way? Is there any advice you could give to a newcomer about avoiding the disadvantages of your position?

Personal Qualities: What are the most important personal qualities people should have to succeed in this line of work?

General: Do you have any particular advice for me if I become interested in entering this career—contacts I should make, experience I should seek? Can you advise me on how to think about the impact of mergers and downsizing in this field? What are the smart steps to take to ensure that I will always have a job?

In the best of all possible worlds your final step in exploring the world of work is actually doing a little of the work that interests you—finding a job in your career field or fields. If medicine is for you, volunteer in a hospital, clinic, or nursing home. If business beckons, get into the world of commerce, even if it means taking a job as a waitress or waiter, sales clerk, shipper, or factory worker. You will look back on these experiences some day as a hospital director or company manager. They will give you insight into your decisions and increase the chances you make the right ones.

THE "MAJOR" QUESTION

Ideally your college major will be determined by the intersection of your intellectual interest and your career aspirations. Sometimes, however, you have to do a little work to synchronize your intellectual curiosity with your career goals. To facilitate this process, you should plan to take a wide range of courses during your first two years of college and then try to focus in on a particular field of study. That field of study need not have a direct relationship to your career, either; it may be complementary. For instance, your uncle, a doctor, may encourage you to study psychology in college prior to going to medical school. His argument runs: "Psychology will enable you to deal with the enormous variety of people and anxieties you will encounter as a doctor." Likewise, a future pilot may want to develop an expertise in electronics before moving on to the special skills required to fly a Boeing 777. A budding journalist may be wise to continue with his love for mathematics as a college major because of the need for technological and scientific writers in the year 2010.

In choosing your college major, it is the relationship of major to career that counts. The less certain you are of your career goals, the more you should focus on choosing a major that will allow the flexibility to explore other areas of knowledge on the way to your ultimate career. While in high school, you can also take courses that may give you an indication of what a particular college major might involve. Talk to your guidance counselor about what choice of courses might be open to you.

Once you have selected a college major or two, consult the *Index to Majors,* published by the College Board, or the special section on majors in *Peterson's Guide to Four-Year Colleges.* Both of these volumes can be ordered on line at http://www.collegeboard.org and http://www.collegequest.com, respectively. They will identify the colleges that offer a particular major, and then you can develop a list of questions about studying a particular major at each college you select. Plan to ask these questions of college admissions officers or faculty members when you visit the college.

- What skills are needed to pursue this major successfully—linguistic, writing, technological? What high school courses will help me prepare myself? (This is a good question to ask if you interview as a junior, because you have time to change your course schedule.)
- What fields of work do students in this major enter?
- What are the combinations of majors and minors for students in this field? For instance, if I am a history major, will I be encouraged to take economics or political science or statistics?
- Are there any special programs within this major such as internships or travel and study that could help me perfect my skills and follow my interests?
- To what extent is graduate school necessary to acquire real competence in this major? What is the graduate school placement pattern for this major?
- What satisfactions and dissatisfactions might I expect as a student in this major at this college?
- What kinds of students and groups of students typically enter this major and do well in it? (Think back to the "party" and the kinds of groups you like to belong to.)

THINKING ABOUT COLLEGE

When you visit college admissions officers or talk to alumni or current students, make sure you ask these questions and record their answers. Also try to discover how closely your interests, personality, values, and aspirations coincide with those of the students who major in the fields you are exploring. If you detect dissonance or lack of agreement, then you should perhaps consider another school or another major. Remember, the learning environment is critical to your success. You need to find a good match of your interests, personality, and values with a particular major in an appropriate school.

Let's look at how George Matthews went about self-assessment and ultimate choice of a major. George is 17, has a keen interest in history, and wants to be a lawyer. He is a Group D person—likes to work with others to inform, enlighten, and cure them. Using the College Majors list in *Peterson's Guide to Four-Year Colleges,* George centers on Donaldson College. He is pleased to hear that 60 percent of the history department's graduates took the Law School Admission Test last spring and did well. He is equally impressed by several courses he found on the Donaldson history department Web site about the role of law in society. He makes a list of the skills he would need to be successful in history, and ultimately, law: strong writing ability, equally strong analytical ability, and a facility with organizing data and making hypotheses. He also knows that his note-taking skills are not that strong, and Donaldson's lecture format will require him to improve in this area.

George has already taken two history courses in high school and has developed a taste for political science. At Donaldson, he discovers he can easily minor in political science. He also notes that he could take an economics course and count it toward his history major. Furthermore, George learns from the history department Web site that the best teaching award at Donaldson has gone to a member of the history department for the past three years. He also notes that several professors require student teams to produce papers and reports. Since he is a Group D person, this resonates with George's desire to work with others.

Finally, George looks carefully at Donaldson's mission statement and motto. The latter says "docere principes et aliis servire"—to teach principles and service to others. This harmonizes with George's value auction in which he put honesty near the top of his list and charity toward others a little further down. He decides to apply to Donaldson College as a history major.

THE OTHER YOU: EXTRACURRICULAR LIFE AND INTERESTS

A similar thoughtful analysis of your extracurricular interests and skills makes up the next phase of your self-assessment. You need to understand what you want to learn and experience outside the classroom as well as inside the classroom. Refer back to your skills inventory on page 2, and make a list of the outside activities you want to continue in college as well as those you want to begin in college. Think about breaking out of the mold of your high school experience and doing some new things. Remember, you can assume a new identity in college. The football player who had to give up the trumpet in order to play tackle in high school might want to make sure that the colleges he chooses have music programs that welcome amateur musicians. The young woman who starred in the Debating Society in high school and wants to pursue a legal career might also want to join the Wilderness Club because she has never had much experience in that area.

You also may want to continue some of your extracurricular activities in college; in that case you need to apply a higher standard. Not only should the colleges you choose have the activity, but the activity should have the scope and depth to allow you to continue to improve your skills. If you are a champion track person, it is not enough to choose a school on the basis of its good history department and the "availability" of a track team. You will need to know if the track team will be sufficiently challenging for a person of your ability and accomplishment. When the time comes, you will want to prepare an athletic data sheet, talk to college coaches, and compare your times with those of the college's team. In the meantime, you might want to look on the colleges' Web sites and see what you can learn about the performance of sports teams, and for that matter, the other extracurricular activities you are interested in.

As you conduct this portion of your assessment, remember that there are many other experiences that you may have in college that cannot be predicted. The football player may not make the team and instead tries out for and makes the final cut in the band. He then becomes the liaison person between the band and the team and develops negotiating and interpersonal skills he never thought he would need. Another student might have a work-study job in the dining hall and progress through the ranks to become the student administrator of the dining hall system by the time she graduates. She then parlays this experience into a fast-track job in a hotel management company after graduation. The lesson: carry out your assessment, but leave yourself open for new possibilities, too.

ACADEMIC ASSESSMENT

By now you have assessed your personality, your career interests, your extracurricular interests, and your potential major. Next you need to engage in an academic self-analysis. Be honest with yourself and as you turn up areas of weakness, plan to concentrate on eliminating these weaknesses during your remaining time in high school. The following list of skills will be crucial to your success in college, and you may be well on the way to mastering them already.

Note-taking

Not only should you be able to take notes on a lecture, you should be able to capture the main ideas in a reading assignment: summarize the message, identify key terms and events, understand the author's point of view, and relate the message to the broad themes of the course.

Research and Writing Analytical Papers

This is the stuff and substance of higher education, and you need to get a running start in high school. Make sure you take a course that asks you to use primary sources (written and electronic), make note cards, develop a thesis, outline a written demonstration of that thesis, and do so in an articulate and even interesting way. Also make sure that you develop a clear understanding of plagiarism—using another's work as your own without telling the reader—while in high school. Colleges and universities today are experiencing difficulties with students who do not understand what plagiarism is.

Oral Skills

Although many college courses are taught in the large lecture format, most students look forward to special, small sections of classes for freshmen and seminars in their major.

A fundamental oral skill is the ability to speak clearly and simply: to state your main point, relate it to what has been said, define any special terms you are introducing, and then relate your argument to the main theme or point of the class. Using slang or frequent spacers like "you know" really detracts from your point.

Another critical oral skill is the ability to keep your mind focused on the main point of the question or the conversation and not be distracted. One role you can play in a conversation is that of the person who asks fellow students to define terms, or to restate the essence of their point after a long-winded response, or, in a nice way, to state the relevance of their point to the issue under discussion.

An ability to present ideas that may contradict, without alienating others, is a third vital oral skill to perfect in high school if possible. Reacting positively to what you agree with in the other person's statement is the first step; finding the language to rebut what you don't agree with is the second step. Some of the commentators on Public Broadcasting provide useful models of this skill.

Finally, the skill of synthesizing—bringing everyone's ideas together—and perhaps posing some new questions is a skill worth working on.

Not all of these techniques come easily. They will take time. Still it is important to master them and not undervalue the role of the spoken word in your educational growth. Whether in an all-night bull session or in an introductory course in economics with a Nobel laureate, your oral skills will help you clarify your own ideas, assimilate new ones, and present yourself to college interviewers, job recruiters, and your fellow workers in the global network later on.

Basic Writing Skills

While oral skills are necessary for the intake of knowledge, written skills are necessary for the expression of it. Good writing is the "coin of the realm" in high school, in college, and in life. Too few of today's high school students have mastered the ability to write with clarity, coherence, and style. High school curricula have shifted the emphasis away from writing courses, and large classes make it burdensome for teachers to ask for sufficient written work from their students. Television stresses the sound bite rather than the thoughtful written paragraph.

High school students should seek a conference with their English teacher as the first step to improving their writing skills. Ask your teacher to help you identify any weaknesses you may have and suggest ways to remedy them. Perhaps the teacher will mention something as simple as the proper syntax for who and whom or remind you not to split infinitives. Or the suggestions may involve more complicated tasks such as vocabulary building, making an outline of your thoughts, or studying the various ways of subordinating ideas in a sentence.

For an indication of your level of writing ability, look at a pamphlet called *Taking the SAT II Subject Tests* (published by the College Board and available in your guidance office). Under the section on the Writing Test, you will find sample essay questions from the exam. One recent version asks students to formulate a written response to the proposition: "People seldom stand up for what they truly believe in: instead they merely go along with the popular view." Write a short response to this statement without reading further. Then look at the examples of good to not-so-good responses. See where you fall. Ask your English teacher to look at your essay and analyze it in terms of the College Board norms.

Word Processing, Computer, and Internet Skills

If you have not had a keyboarding course and if you are not in the habit of producing your papers on a word processor, turn your attention to developing those skills right away. They will be crucial in college. Moreover, many colleges and universities will require that papers—and accompanying diagrams and spreadsheets—be submitted electronically. In college you will operate in a virtual environment. You will not even put your thoughts on paper. You will "write" them on a screen and then send them in the form of an electronic document, via the local area network, to your professor. He or she will evaluate your work, make comments (in bold face or italics) in your text, and then mail it back to you to read on your computer. You will keep it on disk and look at it again at exam time.

High school students should therefore make every effort to gain access to and proficiency in computer use while in school. In addition to the writing function, students should try to gain experience in using computers to analyze data. Potential history majors may want to complete a term paper analyzing the demography of their local community and suggest why people moved out of or into a particular area. Political scientists may want to anticipate college work by looking at voting and attitude patterns. Chemists may want to plot graphs on their computer instead of in the workbook. Spreadsheet proficiency will be useful to the student who plans to major in economics. Often most of these skills can be learned by a simple trial and error method and by asking friends, "How did you do it?"

Using the computer leads naturally to an understanding of the Internet and various search engines that can be used to access data. Students should explore the Internet whenever their assignments will allow them to do so. Gaining familiarity with the various databases that you may be returning to in college will give you an advantage. Some high school students will not

THE INSIDER'S GUIDE TO COLLEGE ADMISSIONS

have to be concerned about acquiring computer and Internet skills. Their high schools will have the equipment and the expertise to expose them to the computer and the Internet and to train them well. Other students may attend schools that have computer equipment but do not use it in an active way. In this instance, students should seek out teachers and librarians who know how to use the computer and try to learn as much as they can.

If high school students can learn to use the computer to accomplish word processing and to collect data, they will develop skills they will need in college, and they will be doing themselves a real service. If their parents can help by purchasing equipment for the home, all the better. The computer will define your college experience.

ASSESSING THE FAMILY

No self-evaluation, however honest and far-reaching, should ignore the importance of your family in shaping the college decision. Thinking about college involves thinking about your family: your parents' expectations—hopes and dreams—for you, the number of children in the family they will have to educate and what their respective needs are, and the family's financial situation. Students should plan for some long discussions with their parents and any others who may be involved in paying for their college education.

In these conversations, students often find that parents have very high expectations for them, or they wish their children to pursue a career that does not interest them, or they want their son or daughter to attend a particular college or university. Students invariably find out that parents want to know more about the details and the reality of gaining admission to some colleges today. Therefore, it is sometimes a useful first step for parents to schedule a meeting with the college guidance counselor and get a non-family perspective on you, your plans, and the possibility for you to achieve your goals.

On the other hand, some parents may not see the potential for their children's success. They may want to de-emphasize the college search process, saying any school will do, as long as it is inexpensive. In this instance, the guidance counselor can inform the parents of the importance of choosing the right college and perhaps even suggest that they should think about their child going to graduate school after college.

One topic that should be covered in the early conversation with your parents is the importance of a liberal arts education. Most professionals in law, business, and medicine agree that a four-year liberal arts education surrounding a solid preparation in a particular major is the best preparation for later specialization and indeed for the unexpected and complex challenges students will face in their professional careers.

Another topic needing frank discussion is the cost of college: who will pay, how loans will be financed, and how the price of a given school will affect the choice of that school. In discussing these and other topics that will surface as parents and students talk about college, both parties should take breaks to gather information, from books like this, from the Web, and from friends and guidance counselors, so that they can make reasonable and informed decisions.

Students can look forward to the outcome of a thorough college conversation with their parents, because once agreements are reached, parents invariably will delegate responsibility to the student to make the plans and move ahead. Most parents want to be informed, and they understand that the most supportive role they can play is a subordinate one.

PHILOSOPHICAL CONSIDERATIONS

At the end of the long assessment process, students should take a step back and consider the larger picture behind applying to a specific set of colleges. Some elements of that picture:

- College begins a lifelong process of learning and changing. It is not a finite four-year experience.
- College ideally is a total experience. What you are looking for in a college is not just a solid academic program in which to pursue your major, not only a winning track team or dynamic debating society in which you can star, or even a place where you will meet friends for a lifetime. You are looking for more than the sum of these parts. You want a place that will enhance your capacity to think and act independently, to appreciate the variety and complexity of the world around you, and that will affirm you as a person and enable you to make a contribution to that world.
- College is also the one period in a person's life that will be relatively free of responsibility. Away from home and family, able to set your own schedule of work and play, free to take a wide variety of courses, to engage in any number of social and extracurricular activities, and with luck, free from major financial worries, you will have an unlimited opportunity to construct and furnish an intellectual, spiritual, and social home of your own.

It is important therefore to choose your college or university well, to match your interests and your potential with a school that will enable you to make the most of what it and you have to offer.

At this point an advisory note: College is nothing like high school. You will be on your own, and you will need to have expectations for yourself and reaching your goals, because others may not. At college you will meet students who will be indifferent to the rules and to common sense. They may overindulge in drugs, or alcohol, or sex, and take liberties with academic honesty. Or they may focus so intently on preparing themselves for careers and compiling good grades for graduate school that they will give up the opportunity to share ideas and join in activities with other students. Whatever your particular experience, it will be beneficial to make some decisions about who you are and where you stand as part of your self-assessment. Doing so will enhance the success of your particular college experience.

In the end what really matters is that you know who you are and that you actively choose a college or university that is right for the person and student you are. As long as your decision is a deliberate one and takes into consideration your own skills, interests, and personality and is informed by a realistic self-assessment, then your choice of school will be the right one. Too often we look at only one side of Robert Frost's poem about the two roads that diverged in a yellow wood:

> *I shall be telling this with a sigh*
> *Somewhere ages and ages hence:*
> *Two roads diverged in a wood, and I—*
> *I took the one less traveled by,*
> *And that has made all the difference.*

We are inclined to read this poem as meaning that the less traveled path is the right path. In other words, it is better to be a poet than a banker. But Frost did not say exactly that, for earlier in the poem he wrote:

> *. . . both that morning equally lay*
> *In leaves no step has trodden black.*

Frost is emphasizing the need for free choice in our life's decision and that each choice should be individual and not driven by external forces. Like the poet you will come to many junctions and have to make choices. In each instance you will want to "know thyself"—to engage in self-evaluation, to assess the environment, and then commit to a course (road) of action.

As we peer into the new century, we can readily see that our society will require the maximum development of our human potential. Gaining a college education will be very important to you in practical terms of earning power and in humanitarian terms. A college education is an opportunity as well as a responsibility. The late Ernest Boyer, former head of the Carnegie Foundation for the Advancement of Teaching, explained the task well when he wrote:

> This nation and the world need well-informed, inquisitive, open-minded young people who are both productive and reflective, seeking answers to life's most important question. Above all we need educated men and women who not only pursue their own personal interests but are also prepared to fulfill their social and civic obligations. And it is during the undergraduate experience . . . . that these essential qualities of mind and character are refined. (*College: The Undergraduate Experience,* Ernest L. Boyer. New York: Harper and Row, 1987, p. 7.)

The decision to go to college, then, entails a special commitment to oneself as well as to the larger society. Like all real decisions it represents both a freedom and a responsibility.

TWO

Choosing the Right College

Choosing the right college for yourself involves using both sides of your brain, the rational left side and the instinctive right side, to arrive at a decision about which college or university best suits your needs.

Judith H. Harper, Associate Director of College Counseling, Phillips Exeter Academy

Selecting a college entails blending the factors you have developed through your self-evaluation with the criteria you will develop for your colleges. It combines a look inside yourself with a look beyond yourself. In the previous chapter, you had an opportunity to think about your skills, values, learning style, and goals. You may have already chosen a possible field of work and the college major that will best prepare you for it. Or you may be at the point where you want to explore a broad curriculum and discover what intrigues you. In either case, you need to seek the advice of three people.

People in the Field(s) You May Wish to Enter

Let us assume you want to enter the medical field either as a physician or a nurse. If your high school does not have a career day and you can't find out much about this area, sign up to volunteer in a hospital and see how you like the environment. If you do, ask one of the doctors or nurses if you can "shadow" him or her for a day. When the opportunity comes, make sure you discuss the advantages and disadvantages of their work with them. Ask their advice on the best course preparation for the field. Then get their opinions on the best schools and graduate schools. Keep notes.

Your Guidance Counselor

Guidance counselors know a lot. They can steer you to the various electronic and printed directories that describe the requirements for various career fields and help you develop a list of the academic prerequisites you will have to meet in college. Some of the directories you will look at will list the colleges and universities that provide the proper training for the field. You can then go to their Web sites and see what you think. You should also ask your guidance counselor what he or she thinks.

From this conversation you should emerge with a list of undergraduate colleges that will best help you to meet your career goals.

Trusted Friends

Your peers, your adult friends, and your parents can help you judge the fit between you and the schools that appear on this early list. Keep an open mind; listen to their opinions. Ask them to back up their views with facts and experience. Remember not to react too much. You will have plenty of time later to make your own judgments and choices of schools.

FUNDAMENTAL FACTORS TO CONSIDER

Keeping in mind the advice you have received, you will want to make a list of the factors that will guide your selection of schools. With each school, you will want to focus first on the academic program. This is your main criterion.

Does the school offer strong programs in your intended field of interest? Are there small classes in which you can receive individual attention? Are there internship programs that will allow you to gain practical experience? Are there international programs that you may wish to pursue to complement your classroom experience?

Next think about the particular region or location where you want to study—Pacific Northwest, Upper South, Midwest, or near home? Think about the size you want your college to be. Then turn to your extracurricular activities, the ones you want to pursue in college: sports, drama, music, or political action. If you want to join a nationally ranked debate team or soccer team, then be sure to make this fact a criterion. You should also make sure that the school has an interesting array of other activities because you will want to explore new things in college. If you have always wanted to sail, now is the time to write it down.

The matter of college cost and the kind of financial assistance you might receive from a school are concerns to many families (Chapter 7 discusses this in detail). Write down cost as a criterion.

Finally, you should consider the mission and culture of the colleges and universities to which you are going to apply. Make it a point to look up each college's mission and see how it resonates with your goals and values. When you visit a school and talk to others who know it, try to form a judgment on the culture and the environment of the institution. Make sure you like it before applying.

SOFTWARE, BOOKS, AND VIDEOS

Once you have established some basic criteria for your college search, you can turn to the vast mound of information that exists about them. In this process, move from the factual to the impressionistic. Take it as your prime responsibility to get the facts about a school first and then form your conclusions about it.

Software

In digging for data, you have your choice between the printed and the electronic tools. The best known electronic tool is Peterson's CollegeQuest®. This program, available at http://www.collegequest.com, will enable you to plug in your criteria for college size, location, major, cost, sports, and the like and come up with a list of schools. So will the College Board's College Explorer Plus, available at its Web site (http://www.collegeboard.org). Both of these programs have a financial aid/cost section that will enable you to determine the institution's tuition and fees and estimated annual expenses, as well as to ascertain what your Estimated Family Contribution would be.

These programs will probably be available in your college counseling office or in your local library. The guidance office may also have one of the CD-ROM college search programs, such as that put out by College View. These programs present formatted information and images of the colleges that subscribe to College View. For more information as to location and operation of this CD-ROM package, call 800-927-VIEW (toll-free).

Directories

The best known printed directory of the nation's colleges and universities is *Peterson's Guide to Four-Year Colleges*. The College Board's worthy competitor volume is called *The College Handbook*. College guidance offices and libraries have these volumes. Both contain in-depth objective descriptions of colleges and universities, including their entrance standards, majors, activities, costs, and percentage of students who receive financial aid.

College Videos

Once you have established a base of objective information about potential schools, you can move to the less objective media. Most colleges have an admissions video that is available on request. First look in your guidance office, and if the video you want is not there, call the particular school. Some colleges also have CD-ROMs that serve as their video. Again, your guidance office may have a collection of these.

Web Sites

You can get to many college Web sites today by linking through Peterson's or the College Board's sites. Otherwise, try the college's name or initials plus "edu" and see if you can find it. If this fails, call the college and ask for the Web address. In looking over Web sites, remember your criteria. Try not to be distracted. Remember, you want information. Most colleges will have their catalogs and sports teams on line, not to mention their admissions and financial aid offices. For access to extracurricular activities, try "students" or "student life" and roam about.

When your formal tour is complete, you can go back and browse in places that interest you. Student sites will say a lot about the culture and social environment of the school. Most colleges also have student bulletin boards to look at, and there is always the student newspaper to peruse.

Subjective Guides

You may also want to take a look at some of the subjective guides that attempt to evaluate schools and give an opinion of their supposed value, ultimately ending up with a ranking. Once very popular, some of the subjective guides have faded, due to the opportunity for a reader to examine a school "virtually" via the Internet. The *Princeton Review* (http://www.review.com) and *U.S. News & World Report* (http://www.usnews.com) guides are the best known.

CATALOGS AND VIEWBOOKS

Once you have narrowed your list of schools using the sources above, you will want to investigate your "finalist schools" further. Look first for their respective catalogs, either on line or in the school or public library. How well do they respond to the questions mentioned earlier? You may want to develop a spreadsheet for each college according to your criteria. Then write yes or no or a number when you find the answer.

Most colleges won't send you their catalogs. The postage to mail them is very high. They will send you their viewbooks, however, and some of these contain a lot of useful information. You will see the school's mission, pictures of the campus (all pretty), sometimes testimony from students and faculty members, and a brief statement on how many students receive financial assistance. Most viewbooks today will talk about outcomes—that is, what graduate schools students go to and what careers they enter.

Beginning with the catalog, look at the academic program in which you are interested.

- Are there a fairly large number of courses you could take in your academic area? You want to have choices, and you want to be able to specialize.
- Is there a program that enables you to combine majors if you want to? You want to have a preparation that is interesting to you and impressive to potential employers.
- What about internships and international programs? You want to have a chance to apply what you have learned before you start your job search in the junior year.

An answer to these questions for an art history major might go as follows: "Since I want to major in art history and go on to a career as a museum curator, I want a college and university program to involve me with nearby museums. I also want a study-abroad option for my junior year so that I can examine firsthand some of the collections and sites of the world's great art and architecture. I also want to study Italian and to visit Florence and Rome. Finally, because I will someday be managing a museum, I want a school where I can take courses in business management and maybe even do a dual major."

An engineering major would have similar questions. He knows that the rapid pace of engineering will make his undergraduate study outmoded in seven to ten years. He therefore seeks a school that will enable him to prepare for the management career he hopes will follow his engineering career. The young man searches for courses in economics, marketing, and organizational behavior in the catalogs he reads. He becomes interested in schools with 3-2 programs that enable engineers to combine liberal arts and engineering and obtain two degrees. He then checks those schools for internship programs and his favorite sport, golf. Gradually, his list comes into focus.

There is one other criterion that college applicants should apply to the schools they investigate, and this they can do when they have read the catalogs and viewbooks. The criterion is called *access*. Some questions to define and determine access are:

- How accessible will courses, programs, and faculty members be to me?
- What is the average class size and the teacher-student ratio (in general and in my chosen field)?
- Are there freshman seminars taught by leading senior faculty members?
- If I am a science major, how many labs are there for a given course? How many instructors, grad students, and/or professors teach those labs?
- Are professors available outside of class? Do they have required office hours?
- Are professors encouraged by the Dean to keep in touch with students by e-mail? Are they encouraged to meet with students informally in their homes and to mentor them?

GETTING ANSWERS

By reading catalogs, surfing through the Web sites, and examining various pieces of visual and printed information provided by colleges, you can develop some answers to these and other questions. Ultimately you will make a campus visit and see, hear, and listen for yourself. For now, keep in mind that college literature and admissions Web sites attempt to present the school in its most favorable light. You will need to repeat your questions, either face to face in an interview, or by e-mail to the admissions office or to a particular academic department or coach, or even in a letter. Some schools have set up links to alumni or present students to help you find out what you need to know.

As you drill deeper with your academic questions, you will want to know if the college or university grants Advanced Placement (AP) credit for AP courses in high school or for advanced courses you may have taken at a local college. If a college has a progressive policy for AP or college courses, you may be able to amass enough credits to graduate early and save a year's tuition. If this is your plan, you may also want to know if you can take courses at any of the university's graduate schools before graduating from the undergraduate college.

On the other hand, if you are not in a hurry and want to take as much as you can in the four years allotted to you, then look for the breadth of courses outside your major department. If you are impressed, then perhaps you will be able to double major. Talented athletes will have to look carefully at programs with rigid lab requirements and schedules, for they may interfere with team practices.

As you probe further for the depth and flexibility of a college's curriculum, ask the admissions office for a detailed description of the departments you are interested in. Most schools will have fact sheets or descriptive brochures that will describe course offerings and possible combinations of courses that will highlight subspecialties. Fact sheets also identify the special interests and accomplishments of the faculty members and often cite statistics about the placement of students in graduate school. Here is a list of questions for evaluating the vitality of an academic department:

Academic Program

- Do the course descriptions in the catalog sound exciting?
- Is there a commitment to teaching undergraduates? What is the number of professors compared to the number of students in the department? Are there seminars taught by major professors?
- Do the facilities seem adequate: laboratory stations, practice rooms, departmental libraries, computer access to faculty members and resources off campus? For science students, will you be able to use the sophisticated equipment in the laboratories, or is it reserved for graduate students?
- Is the teaching satisfactory or even better? This is a question you have to ask current students. For the moment, you might want to probe the college's Web site and see if there is a student guide to courses that will provide some answers. This publication is frequently photocopied and sold in the college's bookstore. Good student guides assess the difficulty of the course, access to the professors, reasonableness of the grading system, liveliness and content of the readings or assignments, and quality of the professor's teaching and that of the teaching assistants, if any.

Here is another route to the same end, evaluating a department:

- Pick a topic within your field of interest, such as cellular biology, and then ask a professor in the department of biology about the research opportunities for students with that interest.
- Look for publications by the professors in a given department in a national journal. In American history, scan several issues of the *American*

Historical Review or its index. You can also look on the Web site of the Library of Congress and look for the titles of publications by faculty members.
- Contact someone practicing in your career field of interest, and ask them what they know about a particular department. Sometimes your high school teachers will have knowledge about an academic department at a particular school. Certainly the personnel manager at a corporation that hires a number of its graduates would. If you know or can be connected to such a person, ask them what they think of the economics department at College X or University Y.

Academic Resources

Library

Viewbooks and catalogs describe the college and university facilities in rosy terms. As a student, you will want to know how accessible the library's collections are, what the facilities are for study in the library, and use of computers in the library. When you meet students, ask whether there is an adequate reserve collection. Are high-demand volumes available to students? You also should try to make a judgment about the adequacy of the library's collection. Budding political scientists will be interested in whether the *New York Times* is available on microfilm; Asian scholars will have the same question about the *Japan Times*. Musicians will want to see the listings of classical recordings on tape and CD.

The question of library hours is important. You will need to be assured that there is a quiet place for you to study for tests—perhaps open all night! Once you get a chance to see a school's library, you can form a conclusion about its adequacy by looking at the number of study spaces. The rule of thumb is that the capacity of the library should be 10 percent of the student body, otherwise it will be crowded and possibly unusable at exam time.

The larger the institution, the less important the library becomes as a study refuge. There are often department libraries, individual dormitory study spaces, and designated classrooms for quiet study.

Computers

All college students will be using the computer in one form or another, and you will want to determine the number and location of computers for student use. Most colleges have fiber-optic cable in every student room. Most have printing facilities in student dormitories as well as computers there for student use. Some colleges and universities will require students to buy or lease a computer and to submit work electronically. Students will need to know all this in advance of selecting a college. If their expectations for their technological education are high, they should be more than satisfied with the answers they receive.

Laboratories, Studios, and Equipment

If you are interested in science or the arts, you will want to study these resources carefully. If there are, for example, fifty stations in every introductory chemistry lab or fifty soundproof music practice rooms and more than 500 chemistry majors or 500 music majors, then crowding will be severe. Limited access to lab and studio space can take away from that vital time for experimentation and practice that is needed whether you are a planning to be a chemist or an oboist.

Special research equipment that would be appropriate for undergraduate learning is another area of inquiry. Is the new spectrometer in the viewbook actually used by undergraduates? How about that giant stress machine in the engineering building? Do undergraduates get to use it for special projects? Similarly, how about that beautiful Baroque organ from Vienna? Do talented undergraduate organists ever have a chance to play it?

Once you have completed your survey of a college's facilities, you should record your impressions in a notebook. Eventually you will want to refer to these notes as you compare schools with one another.

Extracurricular Activities

Let's be honest, the opportunity to pursue an extracurricular activity can be extremely important to a high school student for legitimate reasons. How many prominent politicians today have shone as track stars, cheerleaders, or champion debaters in college? They may have been good students too, but their activities were important to them. The questions you ask of the data, the literature, and finally the individuals who are connected with a particular school are similar to those we posed for academic programs and resources.

Interaction with Instructors

How much contact is there between individual students and the coach or the director? Can you get a sense of how much the institution (administration) is committed to the particular activity and sees it as educational in its way? What are the opportunities for a team member, orchestra member, or group member to be involved in competition with other schools or to perform before the public? Are there road trips, tournaments, or national competitions?

Facilities
Athletes will want to move beyond the athletic video and make sure there are good to excellent on-campus facilities for their sport. Divers will want to look at the special diving pool and on-deck diving tank. Would-be movie makers will want to explore the sound stage and recording studio and clarinetists, the size and rehearsal spaces for the orchestra. Is there sufficient turnover each year so there are spots for new players? Are there enough practice and ensemble rooms so you can keep up your high level of expertise? Potential actors and actresses will want to examine the main theater and see if there is a practice theater or an experimental theater.

Opportunities for Involvement
Like the exploration of the academic side of the house, students with a talent they want to develop will ask the questions above. If they want to explore other opportunities simultaneously, such as the history major who might want to try a foreign language, they need to look at the range of extracurricular opportunities offered. Then look for programs for beginners, be they athletes, musicians, or debaters. Do they exist? Is there a catch-all orchestra? Is there jayvee soccer? Are there informal cabaret theater or dormitory-centered theater productions in which all are welcome to perform? Be sure there are different levels of a given activity so that you can begin something new in college. That is what college is all about.

Campus Life
College is not all books and activities, either. College is friends, it is fun, and it is "down" time. Therefore you need to give serious thought to the social life of a school and the social climate that you'll find on campus.

The Student Body
What kinds of students attend the particular college or university? Where do they come from? What are their goals and attitudes toward themselves, others, and the institution itself? These questions have no easy answers, but they need to be asked. You may be living with these people for the next four years. It is crucial to discover whether or not you will be happy in their company.

In order to focus on your life as a student at College X, consider the following questions:

- Dormitories. What does the viewbook have to say about dormitories and the variety of the living arrangements, both coeducational and single sex? Is there enough room for everyone? Are there 3 and 4 to a room? Is there a tendency for students to move off campus for some reason—crowding, expense, or both? Is there a chance to change your roommate if you need to, or your housing assignment?
- What about the influence of fraternities and sororities? Are they encouraged or discouraged? What percentage of the students are members? If more than 50 percent, you can assume these groups are a major force in campus social life.
- Food. Does the college or university have a variety of meal plans, and can students experiment with cooperative dining and housing?

Sense of Community

Moving beyond living conditions, you should try to discern what the sense of community is on the campus. The key question is, how do students treat one another in classrooms, on the paths, in the dormitories, and at parties? Is there a tolerant atmosphere? Is there a respect for privacy? Is there an interest in diverse viewpoints? What is the level of honesty in regard to academic work and personal relationships insofar as you can tell? Is there any information about crime by students or abuse of university property? You might also want to inquire about student-faculty relationships outside the classroom. Are they cordial or not? Then there is the relationship between the student body and the neighboring community, town, or city.

The purpose of these questions is to arrive at a sense of the shared values of the community and to see if those values resonate with your own. You do not want to place yourself in a community that is entirely compatible with your views, otherwise you reduce your chances of learning from other people, but you do want to place yourself in a community where you will be treated fairly and your differences will be respected.

Social Life

The key question here is what do students at the college *do* in their free time, and will there be things for you to do? Start this inquiry by looking at a school calendar (available on the Web site) and noting the campuswide events—homecoming, spring carnival, and the like. Find out if most of the students participate in these events, and if not, why not. Ascertain what the role of athletics is on campus—whether it dominates or not. Are there other activities that dominate, such as political action groups? How do you react to those truths?

Develop some sense of the cultural life on campus. Is there a list of visiting lecturers, concerts, and plays? Are students involved in planning these affairs, or are they put on by faculty groups?

Photographs in the catalog and the viewbook will tell you something about the college's social life, but they can be misleading. Often viewbooks misrepresent the facts. An upstate New York school is famous for a viewbook with only two pictures of snow. Another urban school in a residential neighborhood is famous for its pictures of students sipping coffee in a coffeehouse that is actually 3 miles from campus. So it goes. As you glance at photos and read text, try to form a conclusion about the degree to which students are involved in the experiences depicted and in the events that occur. If you attended a particular college, would you be involved in decisions that shaped campus life? When you visit the schools you are most interested in, you will get a much better sense of campus life than any video or viewbook can present. (See Chapter 3 for further guidance.)

COLLEGE COSTS

When you and your family are calculating the cost of the schools on your list, you will need to calculate the total cost to the family, not just the costs given in the viewbook or on the Web site. There are often hidden costs, such as:

- Student activity fees
- Athletic facility fees that are sometimes separate
- Lab fees and music lesson fees
- Computer use fees or electronic network fees
- Deposits for room, lab, or other equipment use. Will these be credited to the student's account during the last semester?
- Parking fees
- Off-campus housing fees
- Fees for taking less than a full load of courses, for taking more than a particular number of courses, and for graduating early

Add these extra fees together, calculate the spending money needed, and then put in the formal charges for tuition, room, and board, and you will discover the actual cost of attendance at the college or university. In this connection, families should ask what the projected increases in tuition and fees are for the next three years. This will enable them to plan for future expenses.

Questions about Financial Aid

If a family is counting on receiving some financial assistance from a college or university, the following set of questions need to be asked. (For a more detailed description of the financial aid system and how many schools award aid, see Chapters 7 and 9.)

- What is the availability of need- and merit-based aid? Need-based aid means aid to meet the need a family demonstrates, according to the formula established by the College Scholarship Service, or CSS (described in Chapter 7). Merit aid is awarded according to a particular talent a student may have. Merit aid can go to students with no demonstrated need as well as to needy students.
- Does the college or university leverage its financial aid, i.e., give different aid packages to students with identical need because the college prefers one student over another?
- Hypothetical #1. Given a need of $10,000, according to CSS, how much would be loan, how much grant, and how much college work-study?
- Hypothetical #2. Assuming the student is awarded a package of $15,000 to meet need, would that package increase as tuition rises, and more important, would the mix of that package (of grant, loan, and work-study) change over the course of the next three years?
- What is the college's policy toward outside scholarships, i.e., scholarships the student wins from the local Lions Club or chapter of the League of Hispanic Youth? Does the college reduce its award when it learns of the student's good fortune, or can the student keep the award and apply it to other college expenses?
- If a family does not qualify for financial aid but needs to finance the cost of college with loans, ask for the literature describing loan programs. Most schools have many loan options to offer and payment plans as well. Also ask if there are merit awards for students beyond the freshman year.

SCHOOL SIZE

Just as you would want shoes to fit securely, so too you want to find a college that does. Size is a factor, but remember, size alone can be misleading. Here are four myths that mislead:

THE INSIDER'S GUIDE TO COLLEGE ADMISSIONS

Myth #1: Large schools are more diverse than smaller ones.
Not necessarily. Some large schools see their mission as serving a particular region or city, so they do not recruit widely, and many of their students come from a similar background. Other large schools are very diverse by design.

Myth #2: Small schools have an advantage when it comes to making friends and meeting people.
It all depends. Some large schools go to great lengths to break down the housing system into small units where students get to know each other very well. They also have an array of activities, and in any one of them students have the chance to form close relationships.

Myth #3: The smaller the school, the greater the access to professors.
You would think so. It is probably generally true, but large schools often have small honors classes and reward good teaching as well as research. Look to see if a university has an official hours policy for professors. Also look for joint student and faculty research.

Myth #4: The smaller the school the greater the access students have to classes and to extracurricular activities.
If you want to play football in the Big 10 and you were junior varsity in high school, then this statement is true. Remember though, that large schools generally have resources to run competitive intramural programs. They are apt to put a good deal of funding into extracurricular activities, such as music, journalism, and theater. They also have larger faculties, so if a course fills up, they can find a way to offer another section. Sometimes a smaller school cannot. Check out the extracurricular and academic facilities of both large and small schools before you decide to apply.

ADMISSIONS DIFFICULTY

The final criterion to consider is the difficulty of admission to the colleges and universities you have chosen. Fortunately there is a fund of admissions information in the directories previously mentioned. *Peterson's Guide to Four-Year Colleges* shows the reader what percentage of the applicants with particular SAT or ACT scores were admitted to the school. Whichever directory you choose, look for the words "of those admitted, 60 percent had an SAT verbal score above 560 . . ."

Another route to admissions information is the university or college Web site. Many will post the admissions profile of the last entering class: SAT scores, average GPA, and number of valedictorians or students in the top 10 percent of their class. For schools that do not publish such information, request it by phone or e-mail.

<u>Your guidance counselor will often have an idea of the entrance requirements of particular schools and may be able to predict your chances of admission based on a school's pattern of accepting certain students from your high school.</u> Your counselor may also know how your particular background or special talent may figure in the admissions equation at College X or University Y.

Beyond discovering statistics from your counselor, you might also ask how folders are read at a particular school (see Chapter 9), what role the interview plays, and what the acceptance rate and yield are at a particular school.

The difficulty factor for you is not just determined by the numbers: how closely your profile lines up with the admitted students at the school. You may have a numerical profile that is quite acceptable, but the more selective the school, the more the non-numerical factors play a role. Because selective colleges have so many applicants, their admissions staffs are looking for students with especially strong personal qualities, such as leadership in a particular area, community service, creativity in the arts, or a "great all-around kid." If you are applying to a selective school, the selection process is more complex than the numbers. You should follow the advice of your counselor and be realistic about your candidacy as well as vigorous in your promotion of it.

THE STRATEGY OF SELECTIVE APPLICATIONS

After following all of the advice in the first two chapters of this book and talking to your guidance counselor, your parents, your friends, and others who know your colleges and the admissions process, you come face to face with the task of actually selecting the schools to which you are going to apply. How do you do that? Which ones do you pick? How many do you pick? Before you make those decisions, consider the strategy of selective applications.

This strategy assumes: (1) you will want to reach high, and you will want to be protected from failure—not having good choices when the process is over; (2) there is only so much time you can allot to this process and money you can spend on it—how many trips can you make, guidebooks can you buy, tests can you take, and applications can you fill out? (3) the senior year of high school is a formative and exciting time and it should not be totally distorted by the college application process; (4) if you do your research on the schools you choose and your parents are involved and understand your choices, you will end up with choices of schools to attend—-and ultimately enroll in the "right" college or university for you.

Here is how the strategy works. You apply to a range of colleges, from difficult to safe. You pick two schools in the difficult category, two in the intermediate category, and two in the safe category. You make sure to pick schools where you can afford to attend, based on your assessment of their financial aid policies. You make an assessment of difficulty based on a realistic appraisal of your credentials, GPA, SAT scores, extracurricular contributions, recommendations, the quality of your application, and your capacity to pay either the full price or the difference between your probable financial aid award and the cost of attendance. In choosing your list of schools—two difficult, two intermediate, and two safe—you expect that you will be admitted to at least three of your choices, and perhaps more. You strive for a 50 percent acceptance rate. If you are admitted to three schools, you will have a choice, which is the object of the exercise.

In establishing your order of preference for your college applications, you are really playing a game of diplomacy. The diplomat going to the conference table makes a list stating what his government wants to gain from the negotiations. Then he makes three or four more lists stating what his government would accept if the primary demands are not met. This is called strategic planning. It combines boldness with realism, and it focuses on coming away from the table with a solution that your government (you) can accept.

In order to engage in this exercise, it will be helpful to develop some kind of rating system for each of the colleges or universities you select. Number 1 will designate the most difficult schools and number 6 the easiest. To set these numbers, create an admissions profile for yourself that you will compare with the admissions profile of the college or university.

First, write down your admissions profile. Now write the colleges that you are interested in down the left-hand margin of a piece of paper, arranging them in descending order of difficulty of admission. Put your

CHOOSING THE RIGHT COLLEGE

Your Admissions Profile

Academic: SAT I Reasoning Test: verbal 640, math 590; SAT II Subject Tests: Writing 620, Math II 700, American History 640; grades in high school: B average (3.6), top 15 percent of the class in a competitive suburban high school. National Merit Semifinalist, National Honor Society. Want to major in history in college and become a lawyer.

Extracurricular: Goalie for boys' varsity soccer team, Life Scout, camp counselor for three summers, construction worker for one summer, play the trumpet well in school band, and won a regional talent show last year. Do some acting and like it, want to continue in college. Also write music and drama reviews for the school's newspaper.

Personal: Liked and admired by friends, enjoy being with people and managing them; also value family, personal integrity, honesty, hard work (according to the values clarification exercise in Chapter 1). While not always a leader, I am conscientious and well organized in everything I do. People turn to me for advice and ask me to take charge.

profile criteria across the top of the page as in the sample chart below: Academic Program, Location, Size, Extracurricular Activities, Cost, Level of Difficulty, and Total. In the first column rate the quality of the academic program of each college on a scale from 1 to 5, with 1 being the strongest and 5 the weakest. Do the same for the attractiveness of the location and the size of the school. If a school is attractive in all respects except that its size is too large for you, then it must receive a size rating of 4 or 5.

School	Academic Program	Location	Size	Extracurricular Activities	Cost	Level of Difficulty	Total
Hanover	1	2	3	2	4	1	13
Gold Coast	2	1	4	2	5	1	15
Central U.	1	1	2	1	3	2	10
Sunbelt U.	3	2	4	4	2	2	17
Midwestern U.	2	2	2	3	3	3	15
Gateway	2	4	1	2	3	4	16
Atheneum	2	3	1	3	3	4	16
State U.	2	4	4	3	1	5	19
Small College	3	5	4	2	2	5	21

Shrinking the List to Six

You are now ready to make distinctions among the colleges and universities on your list. Already you know that Hanover is going to be your toughest school to get into. Last year, the students who were accepted from your high school had SAT scores in the high 600s and were in the top 10 percent of their class, except for the varsity basketball center they took—from the waiting list. Even so, you may be able to impress Hanover with your talent as a musician and with your strong record in the school's toughest courses. You are also widely involved in school life, not just as a soccer player but also as an actor and as a writer for the newspaper.

Now, Gold Coast is expensive and its curriculum is not quite as versatile as Hanover's, but it is right on the Pacific Ocean, and you loved it when you visited there. You decide to apply there as your second "difficult" school.

From the schools you have ranked at the second degree of difficulty, you choose Central University. It has a total score of 10 whereas Sunbelt, the other school in this category, has a high score of 17. Central has the lowest score overall, but it is not your first choice. It should be first according to the rating system, but you have dreamed of attending Hanover since you were little. So Hanover will remain your number one choice! But rating systems can still help. Let's continue.

If you don't make it into Hanover, and the chances are pretty good that you won't, the rating system tells you that Central University is just as good as Hanover except for that intangible emotional factor. In addition, your high school has a particularly good relationship with Central, since alumni from your school have done well there. There is no doubt that Central should be your second choice. Its curriculum allows you to construct an area studies major, which is what you want to do; if you pursue international law, you would be able to focus on one particular area of the world, such as Latin America or Asia.

Initially you liked Sunbelt University, even though it is somewhat small and does not have any special programs for history majors. Although it is easier to get into than Hanover, your enthusiasm for Sunbelt pales now in the light of the ratings you have given Central. You have also learned that Sunbelt's admissions standards are rising due to an intensive marketing campaign that resulted in an increase of 15 percent in the applications for this year. So Sunbelt should be scratched as the number two choice.

Midwestern's case speaks for itself. Although not in the best location, it is an ideal size—around 4,000 students—and its history department is superb, surely better than Sunbelt's. Furthermore, your scores, grades, and the other elements of your profile definitely put you in the group that Midwestern will accept. Your counselor says, "If you keep up your good work, you ought to make it." So you decide to apply.

Although Athenuem has as many points as Gateway, your father graduated from Gateway in 1975. This fact will greatly enhance your admission chances, as will your SAT scores, high school record, and athletic status. As you proceed down your list, it is time to be very realistic and select Gateway as a nearly sure bet.

As your backup or safety school, you select your state university rather than pick Small College, which is located in a picturesque Midwestern town and that may need students come April. State University is very near home; it is less expensive than Small College, even including room and board. So if you have to attend your safety school, you will be able to do so inexpensively and live away from home. Moreover, a closer look at the history department at State U. informs you that there are quite a variety of courses as well as internships in government offices in the state capitol nearby. You decide to apply to State because you feel you would receive more of a challenge in a school of 10,000 than in a small liberal arts college of 1,500. State meets the test of a safety school: "If all else fails, it is a place where I would be willing to go and do my best."

Further Advantages of Selective Application

The first advantage of selective applications is choice of school, and this does not just mean being admitted. For some families, it also means receiving the financial aid needed to attend the school. You also gain peace of mind if you apply selectively, and that mental assurance is important. It rises to the top, so to speak, and gives you the time and the confidence to focus on your top choice—increasing your chances of admission. Look at it this way—selective application forces you to pick a top school and not to try to juggle three or four applications to very competitive colleges. With only one top choice (and a close second), you can say to your top school, "I am not shopping around. I really like this place, and I want to come." If many of the applicants have the same credentials as you do, and the admissions committee knows you will come if accepted, there is an outside chance they will accept you. Remember, colleges like to be liked too. They call it *yield* (see Chapter 9), and they are interested in qualified students who will turn up in September.

In this buyers' market, applicants who have one particular school that interests them should let that school know. There are both formal and informal ways to do this. Let's look at the formal ways in which applicants can take advantage of selective application.

EARLY DECISION

Many colleges and some universities have admission plans that enable you to make a commitment to attend the school if you are accepted. This process of application and admission (or rejection or deferral) comes before the regular deadlines and is called Early Decision. Students submit their credentials early, usually by November 1 of the senior year, and sign a statement that they will accept an offer of admission if tendered and withdraw all other applications. Students then receive word of their status by December 15. If the student is denied Early Decision acceptance, he or she may be deferred to the regular time for evaluation (March) or may be rejected.

Traditionally, Early Decision applicants are well-qualified students with strong test scores, grades, recommendations, and accomplishments. "They are as good as they are going to get," according to one counselor, and they apply. Early Decision is not for students who need a strong senior year, need to have several financial aid offers, or who have any mixed feelings about the school.

Note: *Students applying for Early Decision have to be willing to accept the college's financial aid offer, which is tentative at first because it is based on the year previous to the decision. The offer will later be adjusted according to the family's financial statements for the current year.*

EARLY ACTION

A fair number of colleges and universities offer a program called Early Action. It follows the same calendar as Early Decision but does not require a binding commitment from the candidate when he or she is accepted. Rather, the candidate can then go on and apply to other colleges. Originally offered to help able students gain early admission but not feel bound and to limit their applications to a few other schools, Early Action has led to a proliferation of early applications as students "test the waters." At the moment, Harvard/Radcliffe, Brown, Columbia, Duke, Northwestern, MIT, the University of Chicago, and Georgetown are among the well-known schools offering Early Action, while Dartmouth, Princeton, Yale, and the University of Pennsylvania adhere to Early Decision—along with a host of the small liberal arts colleges.

Students applying Early Action should bear in mind several important features of this plan:

- Early Action is very discriminating. If your record is not superior in every way, you should devote your energies to strengthening it and apply at the regular time.
- You can be rejected under Early Action. Then it is over. Moreover, many of the students deferred under Early Action are ultimately rejected—well over 50 percent at the top schools.
- No financial aid awards accompany acceptance under Early Action, so you might get in, but if you need choices of colleges for financial reasons, your peace of mind may still be unsettled.
- Candidates who really want to attend a particular school should not regard this as a way to show their interest. Early Action is distinctly different from Early Decision in this regard. The reason your good intentions won't matter in the decision is that Early Action schools are so competitive that your desire to attend is not that important to them.

ROLLING ADMISSIONS

Rolling admissions bears a resemblance to Early Action in that if you are admitted, you are not obligated to attend the particular school. Rolling admissions is often used by the large state universities with big applicant pools. Generally a rolling admissions school will admit students as they apply and guarantee a response to an application with a month. Because many rolling admissions schools do not require a deposit until April or May, many ambitious candidates use rolling admissions to gain early acceptance at their safety school and then concentrate on their top choices for regular admissions. Whatever the strategy, students need to be very conscious of deadlines at rolling admissions schools. Make sure you reply to them on time, that you send in housing information and deposits on time, and that you comply with the financial aid deadlines of the institution. And make sure you apply early in the fall to the larger state schools, for when they fill their classes, rolling admissions will stop abruptly, and there will be no more room.

TELLING A SCHOOL THEY ARE YOUR FIRST CHOICE

If a college or university does not have an Early Decision program and they are not in the top tier of schools that really do not have to be concerned with yield—being liked—then you might consider writing a letter to the Dean of Admissions of your first-choice school. You would write this letter after you have carefully written out the application and sent it in and after you have filed your other forms, financial aid, supplementary references, late test scores, and the like. At this point, in early February, you can indicate your sincere interest and desire to attend with a few simple lines.

> 34 Wessex Street
> Moline, Illinois 66043
>
> Ms. Susan M. Hill
> Director of Admissions
> Coburn College
> Hawthorne, New York 13231
>
> Dear Ms. Hill:
>
> I first heard about Coburn when I was a counselor at a canoeing camp in Michigan two summers ago. One of my fellow instructors was a Coburn sophomore and told me I should consider it. Recently I have completed a thorough investigation of a number of colleges and universities, and I distinctly like Coburn over all the others. Your special program for engineering students, your nationally ranked swimming team, and the opportunities for pursuing drama and music particularly appeal to me.
>
> I just wanted you to know at this point, when you are considering my application, that I do really want to become a member of the Coburn community. I will definitely come if accepted. I know I have much to learn, and I think I have something to contribute to Coburn, too.
>
> Yours sincerely,
>
> Ted Rafter

BE WARY OF THE SHOTGUN APPROACH

In this era of "why not try it?" there are a number of students who every year choose to respond to the inconsistencies of the college admissions process by filing a large number of applications in hopes of gaining multiple admissions through sheer luck. This shotgun approach is a recipe for disaster. If followed, the students find out that the college admissions process is much more consistent than they thought. What students may not realize is that by applying to many schools that may be beyond their reach, they are maximizing their rate of rejection rather than increasing their odds of acceptance. When you stop to think of it, schools that are equally difficult to get into will react similarly to candidates whose credentials do not come up to the mark—they will reject them.

In addition, filing a large number of applications across the landscape is expensive. It is also time-consuming. You will not have sufficient time to develop a different approach to each of your schools, an approach tailored to the requirements and the style of each school. You will not have enough time to research each college sufficiently and see if it really does fit your academic and extracurricular goals. The most frequent trap that the shotgun approach opens up is that of submitting the same application essay to all the schools you select. Admissions committees are quick to pick up on generic essays, and they are generally not impressed.

So give yourself a chance to *match* yourself with the colleges to which you are applying. Think next about what your particular *edge* might be and how to exploit that edge over other candidates in your category. The concepts of *match* and *edge* are detailed in Chapter 5. Finally, remember the letter on the previous page. If you apply to too many schools, you will not be able to signal your first choice and to focus on the one school you really want to attend. You may end up with no choice at all. So selective application is the best strategy: five to six schools, spread across a range of difficulty, aggressively pursued.

WHAT IS A QUALITY EDUCATION?

By the time you come to the end of the selection process and have chosen your colleges and universities, you may come to the realization that the distinctions among some of the schools are not that significant and that you could be happy at a number of them. That is a reasonable and proper outcome of this strategy. By educating yourself about the schools on your list, you have made a number of slight distinctions based on academic program, size, location, and degree of admissions difficulty. You have inspected the colleges physically, evaluated them philosophically, and have a pretty good idea about what life at each institution is like. That is good.

When you receive your acceptances and decide which one of the schools you will attend, you will do so with the knowledge that this is the college or university where you are going to carry out the most important responsibility you have had in life thus far: educating yourself. The college or university will provide you with the dynamic environment for learning, but you will take the responsibility for making that learning happen. Jean-Jacques Rousseau once remarked that, "it is not the difference in the quality that matters, it is the quality of the difference." You are going to be making that quality of difference.

Whatever viewbooks and videos and even admissions officers promise, whatever judgments your friends, guidance counselors, and others may pronounce, you will have the final word in making your college experience a success. If you have approached your selection of colleges rationally and diligently and you have relied on your knowledge of yourself, you can be assured that you will make good decisions in selecting your schools and ultimately in enrolling in one of them. So relax and be confident about yourself and the process you have followed. The chances for your success are very high.

THREE

Visiting A College

College visits are a necessary part of the process of applying to schools. You have to touch and feel and breathe the air. Some places just have to be experienced firsthand.

    Thomas J. Wonders, Vice President of Enrollment, Davis & Elkins College

In this day and age of instant information, high-powered imaging, and virtual reality, you might reasonably ask, why visit a college before I apply? It is expensive and time-consuming, and if I have to go in the summer, no students will be there. Fair enough. Here are seven reasons why you should visit the colleges you are considering before you are admitted.

1. Logic. Visiting a school fits into the logical process you have been following to identify the schools that are right for you. It is the logical next step and will enable you to refine your choices further, apply to fewer schools, and end up getting into more of your choices.

2. Experience. You can't just pick schools based on their literature, your analysis of their vital statistics, and the opinions of others. You have to experience them firsthand and ask your questions of real people (students and professors), not just of databases and directories.

3. Qualitative. There is a qualitative dimension to applying to college. Selecting schools carefully is not just amassing the facts and vital statistics. You have to experience the location, buildings, physical surroundings, and the climate in order to make a judgment. In the end, you will bring your qualitative judgments and your quantitative analysis together and determine your choices.

4. Realism. There is a realistic element to visiting colleges, too. During your visit, you will meet people who can be instrumental in helping you gain admission: the admissions officer who interviews you, coaches you may speak with, professors you may encounter, or students and faculty members who head activities in which you are interested. They may have a voice in the admissions process. If you are a marginal admit, they can help.

5. Culture. Only a visit to the campus can give you an indication of the culture of a school. Culture is defined as the way people interact with one another. It describes the values of the institution and the society of faculty members and students. It is suggested in any number of ways: the condition of dormitories, the way people treat bulletin boards and especially the notices for esoteric or unusual events, the way faculty members and students interact outside the classroom (or don't), and the way students greet each other and describe events and people to one another, not just to you. The list goes on, but what you want to ensure by visiting a school is that its culture resonates with your values and goals.

6. Cost. This is a crass consideration, perhaps, but don't you want to be able to make a judgment based on all your research *plus* your personal experience visiting a school as to whether the cost/price is really worth it? In the end, both you and your family have to believe that the colleges to which you apply represent a value that is equal to their price. Otherwise one or all of you are going to be unhappy when those bills roll around and loans have to be repaid.

7. Application. Visiting a school is going to provide you with information and insights that are going to enable you to write a stronger application than if you stayed home. You are going to be able to shape your application with the information you learned and the insights you gained so that you stand out from others who are obliged to write more general applications and essays. Remember too that colleges are no different from people in that they like attention, and the fact that you visited will be a point in your favor.

Now can you imagine answering all these questions when you visited a college or university *after* you were admitted? Some of them yes, but most no. Think of it this way, college is a huge investment, and in order to ensure that you pick the right school, you have to invest in the process of selection. Money spent on visiting a campus is more than recouped afterward in the happy experience you will have at your "right" college.

THE VIRTUAL TOUR

Many students will want to prepare for their on-campus tour and interview by hopping on the Internet and taking a virtual tour on their home or school computer. To use this tool, the computer, efficiently, develop a list of specific questions that you want to ask and follow the same sequence at each school. Resist the temptation to *surf* the site until you have obtained answers to your previously established questions. Then surf the site and follow lateral links to see where they lead.

A sensible approach to exploring a college's Web site is to think of it as a series of *vertical* exercises followed by a sequence of *horizontal* ones. Assume you want answers to some of the questions in Chapter 2, about the academic program and the strength of a particular department. Go to the site, find the department, and move down (vertically) to the faculty—their education, degrees, and specific academic interests. Look for their publications. Do you recognize the journals? Look for their presentations at conferences. Do they sound interesting? And look for their personal information and interests. Does it say anything about the clubs that they advise or trips that they sponsor? While you are on the departmental site, see what it says about graduate school placement and job placement.

Next, let's assume you are interested in a particular extracurricular activity, such as the school newspaper. Move across to extracurricular activities, then "drill down" (vertically) to the paper. Read a recent copy of the paper. Does it appear to be a high-quality student newspaper, one you would be happy working on? Next, see what you can find about the writers. Look for their profiles. Are they similar to yours? Now move down to the page describing any awards the paper may have won. Look also for the "entrance" requirements for reporters and photographers. Does there appear to be an apprenticeship system? Could you learn the journalist's craft on this paper, or would you just be turned loose to pursue your own stories?

A third example might involve exploring financial aid policies at the college. Move to aid, and then down (vertically) to packaging policy. Is the school honest about the way in which it puts together a student's package, saying that students with the same need are sometimes packaged differently? Is that a rumor you heard? Make a note to ask this question when you get to campus. Are there sample packages to ponder for different levels of aid? Look at the work-study page. Does it list the jobs that are available—with pay rates and qualifications? Does it list instructions on how to apply for a job and how your performance is evaluated?

Now it is time for the *horizontal* journey, surfing the site. Let's take "students" as a key word and see where that leads. Perhaps to the admissions office for a profile of the entering class (last year). That is quite interesting. You can match your profile with the entering class. Perhaps the key word will lead to the student council or to student governance. Check that out. Does it sound like students really have a role in the affairs of the college? Is there a student life committee? Perhaps "students" will lead to the student directory. Look up the names of students who live near you, if the directory has a geographical sorting function. Perhaps the student link will lead to a student chat room. Very interesting. You can return to this again and again. Perhaps you want to bookmark it. Remember not to intrude too much into the chat dialog. Just listen at first—and record your thoughts.

You can do a horizontal "surf" on music if that is your interest. Concerts, types of music being played, and musical aficionado clubs will come up. Then perhaps you go to specific names of student bands or student instrumentalists and make direct contact via e-mail with questions you may have about playing your trumpet for fun at Hawthorne. "Music" will probably lead you to the bookstore as well, and you can check out the CD collection there.

In a totally different realm, you might want to try to get a fix on the culture and values of the institution by clicking on "campus ministry" and seeing what you find. Perhaps some of the earlier questions about the values of the community will be hinted at here. Also, there may be a reference to a campus committee or a denominational committee that has or is looking at student life. Perhaps they have posted their preliminary findings on another site to which there is a link here.

The only limit to surfing college Web sites is really your own energy. So make sure to observe the vertical and horizontal dimensions. It is important to search vertically first and stay focused on your interests and priorities. Then you can yield to your curiosity and look more widely. Along the way you can download significant information and pages and add them to your notes about the school. You should refer to these pages and notes before making your actual visit to the campus.

THE ACTUAL VISIT: A CASE STUDY

Martha Prentice was having a busy summer working as a waitress in the local family restaurant and trying to plan for her senior year and the college admissions process. She decided to leave her job as a waitress at the end of

August and visit colleges. She called Coburn College during her break on a June afternoon and said she would like to come for an interview between the 25th and 29th of August. She told the author: "I asked for the last morning tour and inquired as to whether I could have lunch with some students who were working as interns in the admissions office." Then she added: "Since I was reasonably sure that I wanted to enter the engineering field, I asked to speak with one of the engineering profs after lunch, and guess what? They found one for me. After that I scheduled myself for an interview at 3 p.m. I figured I would really know the school by then."

Before hanging up the phone, Martha asked the receptionist if she could e-mail her the names of one or two Coburn undergraduates who lived near her. The next day Martha got the name of a Coburn sophomore named Sarah Chapman who lived in the town next to Martha's in Westchester County. Martha called Sarah, and they arranged to meet on Martha's day off. They liked each other immediately and had a long talk about Coburn. They found that they had several friends in common and that they were both interested in the sciences.

Sarah was majoring in Coburn's special program in animal behavior. She had very favorable things to say about the science department faculty and facilities. Sarah had also played field hockey in high school and was a member of Coburn's varsity. Martha also played field hockey, and she was a member of the basketball team in her high school. However, she wondered if women's sports got the same attention as men's. She did not totally believe the claims Coburn made in its fancy brochure on women's athletics. Sarah was able to reassure Martha that 'the playing field was level' and that she would have a great time playing intercollegiate sports at Coburn.

In the course of their hour-long conversation, Martha was able to get interesting answers to most of her questions. Here is what she asked Sarah.

- What attracted you especially to Coburn? Has it lived up to your expectations? What surprised you about the school? What has disappointed you?
- Do you know any women who are majoring in engineering? What do they say?
- Have you gotten solid academic and career advice at Coburn? How frequently do you see your faculty adviser? Can you change advisers easily if you need to? Have your teachers and adviser suggested courses and research topics that have helped you build a strong application to graduate school in veterinary medicine?

- Tell me about life in the dormitories and the social life in general. I know there are all sorts of living arrangements—single sex, coeducational by floor, and theme houses. But what I really want to know is how you like where you live and if there is sufficient privacy.
- In the same vein, do students treat each other well? Do they care about one another, or are they caught up in the rat race for graduate school and jobs? Is the social life relaxed and interesting, or do you feel pressured into going to football games on Saturday afternoons? What about your other women friends—how do they feel about the climate for women? And men, have you met some nice ones?
- And sports? "Frankly," Martha said, "I don't believe all I read in the Coburn viewbook about 'individualized instruction, spacious and well-equipped facilities' and the 'enthusiasm of fellow players.' What has been your experience as a field hockey player there? Do you feel that women's sports have been relegated to second place, because of the prominence of Coburn's football team? Can you tell me about the actual facilities, the locker rooms, uniforms, and equipment? What about the coaches, are they good and committed?"
- Finally, I just don't think I am going to have the time to play two sports like I do in high school. Of those two, basketball and field hockey, what is your opinion of the quality of the coaching and the level of team performance? Are there intramural sports?

Before long, an hour had flown by, and Sarah had to get back to her job as a lab assistant for a local veterinarian—a job her zoology instructor at Coburn had helped her find. This impressed Martha, as did Sarah's enthusiastic answers to most of her questions. Martha looked forward to visiting Coburn and asking some of the same questions of other Coburn students and her interviewer.

In the course of the next several days Martha thought about some of the questions she might ask the engineering professor with whom she would be meeting on campus. She went to the Coburn Web site again and reviewed the engineering faculty. She thought hard about the various programs Coburn offered and which one really appealed to her. The engineering department at Coburn was strong. It offered four degree options: A Bachelor of Science in Chemical, Civil, Electrical, or Mechanical Engineering; a Bachelor of Science in Engineering Sciences (a more general preparation that allowed for interdisciplinary work); a five-year program that awarded a Bachelor of Arts and a

Bachelor's in Engineering; and an integrated bachelor's and master's degree program that conferred two degrees at the end of five years of study. Martha wasn't sure yet which track she wanted to pursue, so she put together some general questions:

- **The Future.** What advice would you offer someone entering the engineering field today? What specific areas of engineering are crowded? What are the fields, such as aerospace and technology, that need highly trained people in the next twenty years? What about environmental science?
- **Flexibility.** I know that I will enjoy the basic engineering courses in civil and mechanical engineering. My father is a civil engineer for the Highway Department, and a couple of years ago, I helped him restore a 1970s Volkswagen Beetle. But I have lots of interests. I know I want to study economics and accounting and organizational behavior. I want to be qualified to enter the management field when my engineering training becomes outmoded. Which of your four degree programs would be best suited to these interests?
- **Faculty Presence.** The Coburn catalog states that the ratio of students to instructors is 10:1. Could you translate that figure into typical class size in engineering? Roughly what percentage of classes have 10 students or fewer? How many have 100 or more? How do the labs work? How many instructors are available in a lab experiment format? Does the engineering department offer small seminar classes? On a slightly different track, does the engineering faculty play an active role in helping students find internships and jobs?
- **Faculty Quality.** Can you tell me a little about the engineering faculty? I read on the Web site that Professor Frankel won a prize for his research on aluminum under stress. Do students have the opportunity to work with professors?
- **Facilities.** Do you feel that the engineering facilities at Coburn are adequate for the programs you are offering? Are there any facilities that are deficient? What arrangements are made for those students?
- **Undergraduate Life.** What is your feeling about the undergraduates here at Coburn? Do the faculty and students mix informally? Do you enjoy this interaction? Do the students appear pleased with the education they are receiving? Do you sense that students conform to the views of their professors or feel free to express divergent opinions?

Martha jotted all these questions down and filed them away in the manila folder she had designated for Coburn. She knew she would not have time to ask them all. She also knew that some of the questions were quite direct. She also thought to herself: "If I don't get complete or positive answers to all of these questions, Coburn could still be the right school for me. There are lots of elements to choosing a college, after all."

When it came time for her visit in late August, Martha and her mother left early in the morning, with an hour's margin built into their schedule just to be on the safe side. Martha dressed neatly yet casually in clothes that made her feel comfortable rather than formal. When they arrived on the campus at 10:15 a.m., they had time to go to the snack bar, where Martha's mother had a cup of coffee, and her daughter, juice. Then they went off on their campus tour at 10:45 a.m., as scheduled.

The Role of Parents

Every family has its own traditions as far as parents and children (college applicants) are concerned. Each college and university will vary slightly in its approach to parents as well. The larger or more selective the college or university, the less parents are expected to be involved in interacting with admissions officers. The volume of students and families passing through the admissions office on a usual day simply does not permit it.

At many colleges, however, parents are greeted by admissions officers and considered very much a part of the campus visit experience. At some schools, faculty members come to the admissions office so they can answer parents' questions while students are being interviewed.

In a conversation with her parents in the spring of her junior year, Martha had said she wanted to handle the college search and application process herself. Her parents had agreed, so Mrs. Prentice played a subsidiary role as driver, fellow tourer, and friend during the visit to Coburn. Here are some other useful functions parents can perform in the course of visiting a college.

- **Literature.** Read the college's viewbook and other information that is sent to the home.
- **Web Site.** Visit the school's Web site and look at areas that are of interest to you—your own undergraduate major, for instance, or the outside activities that you would like to engage in if you were to go to college again.

- **Financial Aid.** If your family is applying for financial aid, visit the financial aid Web site. When your child visits the college, you may want to make an appointment at the Financial Aid Office and ask questions about how the school views family assets, summer earnings, or outside scholarship.
- **Bulletin Boards.** When your child is having an interview, take a tour of your own and look at bulletin boards. Do the events and messages sound interesting? Read the school's newspaper. If the college or university is large it will probably publish an institutional newspaper. Find a copy in the library or snack bar.
- **People.** Depending on your degree of curiosity, you may want to engage a student in discussion while on your "personal" tour of the campus. Some parents have been known to stroll into academic departments and talk to faculty members who seem to have a few minutes to spare. Others feel more comfortable talking to administrators or workers.

Whatever roles you choose to play while your child is being interviewed will depend on family tradition and agreed-upon strategy. Your tradition may be to encourage your child to visit colleges and universities on his or her own. If this is the case, make sure he or she has enough money. Several years ago, a young man concluded his interview with the grizzled dean of a small college near Philadelphia by asking him for a loan of $20 so he could catch the bus to New York City. It was quite logical. The boy turned to the nearest parent figure to give him a hand.

Martha's Tour

Martha had a few questions for the student tour guide who led Martha, her mother, and fifteen others around the campus. These questions centered on student life and access to facilities. Martha asked about the work load for students, the relationships between students and faculty members, the hours of the library, and the access to computer ports and stations at peak times. She was reassured by some of the answers she received. "There is always room at . . . or if you need to speak to a professor, you can always . . ."

Martha also inspected the gym carefully. Sarah Chapman told her about improvements in the women's locker room. Martha saw them for herself. She asked about the gym's hours. Would she and her friends be able to play an informal game of basketball some evenings in the winter? She looked over the new $15-million field house, which had eight handball and

Preparing for Your Campus Visit

Some tips to make your campus visit a success story.

1. Make sure that you—not your mother or father—contact the admissions office of the college or university and make the arrangements. Ask for directions. Many schools have a special visiting brochure with a map of how to get there. If you have to stay overnight, this brochure or the receptionist will be able to give you the numbers for local motels and inns. The school's Web site—under admissions/visiting the campus—may also contain this information.
2. Request and read the catalog of course and program offerings before visiting. The catalog may be on line, too.
3. Ask for any materials that may be pertinent to your interests. All schools will have athletic brochures; most will have brochures for each academic department. Most will have the campus newspaper. These materials will also be on the college's Web site and may be easier to examine there.
4. Ask for the names of current undergraduates who live near you, like Martha did. Call them or visit with them before you go to campus. They can provide valuable information about programs, but more important, about the quality of teaching, student interaction with faculty members, student interaction with students, and the culture and tone of the campus.
5. Ask for the names of faculty members in your field of interest. The admissions office will probably have a list of faculty members who are willing to talk with prospective applicants and can set up an appointment for you. Obviously, if classes are in session, the Admissions Office can build class visits into your day on campus.
6. Finally, schedule your interview. Put it last in the sequence, if you can, so that you are in possession of as much knowledge about the school as you can gather. This will make your interview more productive from both sides—yours and the college's. When you arrive on campus, ask the receptionist who will interview you, so you will get his or her name correct the first time. Often the names of the admissions officers will be posted in the reception area, and you can check there as well.
7. Dress comfortably and neatly. If in doubt, dress "up," not "down." You only will have one opportunity to make a first impression.

racquetball courts, four squash courts, a 200-meter running track, wrestling and weight rooms, a dance studio, trainers' suites, and men's and women's locker rooms. Very impressive, she thought.

Naturally, Martha visited a dormitory to see a student room and check out the living conditions. If she should decide to live in a coeducational dorm, she found that the coed dorms at Coburn were reasonable (there were separate bathroom and shower facilities for men and women). There was sufficient privacy. Each floor had a small study/computer room in case a roommate's stereo was too loud or the choice of music too outrageous. And the library had a small section on the first floor that was open 24 hours a day.

In the course of her tour Martha asked about interdormitory competition and social affairs, about the faculty and graduate student resident adviser program, and about the relationship between the college students and the residents of the nearby town of Hawthorne (What specific activities bring students and townspeople together? Are there areas of tension? If so, what is being done to alleviate them?)

Finally, Martha looked carefully at Coburn's theater facilities. She had been interested in acting for quite a while but never had the opportunity to pursue it in high school. She wanted to try her hand in college. As the tour group moved through the theater, Martha was impressed by both the main hall for major productions and the so-called 'black box' for experimental student and faculty productions. However, Martha was most interested in the small theater downstairs where informal plays and musicals were put on by the students. This was one of the facilities that would eventually induce her to apply to Coburn.

Martha's visit with the engineering professor went well, and by 3 p.m. she was ready for her interview with David Walenski, Associate Director of Admissions at Coburn. In the course of the interview that follows, Martha tried to adhere to the following guidelines.

GUIDELINES FOR YOUR INTERVIEW

Ask analytical questions, not factual ones. Try not to waste time with who, what, and when questions, and concentrate on those that begin with why or how. For example, Martha might say: "How would you characterize faculty and student interaction here at Coburn?" Or, "How is Coburn's curriculum changing to reflect the needs of students entering the workforce in the first decade of our new century?" The point is to ask the interviewer to interpret the facts you already know or course descriptions you have already seen.

It is also fair to ask about alcohol and drug use on campus or student attitudes toward each other and toward the school itself. You might want to inquire about the diversity of opinion. At some schools a particular ideology rules, and you want to make sure you think about that. "Do students get involved in the decision making at the college? How well does that work?" These are fair questions for an interview. You may also want to focus on your intended major and check out the flexibility you need to take all the courses that interest you. "How do students in engineering that want to take economics, history, and humanities put together a plan of study?" This is a sensible question to ask.

Assert yourself during your interview. Make sure your interviewer knows not only who you are, but what you have done in your high school. Very often the interviewer will ask you about your courses. You may even give him or her a copy of your transcript. Know your transcript well. Be able to articulate your strengths in the classroom, on the playing fields, and in extracurricular activities. Be enthusiastic about the activities that interest you and in which you have done well. Indicate your interest in continuing with certain activities while in college and also reaching out to new areas. Try to convey your enthusiasm in a way that shows why you like a certain sport or activity.

Use the interview process to probe the nature of the educational and social experience at the college. Make your interviewer work. For example, Coburn has 3,200 students and is considered a midsize school. Martha might ask what the interviewer thinks the advantages are of a school this size, compared with those of a small school with 1,500 undergraduates, or a large campus, such as Berkeley with 35,000 students. Martha might also ask which are the better academic departments at Coburn and how the interviewer would characterize the status of women's sports at the school. Another question she might ask is: "What kind of student really gets the most out of a school like Coburn?"

Find out about your interviewer. An interview should resemble a polite and interesting conversation. It is polite and reasonable to ask the other person about himself or herself. Try to establish some sort of relationship with your interviewer without distorting the normal flow of the interview or pushing the bounds of what is personal and what is appropriate for a formal meeting. Some sample questions should turn up who your interviewer is, whether he or she is a graduate of the school, and if so, what were the most rewarding experiences at the college. You might want to ask about the interviewer's college major, and if it is natural, the activities he or she pursued in college, especially if they are similar to yours. The end result of asking about the interviewer is to establish yourself as an outgoing person who genuinely is interested in other people, and perhaps to remind the interviewer of similarities between the two of you. If you can establish some kind of connection with your interviewer, you may be remembered.

Make the match between yourself and the college. This is the main object of the interview: establishing yourself as someone who is qualified and interested in making a contribution to the college. Martha Prentice is an example of a person with much to offer. She is an able student who knows what she wants to study. She has a strong transcript and test scores. She is a good athlete, and her interest in dramatics may ultimately translate into a skill that will enliven the Coburn community.

You can introduce evidence of your academic ability into the interview quite naturally by taking a copy of your high school transcript. This will show the success you have had in the courses you have taken. Many transcripts also include scores on the SAT I, SAT II Subject, ACT, and Advanced Placement tests. A transcript gives the interviewer something to react to, and many interviewers will give a frank assessment of your chances for admission once they have examined your transcript.

To make the match for your extracurricular contributions to the college, you can ask: "How difficult would it be for me to make the varsity soccer team?" You can then direct the discussion toward your abilities as a field hockey, soccer, or basketball player. You can also prepare an athletic data sheet (discussed in Chapter 6) to show to the coaches you may meet during your visit. Whatever area you excel in, begin by telling the interviewer, "I have acted in plays, and I would like to know . . ." This tells the interviewer of your interest and desire to contribute to this particular area of college life. Remember, admissions officers are looking for all-around contributors, not just scholars or athletes or musicians.

By asking incisive questions and establishing the connections between your talents and the college's needs, you can impress your interviewer in a reasonable and persuasive way.

TIPS FOR BEING A GOOD INTERVIEWEE

1. The interview is a conversation, not a confrontation.

The best interviews are memorable conversations in which the student has an opportunity to present himself or herself as a person and as a candidate with certain credentials and to find out important answers to his or her questions. Most interviewers will proceed from what you have to say. They will be, to a degree, open-ended and follow the course you set with your questions. Your job is to take the initiative and control the content of the conversation.

2. Prepare for your interview.

Know yourself. Know your subject—the college or university. Remember, you know a lot already. This is an opportunity to show what you know and to learn more. Make sure you have read the school's catalog, either in print or on line, and you don't have to ask any of those "what" questions. According to one report, only one in five students is well prepared for the college interview.[1] If you are prepared, you will be exceptional.

3. Listen to what is being said.

We spend most of our lives trying to perfect our listening skills. The interview is a good place to remember that. If the interviewer asks an ambiguous question, don't be afraid to ask for clarification. Break complex questions down into subordinate parts, and answer each separately. Treat every question as important, but not entirely at the expense of humor. Try to see all the implications of a question—academic, social, psychological, and cultural. Then pick the elements you want to respond to.

4. Be honest.

Often, admitting a weakness can be disarming and may help the interviewer relate to you better. After all, the interviewer is not perfect either. Honesty is the beginning of learning, so it is a value that colleges appreciate. Nevertheless, your honesty need not take the form of an apology, nor should your honesty be overly self-critical. When you relate facts or incidents that may have been embarrassing or perhaps worse, college interviewers will be interested not so much in what you did as in what you learned.

---

[1] Don Dickason, "The College Interview and How to Make it Work for You." (Peterson's Guides, 1994).

VISITING A COLLEGE

5. Pauses can be refreshing.
All too often first-time interviewees rush ahead with their conversation in fear that a pause may create the impression that they are ignorant or insecure. Wrong. Consider the following example.

> On December 12, 1941, General George C. Marshall, the Chief of Staff of the U.S. Army, called in Colonel Dwight D. Eisenhower, who had served in the Philippines, and asked him for his on-the-spot opinion of the best strategy to follow in responding to the disastrous attack on Pearl Harbor five days before. Instead of answering at once, Eisenhower asked for 3 hours to consider the matter, promising to return in the afternoon with his written response. Marshall was a bit taken aback but agreed. As he thought about it, he became very impressed that Eisenhower took his question so seriously that he asked for time to prepare the most careful answer he could. From then on Marshall took a keen interest in the career of this intelligent young officer, who *thought before speaking*.

Eisenhower carried the pause further than a student in a college interview can, but the point is the same. Pause to think before responding. Use the pause to ask for clarification. Use it to gather your thoughts before moving on. Pause after each point when you are trying to build a case. That helps your points stand out and not get blurred in a rush of speech.

6. Look for the telltale signs that it is time to shift your tactics.
You will most likely see the signs to shift the topic, or let the interviewer speak, in the body language of the interviewer. Fidgeting, clenching and unclenching the hands, crossing and uncrossing the legs, and a faraway look in the eye are signs to change your tactics. When this happens, bring your response to a close in two sentences. Allow a natural pause to take place, and if you are not asked a question, move the conversation in a different direction.

7. Eye contact.
Some people will tell you that it is essential to maintain eye contact in an interview. Not so. Clearly, when you are meeting and saying goodbye, it is essential, and it is desirable to maintain natural eye contact during the course of the conversation. But not all the time. Sometimes when people are not sure of themselves or are trying to make a complex point, their eyes will

wander to the side—this is all right. On the other hand, if you see your interviewer looking to the side or at the ceiling, the message being conveyed is boredom or disagreement. By contrast, when speakers look directly at you, they are frequently confident of what they are saying and are seeking confirmation from you. They are also letting you know that at the end of their thoughts, you can respond to them, and they are eager to hear your ideas.

MARTHA PRENTICE'S INTERVIEW

Martha's interview with David Walenski, Associate Director of Admissions, went like this:

Walenski: Well, how did your tour and lunch with the students go? Did any questions come up that I could answer?

Martha: Yes, I enjoyed the tour and my talk with the students. Both experiences answered many of the questions I had, but I still do want to find out from you what you feel to be the advantages for an undergraduate education at a midsize school like Coburn?

Walenski: I'd say there are two or three distinct advantages to this institution.

First, the size of Coburn is ideal. With 3,200 students we can put together a class that has real variety and quality in a way that a small college with half as many students cannot. So what you have here is a genuinely diverse student body that is neither too big nor too small. You are going to get to know all sorts of different, talented people here, and you will learn almost as much from them as you do inside the classroom.

Second, I think the facilities at Coburn are exceptional. Did you see that field house? The unlimited access to the library, the fiber-optic cable strung to every student room, and the three different theaters, not to mention the labs over at the engineering school, really do impress me, even though I am used to them. Smaller schools have a tougher time raising money for such facilities, and at larger ones, often the facilities are restricted to varsity teams or graduate students.

Third, I think that your contact with the faculty here will be of genuine and lasting value to you. The teachers here are just

VISITING A COLLEGE

that—teachers. They like students. They want to spend time with them. If their primary objective were to publish, they would be at the big universities, where they would only have one teaching preparation a term and lots of time for their own research and study. The faculty members at Coburn come here because they want to be with young people and do collaborative research with them in many cases. You will see a lot of your teachers at Coburn. They are available outside office hours. They will guide you toward graduate school and the workforce. They really want you to do well and to succeed in life.

Martha: You mention that you are used to the facilities here. How long have you been here, and what has been your experience with the students and the faculty?

Walenski: I came to Coburn seven years ago as an undergraduate. I had been picked up on a football scholarship. I had never heard of Coburn until one of the leading businessmen in my community of Altoona, Pennsylvania, suggested that I apply. He was a graduate. He knew I had done pretty well academically in high school, and the football coach here took an interest in my case after I sent him some newspaper clippings. At any rate, I came, majored in political science, and worked for a year in Washington at a job I got through a summer internship here. Two years ago I decided to come back and work in the admissions department.

    I may go off to graduate school in a year or so, but I'm going to have to wait for my wife to finish her nurse's training at the hospital in Buffalo. But you asked what my experience has been? Answer—I love this place. I came from a small-town background. Neither of my parents attended college. I was grateful for the scholarship I received here. I worked very hard and feel that the school has done me a lot of good personally and academically.

    The central experience for me here was meeting all the different people—from around the world, from small towns like mine, and from the big cities and suburbs of America. One of my roommates was a champion swimmer from Winnetka, Illinois. Another one was a science wizard from one of those science high schools in New York City. The third one was from Japan. His father worked for Honda. I learned a lot from those guys. I also learned a lot from my classes. I took a variety of courses, some in fields I never knew existed. I even took that special Japanese history course for nonmajors. I took French—started it from scratch—and ended up spending three months in Paris. (Coburn belongs to a consortium of colleges, which owns a study center there.) I think, however, at a big university I would have been lost. I would not have gotten to know so many people or had a chance to excel in class or play varsity football. Here I got to shine in a couple of areas, and I met great people who will be my friends for life.

Martha: That is quite a speech. I believe you. Many of the things you said are of interest to me. I want to get to know new people. I want to take a variety of courses, but I also want to finish here with a special skill in at least one area. Can you tell me which are the strong departments here, and which are the weak ones? Is engineering really that strong?

Walenski: To be honest, I don't think that music is terribly strong here. The department has failed to obtain a couple of grants that would have helped it a great deal, and several of the younger, more promising professors have left. However, I think you are in good shape if you pursue engineering with a minor in economics. Several of the engineering professors have had nationally acclaimed articles in the *Journal of Professional Engineers.* Because our engineering facilities are not as extensive as those at, say, a place like the University of Michigan, we do not get all that government money to build a mock-up of the lunar capsule. However, our engineering professors are nationally recognized—at least several of them are. I would add that the college's Glockenspiel Award for distinguished teaching has gone to a member of the engineering department in two of the past five years. That is really something.

Martha: I am certainly impressed with that statistic. However, could I shift the subject for a moment? I would like to find out a little something about the social life here. I know it may be hard for you to answer, but what is your impression of the role of women here? Have they been fully integrated into the teaching faculty and administration? How about the fraternities and sororities. Do they dominate the social life here—and with what impact on women?

Walenski: Let me answer the latter question first. Fraternities and sororities exist here on a take-it-or-leave-it basis. About half the students belong to a fraternity or sorority, but since freshmen all have to live together in three dormitories, and since there is not sufficient room for all the fraternity and sorority members to live in their houses, students do not break off into frat house cliques. If you do not want to join a sorority, fine. You'll probably get invited to many of their parties anyway. I wouldn't worry about fraternity or sorority domination one bit.

Now the question about the role of women here. That is pretty hard for me to answer, and figures do not tell the whole story. We have been coeducational for fifteen years. Over 50 percent of the undergraduates are women, and when it comes to retaining students, more women stay the four consecutive years than men. When I was an undergraduate here, I did not sense any discrimination toward women, and I don't now. Since the competition for places is keener for women than for men, the women tend to be a little bit brighter and dynamic than the men. So they more than hold their own. Last year our Class Day's Phi Beta Kappa speaker was a woman. She was the third in the past six years. So on the undergraduate front, I think things are normal and relaxed and tolerant.

On the faculty front, Coburn has had some difficulty attracting women faculty members. Perhaps it is our rural location. Some of those we've attracted have not stayed for some reason or other. So we still need to make progress in retaining women faculty members. For instance, no woman has yet won the undergraduate teaching prize for faculty members. Overall, there are just not enough women on the faculty.

Martha: Just what is that ratio, anyway?

Walenski: Actually it is about 20 percent women, and as you can see, this is well under half of the percentage of women students. So what this boils down to is that there is an insufficient number of role models for the women students here. That said, I would say that women here do have a fulfilling experience teaching and as members of the community. They advise undergraduate women as resident advisers in the dormitories; there are women on all the major committees, a woman dean of the faculty, and, incidentally, five women on the Board of Trustees of twenty-two people. In addition, in the special events and lecture series on campus, women artists and scholars are emphasized. Alice Rivlin, Undersecretary of the Treasury, was here a year ago, and Donna Shalala is supposed to receive an honorary degree this spring, according to rumor.

Martha: From what you say, I gather that the role of women at Coburn is not a pressing issue. What are the social and academic issues that have come up on the campus during the past year?

Walenski: I would say that the role of women is an issue, and one that the school is sensitive about. That there has not been a public outcry about women's rights should not obscure the fact that the administration cares very deeply about according women an equal place on this campus. You can see that from the special pamphlet on women's athletics that was sent to you along with the catalog.

If you looked at the campus newspaper, you probably know that the big issue last year was the investment of Coburn funds in tobacco companies and the purchase by the bookstore of athletic clothes made in the sweatshops of Southeast Asia.

Martha: I saw those articles, and how has the Coburn administration responded to them?

Walenski: After a series of articles in the student press that were picked up by the regional papers, the Trustees met to debate the tobacco issue. They decided to sell their tobacco stock and announced it at a big student rally, much to everyone's satisfaction. On the Southeast Asia sweatshops, the Trustees asked for a committee to be set up to see if it could trace the actual sources of Coburn athletic gear, both the fibers and the finished products. Students and professors are making a kind of academic exercise out of this task, and the committee plans to report its findings

VISITING A COLLEGE

and make recommendations to the Trustees at their December meeting. I think the matter will be resolved in a reasonable way. You can check the President's section of the Web site for an update on this issue.

Martha: I think that the debate over the sweatshop clothing is fascinating, but the school ought to go slowly.

Walenski: You do? Why not with all deliberate speed?

Martha: I feel that the maintenance or withdrawal of trade with a particular county is a proper concern of governments, not educational institutions. I think if the President and the Treasury Department and the Secretary of State think it is in the U.S. interest to withdraw trade from a particular country, well, fine. But remember when you do that, you effectively end the relationship with the country, which may engage in more destructive labor practices after the U.S. leaves. I believe in creating as much leverage as you can and looking for gradual improvement in those awful labor conditions. Colleges, I think, should be as nonpolitical as they can be and should coordinate their efforts with our government in cases like this. You never know, leaving the investments in place and threatening sanctions may do more good than pulling the investments and contracts out.

Walenski: You have a point there, and I don't know that I had thought about it quite that way before.

Martha: Well (Laughing) when I get in, I can change Coburn's position. (Pause) I have another question that relates to one of my interests: field hockey. If I were admitted to Coburn, how difficult would it be for me to win a place on the freshman field hockey team? We play pretty good field hockey at Westchester High. Last year our team made the state semifinals. But I have heard that Coburn's field hockey team is pretty good, too.

Walenski: Yes, it is. Last year the Coburn team went up to the semifinals in the regional, tristate playoffs and managed to get into the first round of the nationals at Mt. Holyoke. If you are as good as you say you are, and your position is not overcrowded with candidates, I think that you could make the freshman team and plan to play about a third of the time. If you hang in there, you would probably make the varsity team the following year, when some of the kids drop out because of academic or other interests. I will ask Sharon Cushman, the varsity coach, to drop you a line. Meantime you can look up the team's recent accomplishments on the athletic Web page. It is updated daily.

Martha: Thanks. If I am a potential field hockey player, will that enhance my chances for admission?

Walenski: Definitely. Each year we try to take a handful of people for each varsity sport. There is no formal rating system or quota system for the coaches as you might have at a large state school, but athletic ability is a distinct plus. If Sharon backs you, it will help.

Martha: In that connection, I hope you do not think me too bold when I ask how I look as a candidate for Coburn? Here is my transcript for you to look at before you give me an answer.

Walenski: I can say frankly from our conversation here today that you are a reasonably strong candidate. Let me see what courses you have had in high school (Looks over the transcript). This transcript looks pretty strong to me. You have paid close attention to college prep courses, and that's what we look for: English, a foreign language, math through calculus, and three lab sciences. Do you plan to take another semester of chemistry—the course in organic?

Martha: Chemistry is not my best subject, and my physics course is very hard, so I was considering putting off the organic chemistry until college. I will also be in AP French in the fall in addition to my other courses in English, history, and physics.

Walenski: Those are tough courses all right, but I would still advise the organic chemistry in the spring of your senior year. By then your grades for college will be submitted to us, and if you are admitted and don't do well in chemistry, we will not penalize you for it. Having those chemistry concepts under your belt before tackling college chemistry would be a big help. (Pause)

Let me say something about your testing. It looks good. We will be looking for three SAT II Subject tests as you know, and one or two of them should be science or math. If you get low 600 scores on those tests, you will look pretty good to the Admissions Committee.

Martha: I will consider your suggestion seriously. Is there anything besides grades, scores, and an ability to contribute to athletics and extracurricular activities that you and the committee are looking for in an applicant to Coburn?

Walenski: I'd say that we are definitely looking for an intangible quality of dynamism in a candidate. That can come out in a field hockey game, in an aggressive hook shot from the center of the field that catches the goalie off guard. But we really hope it will come out in the classroom, when a student says: "I am sorry, Professor So and So, I really don't understand what you just said. Could you state that again?"

Or it could be a statement in a student faculty forum, such as the one you made a moment ago, urging caution on withdrawing the college's investments from Southeast Asia. You said in essence: "I wonder if it is the responsibility of a midsize college in central New York State to withdraw its investments for Southeast Asia unilaterally when it perceives that the civil rights and working conditions of a group of laborers may have been violated. I wonder if we ought to heed the advice and guidance of the State Department and Treasury, and consult with our fellow institutions before attempting to deal with a social and economic injustice 15,000 miles away."

In short, we are looking for people with the vitality, imagination, and sense of responsibility, to themselves and to the community, to speak the truth as they see it and do so reasonably. I always remember a line from Alfred North Whitehead, who said: "The task of a university or college is to weld together imagination and experience." The professors, the libraries, and the facilities here all add up to experience. What we in the admissions office are looking for is a group of students with imagination and a constructive interest in challenging themselves and their teachers as they move through the institution. If we can bring together a class of varied and bright individuals who can challenge each other and us, then we have done our job.

Martha: Thanks. In my application I will give serious thought to the points you have raised.

Walenski: Well, thank you too for coming up today. I think we have to wind up this interview because we have gone into overtime. I am very glad to have had the chance to talk with you. I shall look forward to reading your application. In the meantime, if there are any questions you have, please get in touch with me by phone or e-mail. Here is my card.

Martha: Thanks again, Mr. Walenski.

Alumni Interviews

Because the time and expense of interviewing students is not insignificant, many colleges and universities have enlisted their alumni in interviewing candidates. If an alumni interview is offered to you, by all means accept the opportunity. You should visit the campus nonetheless, and accomplish the tasks suggested. The only difference is that you would be interviewed by an alumnus near your home.

Theoretically alumni interviews should not be different from one on the college's campus, but in fact they are. One cannot expect the alumnus to be as well versed in reading transcripts and knowing high schools as a college admissions officer is. Also, the alumnus may not be as familiar with students your age—with their tastes and styles—as the typical college admissions officer is. Here are a few tips for an alumni interview:

- Dress more formally than you would for an on-campus interview. Chances are you will be invited to the alumnus's office for the interview.
- Do not go into as much detail about your high school courses and test scores unless you are asked to do so. Focus more on your plans for college.
- Make sure you ask the alumnus what his or her experience was at the college, and then try to make some connections to your own thoughts about your experience there. This is a good way to begin the conversation. All of us like to tell stories about our youth, and alumni, whether in pinstripes or jeans, are no exception.
- Make sure you say honest, favorable things about the college or university the interviewer attended. You questions should not be quite so sharp as Martha Prentice's were.

- Know the vital facts about the college, but make sure not to strain the alumnus's knowledge of the school with your questions. One topic an alumnus cannot be expected to know a lot about is the ever-changing patterns in financial aid. After all, the alumnus cannot know as much as David Walenski, who is living and breathing Coburn every day.
- Be prepared for the conversation to be a little more wide-ranging than one in the admissions office. Remember the word "conversation." An alumnus may have as his goal merely to get to know you and see if you would fit into the school he remembers and loves. He may not concern himself too much with your academic credentials.
- Last, you cannot place as much stock in an alumni prediction of your chances of admission as you can that of an on-campus admissions officer.

HOW INTERVIEWS REALLY WORK

By now you know that interviews will vary enormously in their style and content. You can only hope that they proceed as smoothly as the one between Martha Prentice and David Walenski. Even though they might not, a weak interview will probably not have a severely negative effect on your chances for admission. On the other hand, a really positive interview that makes you memorable to the admissions officer could help you if you are at the margin of admission.

You should keep in mind that a wonderful interview will not guarantee you admission to any college or university if your other credentials are not strong. A good interview cannot overcome a poor academic record, weak teacher and school recommendations, and minimal involvement in extracurricular activities. Colleges want to enroll students who have made the most of their educational opportunities rather than those who only show charm and an ability to converse with adults.

Nevertheless, you should think about your college interviews as opportunities to present your unique personality and academic and other talents to the school. In addition, remember that the request for an interview itself and making the long journey to the college are statements of interest in the college, and these statements are not forgotten, either. In fact, the interview from the college's point of view is also an opportunity to market its products, so to speak, and to recruit students. It provides a chance for the college to remind prospective students of its strong programs, talented faculty, diverse student body, vigorous athletic program, and second-to-none facilities for art, drama, and computing. So one way to look at an interview is to see it as a very civilized "show and tell" encounter in which you try to make sure your "show" is the best that it can be.

For the very selective schools, one admissions officer put it this way: "I look on the interview as the first and last opportunity a lot of kids will have to make contact with my school. I want the opportunity to be as pleasant and productive as can be."

Given the opportunity for a college or university interview, show a natural enthusiasm about yourself and your credentials, try to control the flow of the conversation, listen carefully to your interviewer, take time to formulate your responses, and, above all, be honest about everything you say. Remember, the interview presents a vital chance to learn something more about the school and maybe even yourself. In Martha's conversation with David Walenski, the digression about Coburn's purchases in Southeast Asia brought both interviewer and interviewee to a new level of understanding. Walenski discovered that the neatly attired, upper-middle-class girl from a wealthy suburb of New York had a mind of her own and wasn't afraid to speak it. And on Martha's account? She came to understand that the "climate of free discussion" described in the Coburn viewbook really did exist at Coburn. She found Walenski's reaction to her statement a reasonable one, and that really impressed her.

After Martha left the room, David Walenski jotted down a few notes on Martha's interview report form: "Sensitive, intelligent, mature young woman who knows what she wants but is open to the ideas of others. Reasonable scores, very good grades, probably a contributor to field hockey, and may also turn up in student theater productions. I was impressed with her. I hope she applies and we can find a place for her."

Martha's interview did go well. Her visit to Coburn was a success. She made the visit her opportunity to get a "feel for the place." She knew that she was not just going to college to study, and she wanted to be sure that the values of Coburn, the nonacademic opportunities she would have, and the people she would be with all resonated with her best instincts and her goals. She was favorably impressed. It was a win-win situation. She decided to apply.

FOUR

Talking, Testing, Planning

The middle school and junior high years are a pivotal time to develop the academic planning, preparation, and motivation needed for higher education.

Eileen R. Matthey, *Counseling for College,* Peterson's Guides, 1995

Some readers may be surprised to hear that a little college planning in the ninth grade goes a long way toward smoothing the college search and application process. It is true, though, because like a building, the foundation is what determines the stability of the final structure.

THE FRESHMAN YEAR—TALKING AND AWARENESS

Before you even have settled into the routine of ninth grade, you should think very seriously about the courses you plan to take in your first year of high school. Simply stated, they should all be college preparatory. When you register for your courses, make sure your counselor knows you are college bound and will be checking in with him or her from time to time.

Your selection of courses should be part of a larger exercise of self-examination. You also need to think about what activities you want to pursue in high school. These will be the ones that give you special pleasure and excitement. It may be a sport, it may be music, or it may be debate. Whatever it is, make plans to pursue your interest in school.

By the ninth grade some students spend a good deal of their time working, so they may wonder how they can follow this advice. Work sometimes provides an opportunity to express your creativity and to develop your skills. Rebecca Liczko is one student we know who helps her mother with her expanding catering business. Not only does Rebecca love doing the cooking, but she also has developed good phone manners, and since she is a whiz at math, she does all the bookkeeping on Quicken. In the ninth grade Rebecca is taking an optional cooking course in her free period. She has also found a Web site where she can converse with other catering people and relay good ideas for the business to her mother. In making these decisions Rebecca is taking some initiative concerning her future. Perhaps someday she will bring together in her college program her talent for math, her experience in food preparation, and her knowledge of a particular business.

Talk with Older Students

As a ninth grader you may also want to talk to older friends and family members who may be in college and find out what it is like. Ask them what they would have done differently if they were just starting high school now—what advice they would give freshmen like yourself. Here are a series of responses from a group of college students to whom I recently asked this question:

- "I would certainly have gone to see my guidance counselor more."
- "Yeah, I would have read one of those 'how to' books."
- "I would have gone and looked at a college and tried to picture myself there. I never saw my college until I got there."
- "It may sound ridiculous, but the more reading of all that stuff they send you, the better off you are."
- "Yup, there are videos and CD-ROMs the colleges will send you, if you just ask. Sometimes you can find them right in the library of the counseling center, or in the public library."
- "And of course there is the Web. I would have done a lot more 'surfing.'"

Talk with Your Parents

You should have some conversations with your parents, too. This is the time, before college looms, to make sure you and your parents set up a basis of understanding.

You will want to know if your parents have saved enough for college and whether you need to help. You will want to know whether your parents want you to go to a particular school because of cost or because they think the education there is superior. They may also have a particular college in mind because they think it suits your strengths and you would be happy there.

These conversations can be very productive because your parents sometimes know your strengths and weaknesses better than you do. If it happens that there is a difference of opinion, perhaps the family could agree to visit a few colleges on a "drive through" basis over the course of next summer's vacation. Combine these visits with information from the colleges' Web sites and agree to keep talking about this important decision.

At some point you will need to talk with your parents frankly about finances.

- Have they been planning for the cost of your college education?
- How do they plan to deal with the cost of educating other siblings or stepsiblings?
- What can you do to help, not just in a financial way, but also in finding out information that may be helpful to your family, such as financing college costs and special outside scholarships?

In Chapter 7 we discuss the financial side of college—the costs and the types of loans, scholarships, and awards that may be available to you. When you have had a talk with your parents, with college students, and with your counselor and made some decisions about courses and activities you will be engaged in, you will have a good start toward college. Time now to go back and start enjoying your freshman year!

THE SOPHOMORE YEAR

The tenth grade is an ideal time to start exploring your interests and your dreams about your future and to begin to focus on a possible career or careers. Start the tenth-grade year with an interview with your guidance counselor. Ask about computer-based preference tests, values assessments, and career information. If the material is not on the computer, it may be available on paper. Taking some of these tests can be fun because you find out more about who you are and where you might be headed. You learn what your underlying talents and dominant personality traits are. You learn how you approach challenges and what situations bring out the best in you.

You might also want to stop at the local library and see what programs it has along these lines. Libraries and schools have access to large state databases where many interesting programs are stored. *Career Options* from Peterson's is one of them. Take some time to pore over the books and software you turn up. Get a feel for the careers that interest you; study the qualifications necessary to get started in them and the type of work that is involved. Try to get a feel for the work environment. You may know a little about these careers already, but now it's time to get a bit more serious.

Take Some Tests

During the sophomore year you should also be thinking about the college admission testing process itself. Although a few colleges do not require the standardized entrance tests, most do, so you should plan to take the PSAT or the Preliminary ACT (P-ACT+). Ask your counselor for advice and for the application forms for one of these tests. Neither of these tests goes to the colleges. Both have very explicit instruction books with sample questions, and they will acclimate you to the testing experience.

Beyond these tests lie the SAT I, offered by the College Board, and the ACT Assessment Test, offered by American College Testing, Inc. Most schools will accept either one. The SAT II Subject Tests assess your knowledge of particular subjects and are required by some selective colleges and universities. Some students in the tenth grade are in sufficiently advanced courses to take one or more SAT II Subject Tests. Ask your counselor for advice.

The P-ACT+

The P-ACT+ is offered by American College Testing, Inc. The "P" stands for Preliminary. This test helps students become familiar with the testing format—the way questions are put, how test sections appear, and how students can work out their answers to questions and fill in their answer sheets properly.

The PSAT

The Preliminary SAT/National Merit Scholarship Qualifying Test (PSAT/NMSQT) is given in late October as practice for the SAT I. It is a crucial test for good students because it serves as the qualifying test for the National Merit Scholarship Program. Even if you don't win a scholarship (few do), just being a semifinalist brings you recruitment letters from the best colleges and universities. Guidance offices have the registration forms for the tests, and when the results come back in the winter, your counselor can interpret the results for you. The pamphlet accompanying the test results is very helpful in interpreting your scores as well.

The Web

The sophomore year is the time to spend some hours on the Web in two different areas. First, you can find out a good deal about tests by going to

TALKING, TESTING, PLANNING

http://www.petersons.com and looking at the section on testing, and in particular "Taking the SAT's." Likewise, the College Board has a sector of its site, http://www.collegeboard.org, devoted to testing that is worth looking at. The two major test-preparation companies also have sites, and each will allow you to sample a few trial SAT questions. Look for the Princeton Review at http://www.review.com and Kaplan Test Preparation Company at http://www.kaplan.com.

A second line of inquiry will take you to the colleges and universities themselves. Just follow your curiosity and look for things that you are interested in at say, six schools: three colleges and three universities. Perhaps it is just athletic scores you want to know. At most places, those are posted every day. This investigation of colleges need not be a formal one. (That is described in Chapter 2.) The point is to get used to the Web as a tool for learning about schools.

Parents—Talk

During your sophomore year you should have a more extensive conversation with your parents than you had last year. Relate to them what your guidance counselor has said about your courses and your general college plans. Tell them what courses you plan to take and why and what tests you have lined up. You also need to be specific about who is going to pay for the cost of college and see what role you are expected to play. Perhaps it is time for you to think about a job after school or making some money next summer.

College Directories

In this electronic age one still needs books. You should begin to build up a small library about colleges and universities. Concentrate first on buying one of the major reference works, either *Peterson's Guide to Four-Year Colleges* or *The College Handbook,* published by the College Board. Both are comprehensive, informative, and relatively inexpensive. The Peterson's volume contains a useful index to majors that enables you to look up schools according to the major subject you are interested in studying.

THE JUNIOR YEAR: SETTING STRATEGY

The plot thickens in the junior year. Now is the time to get serious about college planning. If you did not do what is suggested above for the

THE INSIDER'S GUIDE TO COLLEGE ADMISSIONS

sophomore year, do it in the fall of your junior year. The most important exercise is to organize your testing program.

- Time your SAT I test so that it does not interfere with an SAT II Subject Test. Generally speaking, you should take the SAT I in January or March. Usually you would take the SAT II Subject Tests in June in subjects that coincide with the test requirements. For instance, you might take the writing test in June at the end of an intensive English course that stressed writing. Also, you might take the American history test if you have just completed the junior-year course in American history. If you are taking a chemistry-physics sequence over a two-year period, you would not attempt the chemistry test until the following year.

- Remember not to take the tests too many times in hopes of improving your scores. Your scores on the SAT I may rise 10 to 15 percent from the first to the second time you take them, but they will probably not rise after that. Follow this rule of thumb. *Take the SAT I or the ACT twice, and leave it at that. Take the SAT II Subject Tests once at the right time.* Remember, there are other things to do on Saturday mornings besides taking tests.

- Trial testing. If you are worried about the test-taking process, you should go to one of the Web sites just mentioned and take a trial test to see how you do. You should also read the pamphlet *Taking the SAT I,* which is available in your college guidance office, and take the trial test in the back. When you have checked and scored your test, there is a chart that will enable you to convert your raw score into an SAT I score. There is also a book called *10 Real SATs,* published by the College Board, with actual tests for you to sample.

A College Planning Calendar for Your Junior Year

October—Take the PSAT, and if you have not already done so, read the materials describing the content of the test. When you get your results, discuss them with your counselor, who has additional materials to help interpret your scores.

January—Take the SAT I, or if required by the schools you are interested in, the SAT II in subjects you have completed in the first semester of your junior year. For specific information on the eighteen tests covered by the SAT II, consult the pamphlet *Taking the SAT II: Subject Tests,* available in your guidance office. For the SAT I test, there is a similar, useful pamphlet, *Taking the SAT I: Reasoning Test.* It is also available in your guidance office.

TALKING, TESTING, PLANNING

February—Take the ACT if you think it will be a better indicator of your strengths than the SAT I or if any of your colleges or universities require it. A quick check of *Peterson's Guide to Four-Year Colleges* or *The College Handbook* will tell you if they do. If you take the ACT, ask for a pamphlet called *Preparing for the ACT Assessment* at your guidance office. Review the suggestions for the subject area tests and the sample questions.

March/April—Familiarize yourself with your school's guidance library, both printed and electronic. If there are gaps, check your public library. Using your fingers to go through one of the two directories, *Peterson's Guide to Four-Year Colleges* or the College Board's *Index to Majors,* locate the colleges and universities that offer majors you are interested in pursuing. Or use your fingers to look on the Web at http://www.petersons.com or http://www.collegeboard.org to conduct the same search. While you are on these Web sites, you will learn that Peterson's offers a college selection and application service called CollegeQuest that covers the whole range of decisions you will have to make. It is well worth learning more about the financial, counseling, and management dimensions of this program before moving on. The College Board offers a parallel program called College Explorer Plus that is also worth looking at carefully.

During this time period in your junior year, you should consider taking the ACT if you missed it in February.

April and March also present opportunities to make preliminary visits to colleges near your home. Perhaps you could go on your own or with a group of friends, just to get a sense of the campus, or drop in on a class, and pick up any literature that is available. Whenever possible, talk to students who are presently attending the school. At this point you should definitely write or e-mail the colleges and universities in which you are interested. Ask to be put on their mailing lists and for any information you may lack. Once you are on the mailing list, they will send you newsletters and applications when the time comes.

May—Take the Advanced Placement tests if you are enrolled in advanced courses and your teachers approve. The AP tests are expensive and often involve some preparation, but the payoff can be significant. Often, good scores on the APs will allow you to advance in a college's curriculum, avoiding entry-level prerequisites, and perhaps even to graduate early and save a year's tuition. AP tests, while not a formal part of the admissions criteria of most schools, are still carefully noted by admissions officers, who are properly impressed by students capable of advanced work. AP test taking is on the rise. In 1998 more than a million tests were taken by high school juniors and seniors around the world.

June—There are now eighteen different SAT II Subject Tests, and it is important to consult the College Board's test schedule (posted in your guidance office) so that you take the SAT II tests in subjects you will not be continuing in your senior year. Consult each of your teachers first for advice on whether or not you should take a particular exam and when to take them. If you do not take any SAT II tests in June, you may want to take the SAT again, but do so only if you feel you can better your first score significantly. June offers another ACT test date.

Summer Vacation—Plan to visit and have interviews at the colleges that interest you the most and are located too far from your home to be visited when classes are in session in the fall. (See Chapter 3 for how to make the most of your campus interview and visit.)

THE SENIOR YEAR—ACTIVE ENGAGEMENT

The last year of high school is the time when you need to do your best at everything, particularly in the academic department. You need to get good grades in school. Outside activities and leadership positions are important, but colleges will definitely want to see a strong record in the senior year, particularly if you have a less than stellar record in any previous year. This is the time to take that course in integral calculus or the fourth year of French even though you did well on the SAT II. It may also be time to take a leap into a new area and take a course in art history or economics, if your school offers one, or to take a course at the local college and double count the credit, both for high school and college.[1] If you need advice on course choice, ask the colleges you may be applying to, either by e-mail or in your interviews in the summer. Your college counselor will have an opinion worth hearing, too.

Recognizing that the senior year can and should be a growing and learning experience, you will want to extend yourself: leading your athletic team, heading up the social service organization of your school or church, or

---

[1] This arrangement is possible in some states, but you generally cannot "export" the course to an out-of-state school.

TALKING, TESTING, PLANNING

even thinking about an exchange program with a high school abroad. Thinking about your senior year before it happens will help you make the most of the possibilities it holds.

September/October. Make sure you have requested all the materials you need from the colleges you are applying to, including applications, viewbooks, course catalogs, athletic brochures, and financial aid applications. Use e-mail or the school's toll-free number, and procure what you need to apply.

During these months set up Friday–Saturday visits to the schools near you and have tours and interviews—and be sure to visit classes. Remember also that college representatives will be visiting your high school or your town, and you will want to make contact with them. If you are on the college's mailing list, you will be notified and invited to receptions, along with your parents. Even though you may know a school well and intend to apply, you should still attend these meetings. These encounters give you and your family a chance to ask questions that may come up as you become more familiar with the school.

Keep your college counselor informed of your travels and meetings and of any new developments, such as honors or awards that may come your way. He or she will also be interested in any words of encouragement from college coaches or admissions officers.

During these two months many state schools begin to accept applications. If they do, file early. Often, admissions are calculated on the day your application was received—along with other factors—in state schools with rolling admissions (see Chapter 3). The increased popularity of state schools has caused them to fill well before their published closing dates in January.

This is the time, too, to take the ACT as a senior.

November—If you are an applicant for financial aid, now is the time to pick up an application for the Financial Aid PROFILE in your guidance office. You can apply for this form in the same fashion as you do the SATs, or you can register over the Internet, where you will find it on the College Board's home page at http://www.collegeboard.org. Some of your schools may only ask for the Free Application for Federal Student Aid (FAFSA). Here, too, the application forms are available in guidance offices and public libraries, as well as on the Internet at http://www.fafsa.ed.gov.

November is also the month when most seniors take the SAT I for a second and final time. When the test is over, take a short break and then begin filling out your college applications. Do the easiest parts first. Plan to spend three or four days on each application and to have them all done by Christmas.

December—Most seniors will take their final set of SAT II Subject Tests early in this month. This should conclude the testing process. Once it is over, remember to distribute your teacher recommendations to those teachers who have agreed to help you. Your school report form, a portion of your application for the guidance counselor, should also be submitted to the guidance office. By now you should know that all of these forms have a short section to be completed by you and that you should provide your references with stamped envelopes. Finally, if you are on the ACT track, December has another test day.

January—Send off your final college applications by their due dates, usually no later than January 15. Take a breather, and then if you plan to submit musical tapes or art portfolios, do so by the end of the month. During this month your parents should complete the Financial Aid PROFILE and the FAFSA. It is extremely important that these forms go in on time and arrive by February 1. Tell your parents to estimate their income. They will have an opportunity to file their final tax data with the colleges once you are accepted.

Some students still have testing to complete in January and take either the SAT I or II at the end of the month.

February—Submit your portfolio, if you have one, or any special letters of recommendation that you have been able to drum up (more on this in Chapter 6). Consider writing a letter to the Dean of Admissions at the school you most want to attend, stating that you will come if accepted.

Colleges make their tentative evaluations of students in February, and there may be some feedback to your counselor—and there may not. Listen carefully to what your counselor has to say. Read between the lines. File other applications if the horizon darkens.

March—Nothing to do but wait! Try to avoid agonizing. Don't eat too much or too little. Keep your academic work up to its previous level. Enjoy your courses and activities. If you are placed on a Waiting List, this term will be important. Plan for graduation.

April—Selective colleges and universities notify applicants in early April. Some students may hear earlier from less competitive schools. If you have

TALKING, TESTING, PLANNING

applied to six schools as recommended and are admitted to three or four, declare victory. You still have choices to make, so make plans to return to the schools you liked best. Many will have April Visit Days and invite you to come to campus. If financial aid figures strongly in your ultimate decision, the opportunity to visit campus will give you a chance to visit the financial aid office and go over the figures. If your financial circumstances have changed, bring documentation and ask the financial aid office to reevaluate your aid package. Most offices will, in the light of new information.

May—Reply to the colleges that accepted you, and choose the one you think best fits you, not necessarily the one your parents or friends think you ought to attend. Do listen to their opinions, though. If you are placed on a Waiting List, you should accept an offer of admission from another school and then proceed with your Waiting List strategy. Suggestions on this are in Chapter 10.

TESTS, TESTS, TESTS

Because high school courses and grading standards vary so much from school to school, the SAT "provides a common standard against which students can be compared." There are two separate tests under the SAT umbrella, the SAT I test and the SAT II Subject Tests (eighteen different tests).

SAT I

This test has two parts, verbal and mathematical. Both measure reasoning ability. The verbal part has two 30-minute sections plus one 15-minute section. The types of questions, all detailed in the pamphlet described earlier, consist of analogies, sentence completions, and critical reading questions. There are seventy-eight questions in all. Vocabulary will be tested in the context of the reading passages, not in the much-dreaded antonyms of the earlier test. There are also fewer questions than on the test ten years ago, so students should have enough time to finish both portions.

The mathematics portion of the test has two 30-minute sections plus one 15-minute section. The types of questions are thirty-five standard multiple choice, fifteen 4-choice quantitative comparisons, and ten questions called "student produced," which means you have to calculate the answer and then choose from a list of choices presented. As with the verbal section, the emphasis on the interpretation of data and the application of data to mathematical questions has replaced an interest in specific formulas.

The mathematical section has been shortened in its present version. Students will have 75 minutes for sixty questions.

When to Take the Tests; Whether to Take a Test-Prep Course

Normally your guidance counselor will suggest a sensible schedule for taking both the SAT I and the SAT II tests. If not, you can use the one mentioned previously. Allow yourself two chances at the SAT I, once in the junior year and once in the fall of the senior year. The SAT II test schedule normally involves three to five tests, taken when the courses that prepare you for them are completed.

The subject of the SAT I in particular brings up the question of the various test-preparation courses that are offered to students. The marketing of these courses is very direct, and their Web sites bristle with statistics to support their case and show their success. Still, the lingering faith in individual resolve and study leads this author to be cautious about recommending the test-preparation courses for everyone. The rule of thumb is that for students who have an anxiety about tests and who score on the low side the first time around, the test-preparation courses will probably be of some value. Here are a few considerations to ponder before signing up for a test-preparation course.

- There are a host of test-taking techniques that you can learn yourself (i.e., how and when to guess).
- The SAT I test relies less on memory and more on analytical reasoning than previous tests, so cramming vocabulary and formulas won't help, but analyzing data in your classes will.
- The SAT tests have been *recentered* and the scoring system changed since your parents took the test twenty years ago. This means that the mean or average for the test has risen from the low 400s to 500 for all takers. Your score will be higher and more meaningful than in the past.
- Colleges keep elaborate records on performance according to SAT scores, but they use score ranges. If your scores are well within those of the accepted students in last year's class at a school and you have a strong transcript, you may not need a test-preparation course.
- In selecting students, most colleges consider the SAT I test in the broad context of other testing (SAT II and ACT) and in the context of your high school record. If your record is good and above the level that might be

- expected given your scores, the colleges will be impressed with your hard work and will be inclined to admit you. The reverse is also true. If you have high scores and a mediocre record, you will be in some difficulty in being admitted to selective schools. Simply put, the SAT I is part of a larger picture.
- There is also the phenomenon of score fluctuation from one test to another. The College Board tries to prevent this, but it is not humanly possible. Admissions officers know that the exact numbers you receive on one test are not sufficient for judgment. Normally, scores for the same individual fluctuate 30 points from test to test. If a test-preparation company guarantees a 60-point increase, one half that amount is normal fluctuation.

If you decide to take an SAT prep course, explore the offerings thoroughly on the Internet and take a course that teaches you skills of test taking, learning about analogies, and setting up equations, rather than merely focusing on "beating the system."

IMPROVING YOUR SCORES ON YOUR OWN

There is much that you can do without outside help to improve your scores.

Materials in Print

When you sign up for the SAT, ask your counselor for the pamphlet entitled *Taking the SAT I: Reasoning Test*. It contains a sample test with answers. You can time yourself, score yourself, and then convert your raw score into an SAT score on both the verbal and mathematical sections of the test. There are numerous test-taking tips in the margins of the pamphlet as well. Then you can move on to books like *Word Flash* and *Math Flash* from Peterson's. There are also other specialized books from Peterson's, such as *SAT Word Flash* and *Panic Plan for the SAT* (a two-week crash course), as well as parallel books helping you prepare for the ACT, such as *ACT Success, ACT Word Flash,* and *ACT Math Flash*. Another good book is *10 Real SATs*, published by the College Board.

Electronic Tools

A brief jump to the following Web sites will bring more information and assistance on taking tests successfully than you might have imagined.

http://www.collegeboard.org Here you can register for the SAT I and SAT II electronically, and you will find an array of buttons for question types, tips, use of calculators, and other test-preparation topics.

http://www.petersons.com In addition to a listing of all of Peterson's products, the site offers an opportunity to register for membership in CollegeQuest, Peterson's full-service college center. There you will find an SAT section that contains a page of useful test-taking tips for both the verbal and mathematical sections, as well as for the test overall. Another page has a chart of the software the company produces. SAT Success is a complete package of software that leads you through the SAT I test and allows you to score your results. In addition, Peterson's SAT preparation books listed on the previous page are also available as software.

http://www.kaplan.com The introduction to the Kaplan site invites the visitor to take a "test drive" of a typical SAT test and then have Kaplan send the respondent his or her scores and some suggestions for improvements, all free. This site also contains the locations, times, and costs of the famous Kaplan test-preparation courses for all types of tests, including the SAT. It also lists the software that students can use to study for the PSAT and SAT tests and another that focuses just on the ACT and SAT. Kaplan also offers software for self-study of the most frequently taken SAT II Subject Tests.

http://www.review.com This address reveals the Princeton Review's test-preparation site. Here you can buy software that helps you prepare for the PSAT, SAT I and SAT II, and ACT. There are full-length practice tests and correction mechanisms that enable you to identify your weaknesses and focus on them. Princeton Review publishes other software that guides you through your high school studies. One software package called the Math Library focuses on the 200 essential math topics and several hundred related problems that high school students should be able to solve by the time they take the SAT tests.

Evaluating Electronic Programs

Here are a few suggestions on how to get the best software program and extract the most from it:

1. Share the program with others to save on the cost side.
2. Make sure the program is designed in such a way that students will know when and why they got wrong answers.
3. Ideally the program should have sound and graphics that make the learning process visual and humorous at times.

4. Make sure there are accompanying materials such as workbooks, practice tests, and perhaps a manual that complement the program and provide the student with a written record of his or her progress.

Common Sense

Aside from your formal preparation for the test, which you may or may not like to do, remember that the SAT I is not unrelated to what you are studying in your mathematics, English, and other classes. Continuing to strive to do well academically will reap rewards on testing Saturdays. In addition, striving to do well in your classes will prepare you to score well on your SAT II Subject Tests. It may well turn out that those scores are higher than your SAT I testing, and that pattern will have a positive effect on your admission to selective schools. Remember, too, that some of the analytical skills and insights the test makers are looking for will come to you as a byproduct of growing and maturing. Relax if you can, and try not to make testing the center of your college application universe.

Also remember that intelligent scheduling of the tests will eliminate some of your anxiety. Synchronize the tests with your course work. Leave intervals so that if you are not satisfied with your results, you have time to do something about it.

Make sure you keep in touch with your guidance counselor regarding your test results. He or she can give you helpful advice about test preparation and how certain colleges might react to your scores. Listen to what he or she says. Try not to make the mistake of "applying over your head" and seeking admission to colleges where your scores place you at a distinct disadvantage. Being realistic about your scores in the fall will help you develop your top, middle, and bottom choices of college and help you ensure admission to several of them in the spring. Being realistic about your scores helps turn the college admission process from a game of chance into a game of choice.

SAT II Subject Tests

The SAT II Subject Tests measure your mastery of a particular subject, such as calculus, English, or American history. There are eighteen different tests, and normally a student would not be expected to present more than three Subject Tests for admission to a college or university. Still, some of those schools may have specific Subject Tests that they require for admission. Check Web sites and catalogs to be sure.

In planning for your SAT II Subject Tests remember to schedule the tests so that they coincide with the courses that cover their content. Your teachers will advise you. Students should not plan to repeat the Subject Tests as they might the SAT I test.

If you plan to take the Math Level IIC exam, for instance, do so soon after you've finished your class sequence in algebra, solid and coordinate geometry, trigonometry, and functions—and when you can do simple graphing on your calculator—not when you are halfway through your study of calculus!

Likewise, you should take the French Subject Test after you've covered all of French grammar, most standard French vocabulary, and the various styles and levels of written French. In other words, you should be able to read French quickly and understand the author's point of view, the feelings of the characters, and the mood and tone of the work. Moreover, you will need to schedule the listening portion of the test in November, for French is now one of the six languages that has a listening component. So you should not attempt to take the French Subject Test before you have completed two years of intensive study of the subject. Three years would be better. At the same time, deferring the French Subject Test until you have reached the Advanced Placement level is too long. By this time you would have gone beyond the study of spoken French and risk not doing well on the speaking portion of the Subject Test. Your memory of the proper grammatical forms may also have been clouded by the fact you have been reading, not speaking, French for over a year.

The pamphlet *Taking the SAT II: Subject Tests,* available in your guidance office, describes the material for each Subject Test and contains sample test questions and answers. The final decision as to when to take a given Subject Test rests with your teachers. They know which of your school's courses best prepares students for the test. They also know what outside preparation may be necessary for real success on a particular test. Some high school courses intentionally do not parallel the content of the Subject Test. The most prominent example is American history, where many teachers focus on analyzing documents, exploring themes, and developing hypotheses, rather than having students commit a lot of factual material to memory. Students in those kinds of courses will have to be prepared to do some extra work to brush up on the factual side of American history before tackling the test. Sometimes teachers will even run a few practice sessions to make sure their students are properly prepared for the test.

TALKING, TESTING, PLANNING

If you take a Subject Test at the proper point in your course of study and get a good score, you should not take the test again. If you want to try taking the test a second time, answer these few questions first:

- Are you completing another course in the same subject? If yes, take the test again. If you took the French Subject Test a year ago and scored a 600, for example, and now you are in French IV, French playwrights and poets, then you could take the test a second time and hope for better results. By contrast, if you are in Physiology I and are dissatisfied with your Biology Subject Test score of 600 a year ago, you are not going to do any better taking the test again. In fact, you might do worse.
- How will the Subject Test relate to your college major? If you plan to select your college major from the same area as the material covered by the test, and you believe you can improve your score by a second attempt, take the test a second time. In the case of a premed candidate, even though she is in physiology, she should take an intensive review course in biology and try to improve her score of 600.
- Did you get a strangely low score? If you have achieved a score of 700 on a Subject Test, rejoice and be satisfied. If you liked the subject and got a B or better in the course and got a 500 or less on the test, you probably should take the test again. Demanding schools will look askance at scores below 500, even if they are not in the area of your intended major.

If you are really worried about your test results and sequence, you can always call the admissions office of the colleges to which you are applying. Two calls will probably produce the same advice. Follow it and realize that there are points in the college admissions process in which you have to be satisfied that you have done the best you could.

ACT Assessment Test

If you are considering taking the ACT, get a copy of the pamphlet *Preparing for the ACT Assessment* from your guidance counselor, or you can register on line for the pamphlet to be mailed to you. The address is http://www.act.org. The pamphlet will be helpful because it gives a detailed description of sample questions accompanied by an explanation of the correct and incorrect answers. It also gives strategies and activities that are useful in preparing for the test.

The ACT itself is given five times a year, in October, December, February, April, and June. It is divided into four sections: English, Reading,

Mathematics, and Science Reasoning. It also has a career inventory section that is quite helpful. On its Web site, ACT lists a set of tips for each of its four sections. The site and the pamphlet also give the percentage of questions on a particular field, so that if you are weak in one area, you will know in advance what that will "cost" you in taking the test.

The English Test is a seventy-five question, 45-minute test that measures understanding of standard written English, (punctuation, grammar, and usage). It has five prose passages, with multiple-choice questions on each (forty questions). There is also a rhetorical section that assesses your ability to grasp strategy, organization, and style (thirty-five questions).

The Reading Test is a forty-question, 35-minute segment that assesses your comprehension. It expects students to derive meaning from several texts by asking them to show the implicit meaning of underlined portions of a passage. The reading test has four passages—in the arts and literature, natural sciences, social sciences, and prose fiction and humanities. There is a sub-score rendered for each of these passages.

The Mathematics Test has sixty questions and takes an hour. Multiple-choice questions "require you to use reasoning skills to solve practical problems." Knowledge of basic formulas and computational skills are assumed; students can use calculators (rules explained on the Web site). The math test yields four sub-scores: overall, pre-algebra, intermediate algebra/coordinate geometry, and plane geometry/trigonometry.

The Science Reasoning Test has forty questions and takes 35 minutes. It measures your ability to analyze, interpret, evaluate, and reason with scientific data and concepts. It also looks at problem-solving skills. Graphs, charts, tables, and research summaries are used to present information, and students are expected to recognize conflicting hypotheses and viewpoints and to examine them critically. No calculators are permitted.

REGISTRATION FOR SAT AND ACT

This is not a difficult task. Each organization puts out a pamphlet with your registration form and an envelope to enclose it in. The pamphlets, called *The SAT Program* by the College Board and *The ACT Assessment* by ACT, also contains the codes for the various colleges and universities to which you will want the results sent, the fee structure, and the codes for your intended college major. Both have some form of a student descriptive questionnaire, which you should complete the first time you take a test. This enables the testing agencies to understand the different backgrounds and goals of the

TALKING, TESTING, PLANNING

students taking the tests. Sometimes colleges and universities will purchase this information from the testing service and write to you, so filling out the form could open a window.

There are any number of special circumstances that surround college entrance tests: religious beliefs, inability to afford the fees, crowded test centers, and individual student disabilities. *The SAT Program* covers all of these situations. Options for students with disabilities follow.

> **Test Options for Students with Disabilities**
> Students with a documented disability are permitted to take an SAT I or SAT II test with accommodations appropriate to that disability. Those students need to procure a copy of *SAT Services for Students with Disabilities* by writing to P.O. Box 6226, Princeton, New Jersey 08541-6226, or by asking their counselor to call for one. In addition to filing the regular application for a particular test, students with disabilities are asked to file a supplementary form that comes with the pamphlet. They also need to ask their school counselor to write on their behalf and request the particular accommodations they need. Those might include a wheelchair-accessible desk, photo-enlarged test book, the opportunity to take necessary medication, a large-block answer sheet, or audio equipment so that they can hear oral instructions.

DEALING WITH TEST ANXIETY

With registration details out of the way and your test-preparation program settled, you can now turn your attention to the matter of preparing yourself for the actual test situation. Ask yourself three questions:

1. How do I really feel about taking tests? Am I generally relaxed and efficient and usually score well? If the answer is yes, you can skip this section.
2. Am I nervous in a test situation, so nervous that I waste time with instructions, get confused by questions, or fixate on getting the answer to every one, unable to move on until I do?
3. What special skills will I need to work on in order to improve my test performance?

THE INSIDER'S GUIDE TO COLLEGE ADMISSIONS

Recently, a group of students spoke candidly with Peterson's about their first reactions to the college admission tests:

- "Well, I feel fine about tests until I am in one, and I encounter the first question I can't answer. Then I just tighten up, and at the same time have trouble focusing on the question that is blocking me. I worry that I'll never get anywhere in life."
- "When it comes to tests, I am the kind of person who gets hypnotized by the clock. I watch the minutes tick away and become more and more tense until I can't work anymore. Consequently I never finish tests on time, and always leave them with a sense of deep frustration."
- "It's funny; I have worked hard and performed pretty well in my high school classes, and on the tests we have every week in class. However, I have never been able to transfer that success over to the standardized tests. I just wish I didn't have to be judged by how well I do on tests, and that people would just accept me for who I am."
- "In test situations I just can't focus on the test! I keep thinking of how much fun I am going to have next Saturday afternoon as the center on the girls' basketball team, playing in the state championships in Springfield."

These comments all relate to various forms of test anxiety, and it is important to deal with their sources:

1. Concerns about self-image (the first example)
2. Concerns about how others will treat you if you do poorly (third example)
3. Worry about future security (first example)
4. Concern about ability to focus (fourth example), or focus on the wrong task (second example)

If you fall into one or more of these groups, try to take up your situation with your guidance counselor. He or she may suggest that you write down the features of your anxiety and build up a behavior modification scheme.

If you are worried about your *future security,* remember your non-college-educated grandmother who said she never did well on tests but somehow rose through the ranks of the department store where she worked and retired as head buyer, with a nice pension.

If you clutch *(inability to focus)* when you go into a test, remember how you overcame other challenges in your life, like your first dive into the local

TALKING, TESTING, PLANNING

swimming pool. You talked to yourself, right? Do this again, and persuade yourself to look at the questions in a relaxed and thoughtful manner.

If the clock intimidates you *(focusing on the wrong thing),* then practice with your software or test-preparation book, using a kitchen timer. When the timer rings, reset it and move on to the next question no matter what. You will get used to thinking more efficiently and quickly.

"Difficult questions make me *panic"* (first response). If this is the case, then the appropriate strategy would be to skip the difficult questions. On the SAT tests, we know that some of the responses are more difficult than others, and we also know that each response counts the same. Think of the fact that if you correctly skip the few difficult questions on the test and get all the others right, you are going to do very well. As added inducement, remember that a wrong answer counts for a quarter-point deduction from the number of right answers, so there is an actual penalty for panicking.

If you have difficulty with a question and pass it by, you can always look at it again if there is time. Faced with four multiple-choice responses to a question you understand, eliminate the one or two obvious wrong answers, then select the response that best answers the question. If you are still puzzled, do not respond to the question at all. Remember not to read too much into a question. Take the test questions at face value. The test makers are not out to trick you, believe it or not.

A Group Approach to Test Anxiety

Sometimes counseling centers will offer group sessions devoted to alleviating test anxiety. The first step requires that all members of the group share their test-taking experiences, including the counselor, and these experiences are condensed and put in the left-hand column on a chalkboard. The group then brainstorms about ways in which each anxiety might be reduced or eliminated. These responses are recorded in a middle column on the board beside the anxiety they are meant to cure.

Next, the group conducts a rehearsal of the test situation itself. This exercise enables students to identify how they react in a test situation. The counselor takes notes on how each student acts as he or she is taking the test. For example, he might write in his notebook: "Dave appeared stone-faced and stared into the middle distance a lot." Or, "Joan bit her nails and her pencil unmercifully." Or, "Tom kept crossing and uncrossing his legs and then scrunched up in the chair, and he kept looking at the clock." When the exercise is over, the counselor reads his comments as he writes them in the third column on the board. The group discusses the chart they have produced on the board and makes recommendations about the behavior of each member. The counselor enters that recommendation in the fourth and final column on the board.

For Dave, the conclusion might be, "Dave should relax and not lift his head and be distracted from his paper. He should focus on head and neck relaxation techniques." For Joan, "She should keep her hands as still as possible and chew gum so that she does not poison herself chewing her pencils." For Tom, the comment is, "He should sit in a more relaxed and upright position and look at the clock only when he has come to the end of a section."

Simple Relaxation Exercises

Once students have identified their particular counterproductive behavior in an exam situation, they will want to think seriously about going through a brief relaxation exercise before taking the SAT or ACT or any other important test for that matter. John Emery of the Human Resources Institute in California has suggested the following muscle-relaxing exercises for people approaching anxious moments in their lives:

1. Settle back in your chair and relax. Take a few deep breaths and begin to let yourself go.
2. Now extend both arms straight out and clench your fists more and more tightly as you count slowly to five. Then relax and let your arms drop. Concentrate on the differences you perceive between the tension phase and the relaxation phase.
3. Focus on your forearms. Extend your arms as above, and push out on a slow five count as before. Relax again. Do the same for your biceps, flexing your arms toward your body and then relaxing after 5 seconds.
4. Concentrate on your forehead. Wrinkle your brow hard on a five count. Relax.
5. Close your eyes tightly as you count to five. Then relax slowly.
6. Do the same for your neck and shoulders, sitting up rigidly, then relaxing. For each exercise, conclude by contemplating the difference between the tense feeling and the relaxed feeling that follows it.
7. Do the same for your stomach muscles. Then let them relax and try to spread this relaxation throughout your entire body.
8. Now move to your thighs. Straighten out your legs and turn your toes up toward your face on a five count and relax.

9. Relax your calf muscles in a similar way, turning your toes away and down as hard as you can as you count to five. Then relax again. Repeat the exercise, turning your toes up this time.
10. Finally, in a relaxed position, close your eyes and review your exercises, trying to spread that relaxed feeling outward from each particular muscle group throughout your whole body.[2]

Rewarding Yourself For "Good Behavior"

Test anxiety can also be handled by inventing a simple game called "Rewarding Yourself for Good Behavior."

- Dave, who blanks out and stares into the middle distance during tests, might promise himself a solid 10-minute break after taking a mock test, if and only if, he does not look up and blank out for 10 minutes while taking the practice test.
- Joan might reward herself by having something decent to eat, if and only if, she is able to abstain from chewing her pencil while taking a practice test.
- Tom could decide to limit his clock watching to two time checks per test session and reinforce this behavior by promising to buy himself a designer shirt he recently admired in a shop downtown, if and only if, he succeeds in controlling his behavior on the practice test.

Whatever strategy you use, the important idea to bear in mind is rewarding good behavior and punishing the undesirable behavior. Make sure the reward and punishment system is reasonable for you. The more it is, the better it will work to reduce your anxiety.

THE REAL THING: TIPS FOR TAKING THE TESTS

Now it is time to go to your test center on a Saturday morning. Here are some reminders:

- Take your ticket with you. Make sure you have made any changes you need to in the correction spaces on the ticket.

---

[2]John R. Emery, Systematic Desensitization: Reducing Test Anxiety. In *Behavioral Counseling/ Case and Techniques,* pp. 270–272, eds. John D. Krumholtz and Carl E. Thoresen. New York: Holt, Rinehart, and Winston, 1969.

- Take two or three sharpened number 2 pencils unless you are going to take the test electronically. Make sure they all have adequate erasers.
- Take at least one photo identification card, such as driver's license or a student identification card, issued to you by your school. If you do not have either of these documents or a passport, ask your guidance counselor for advice. Your counselor may be proctoring the examination, in which case you need not worry.
- Plan to arrive early—at least 15 minutes before the scheduled time. If you are unfamiliar with the test center, be there 30 minutes before the test. You may find that only one door to the test center is open on a Saturday morning, or you may have to walk through an unfamiliar neighborhood to reach the test center. Allow time for such contingencies. Call in advance and ask for directions if you need to. Ask for the name of the person to report to if you have a disability or are walking into the test without a prior registration.

At the Test Center

Once you arrive at the test center and pass through the registration line, you will be assigned to a particular test room. If you are taking the SAT I or II, you have already read their respective instruction pamphlets and you know what to expect. If you are taking the ACT, you know that there are four sections—two of 35 minutes each, one of 45 minutes, and one of 60 minutes. As with the SAT I and II, there is at least a half hour of oral instructions involved with the test, so the overall experience will take at least 3½ hours, probably 4.

As the test instructions are being read, or earlier if you have time, review your muscle-relaxing exercises. Then go over in your mind the detrimental behaviors that you are tying to limit (stop). Review your reward system. Accentuate the positive. Think of that delicious sundae or colorful shirt or the party invitation you told yourself you would accept only if you can find the courage to skip over the hard questions and finish each section of the test.

Taking the Test

When it is time to start the test, work slowly and methodically. Every ten questions, check to see that you are blacking the answer space that corresponds to the number of the question you are working on. Some

TALKING, TESTING, PLANNING

> **Walk-in or Standby Registration**
>
> Walk-in or standby registration for the SAT I or II tests is a last resort, to be used only when you forget to register in advance. (The ACT does not permit walk-in or standby registration). Students in this predicament should follow these steps:
>
> 1. Get a copy of *The SAT Program* from your school's counseling office. Fill out the registration before going to the test center.
> 2. Write a check for the test fees that you will incur, which are listed on the back page of the *Program* booklet. The check should be made out to the Admissions Testing Program. Most centers will not accept cash.
> 3. Contact the test center in advance. Talk to the person in charge of the test administration and leave your name in the event that he or she has only so many extra tests to distribute. Ask the person in charge about any special directions for standby candidates, such as arriving early or meeting at a particular location within the center.
> 4. Take photo identification with you to the test center.
> 5. Arrive at least 45 minutes early. Standby registration is not guaranteed, and often walk-ins are served on a first-come, first-served basis.

questions will have more response possibilities than others. Do not let that bother you. Blacken each space thoroughly, and avoid fidgeting with the pencil on the test sheet. Extraneous marks might be picked up by the computer. If you need to change an answer, erase thoroughly—otherwise, the computer will record two answers for the question, and you don't want that.

Use the test booklet for any scratch work you want to do. Feel free to underline passages and phrases or to circle words. Scratch work should not be confined to the mathematical part of the SAT I. You may want to underline the main idea of a passage as you read through it or put a question mark beside a section that puzzles you. If you see a group of words that captures the author's point of view, underline them. If you want to jot down a word for the tone of a piece of prose, do so.

Answering the Questions

Remember that on the SAT I you neither gain nor lose points for questions that you do not answer. At the same time, if your answer is wrong, one quarter point is subtracted from the number of right answers. Being smart about what you do not answer is important. If you fail to answer 20 percent of the questions on the SAT I and give correct answers to the remaining 80 percent, then you will score 700 on the test. That is pretty good. On the ACT, by the way, wrong answers do not count.

If you have to guess at an answer, at least be able to split off the two responses that are clearly wrong. They could be extreme statements that are opposed to each other. Then look at your choice and pick the one that seems the most reasonable. Look at the first and last sentences in the paragraph to be sure you have the main idea correctly in mind. Remember that the questions usually follow the order of the selection, and question one will probably be answerable by looking at paragraph one, and so on.

When grappling with sentence completions, make sure you understand what the sentence says and what the missing word has to say for the whole sentence to make sense. If you don't know what a word means, look at the prefix or suffix and see if that will help. Look at the context of the sentence, and make sure to understand what part of speech the word is playing. If it is an adjective or adverb, can you guess from the meaning of the subject and the verb? If it is a noun subject that you don't know, what has "happened" to that noun in the predicate?

When the test is finally over, make sure that there are no extraneous marks on your answer sheet. Double check to be sure that the answer sheet has the same number as your test booklet. If it does not, call the proctor. Then collect your pencils, and you are off, hopefully to enjoy that sundae, that shirt, that party, or perhaps all three.

INTERPRETING YOUR SCORES

SAT I

In three to five weeks you will receive your results on the SAT I on your Student Score Report. Now you, your parents, and your college counselor will want to interpret the results on the report and perhaps revise your college choices somewhat. By looking at the report carefully, you will be able to decide whether you need to retake the test, take a test-preparation

TALKING, TESTING, PLANNING

program and then retake the test, or be satisfied with what you have achieved and move on to other things.

Notice first that your verbal score is broken down into percentiles for reading and vocabulary and that these raw scores are shown as percentiles of college-bound students. Let's assume that your overall verbal score was 640. That is quite good. Look at your reading score; it is 75 and puts you into the 83rd percentile among college-bound students. That means that only 17 percent of the students did better than you.

The next step is to compare these numbers with those of the colleges in which you are interested. You note that at State College, the average verbal score was 550 and the reading percentile was 65. You know that you are in good shape for admission there.

Next, look at your vocabulary score. It places you in the 70th percentile of college-bound seniors, so you can relax a bit. Those lists of words you laboriously compiled in the back of your English notebook have paid off. Finally, you look in the upper right-hand corner and see that your 640 only places you in the 75th percentile of college-bound students in your state, and you desire to attend a selective school there. That news is a bit sobering but not bad by any means.

Your frank appraisal of these numbers suggests that you will probably gain by taking the SAT a second time, especially if you aspire to a selective school and there are others from your high school applying there, too. A little vocabulary study will help over the course of the next few weeks.

Now your math score. It is 600. It is good, but by no means great. This score places you in the 75th percentile of your national high school class, but you remember that at one of the competitive colleges you are considering, the mean math score is 620. Then you notice that within your state your 600 math score places you in the middle of the college-bound high school seniors—50th percentile. This means that you need to brush up on your mathematics skills in a serious way and to take the SAT I again. Your choices are to consult your math teacher for advice, procure a copy of *10 Real SATs* from the College Board bookstore, buy Peterson's *Panic Plan for the SAT,* or go to their Web site and look at their software offerings for the mathematics side of the SAT. When you embark on your own little course of math review, accompanied by a few vocabulary words, you will undoubtedly improve your scores on the verbal and math the second time around. According to the College Board, 65 percent of second-time test takers do.

SAT II Subject Tests

Let's assume you have taken three Subject Tests at various times, and you have your score reports before you. The report gives the results of your three tests: Writing, Mathematics Level I, and American History and Social Science. You can interpret these results just as you did those of the SAT I. The results of the Writing Test are important because that test contained a 20-minute writing sample in addition to the multiple-choice sections. There are sub-scores for both, ranging from 20 to 80. The raw score in writing expresses your ability to express yourself clearly and shows how you compare to the nation's college-bound students. The multiple-choice sub-score will do the same for your ability to recognize faults in usage and structure.

Colleges do focus on the writing score results, so if the score does not meet your expectations, consult with your English teacher and consider taking the test a second time. Normally a little practice on writing short, topical essays will improve the results here.

Say your score for Mathematics Level I is 610—not too good. In the columns to the right of the score, you see that among the college-bound students you are in the 75th percentile, but the mean score on this test for your top colleges is 650. You may have made honors grades in math for the past three years, but you have not done as well as the competition at three of your top schools. At this point seek a conference with your teacher for advice. If you are not going to major in math in college and yet have gone on to calculus and are doing well, then perhaps you can let this test result stand. Perhaps your teacher will advise you to take the Mathematics Level IIC (with calculator). Your teacher will know that although the Math Level IIC is a harder test, the standard deviation is also higher. The mean score nationally on that test is often 100 or more points higher than that of the Math I. Perhaps your teacher will say not to bother to retake either test and offer to write you a college recommendation because you are doing so well in calculus. After seeing your teacher, inform your counselor of your plans. He or she may add to this complicated decision the fact that under College Board rules you can opt to withhold certain scores. (See box on page 97).

Fortunately your American History and Social Science test score of 700 is another matter entirely. It places you in the 85th percentile of the college-bound group taking the test—very good by national standards and by the standards of all of the colleges to which you plan to apply. As you do not plan to major in American history in college, this score will not help you in the admissions process all that much, but it still looks and is good! It also gives you an indication of where some of your abilities lie and suggests that once in college, you should consider taking some history courses as part of your program.

Subject Tests often tell you where your competence lies. You will probably begin as an economics major. You put that on your applications, but you may end as a history or political science major and move toward law and politics rather than business. Who knows?

The ACT

When receiving your ACT results, you will be confronted with a number of different scores aside from your final score. The selective colleges will look carefully at your sub-scores on the ACT. First, the composite score on the ACT runs from 1 to 36. Each of the four subtests is scored on a 1 to 36 scale as well. A score of 18 will be the mean score for the nation. There are also seven sub-scores across the four different subtests. These are scored on a 1 to 18 basis, with a mean score of 9 for the national sample. On the official test report form, you will find the percentages of students who received the same or lower scores than you, both in your home state and the nation at large.

The Score Choice Option

Score Choice is an optional service of the Educational Testing Service. It allows you to request that the Admissions Testing Program hold back your SAT II Subject Test scores until you have had a chance to review them. Once you see how well you did, you can then decide to release a given score into your official record, which is then sent on to the colleges, or you can hold the score back. Exercising this option gives you the opportunity to take the Subject Tests in the early stages of high school and not be penalized by a low score before you have even figured out what colleges you are going to apply to. If you receive a low score, you can then take a more advanced course later on in high school and probably improve your scores considerably. Note that once you have released a score, it cannot be withdrawn or only sent to certain colleges and not others.

Using these scores and percentages, you will be able to ascertain how well you are developing your academic skills and performing in major content areas. By consulting with your guidance counselor and teachers, you can work on the techniques and the material for improvement on the ACT. The ACT is a good predictor of college performance because it tests mastery of content as well as mastery of skills. High scores on skills may suggest certain careers; high scores on content can suggest success in certain courses in college. The predictive validity of the ACT on a recent test was impressive: 78 percent of the students whose scores placed them in the top 20 percent of their class in high school were in fact making A's and B's in their first term in college. As with the SAT I and II, colleges and universities that use the ACT will indicate their mean entering scores on their school profiles.

Once you have analyzed your success on the SAT I and II or the ACT, you are ready to go on to the next step in the testing process: congratulating yourself on your high scores, reviewing your weak areas, and making plans to patch those leaks and retake the tests at the next appropriate time.

FIVE

The Application Makes All the Difference

The application is a golden opportunity that some kids overlook.
William T. Conley, Dean of Admissions, Case Western Reserve University

College candidates today have ample opportunities to talk with college representatives, have tours and interviews, and correspond with college students and faculty via e-mail, but they may be lulled into thinking that their formal written application is not as important as their other communications with a school. Nothing could be further from the truth. The college application process, even though it has been enhanced and accelerated by the computer, is still a *written process*. The most ebullient student is still reduced to a manila folder full of documents that are pored over by a committee—whether the student likes it or not.

So, what do you do about this? Look upon your college application as an opportunity to present yourself to the college, to market yourself, to put all your good points forward, and let the others fall by the wayside. Look upon your college application as an opportunity to control the conversation with the colleges to which you are applying.

The comments that follow will give you some idea of the importance colleges place on students' candid and vigorous presentation of themselves in their applications. These comments are recorded on a rating sheet that compresses all the student's information, recommendations, and judgments of previous readers on one sheet. These particular remarks are the final judgments of the admissions officers at a fine small college in New England.

THE INSIDER'S GUIDE TO COLLEGE ADMISSIONS

- "Nope. Despite A's in summer courses at the Wharton School, and nifty scores, the raves aren't uniform. The *person* is missing in the essay and in the extracurricular activities (Star Wars Games and Model UN). May be brilliant and precocious, but he is also narrow and limited in his outlook on life."
- "Wait List maybe. Proctor (student leader in dormitory), math team, varsity water polo, and New England champion swimmer. Termed "diligent, shy, responsible" by school, less than enthusiastic adjectives. Essays show ambition and drive, but lack the depth or perspective we usually see. A caring kid who takes his job as a proctor seriously. At least he is directed toward others and community minded, even if the essay is flat and non-reflective. A good person. Maybe."
- "Admit this kid! Art, hockey, lacrosse, guitar; a favorite of the counselor who likes her warmth, integrity, and creativity. Perceptive essays show she is a strong person who would make maximum use of the opportunities here. Still growing personally and academically, but impressive application all the same."

These perceptive admissions officers are not only looking for candidates who are academically talented and have other strong attributes, they are seeking applicants who can present themselves convincingly in their applications as potentially strong contributors to the college community.

HOW THE COMPETITIVE PROCESS WORKS

Your first task before beginning your application is to review your academic and extracurricular interests, your thoughts about possible careers, and your personal values. Go back to Chapter 1 and consult your inventories. Think about how your academic and extracurricular interests can be related to your career aspirations and to your personal qualities. How you see yourself as a person, and how you see a particular college's environment as eliciting your personal strengths will help you to formulate your application. Some of the connections you see may be subtle or even tenuous, so don't overdo it. Just keep in mind your strengths and your personality, and where possible, relate both of them to the school to which you are applying. This is called *making the match* between yourself and your school.

If you are applying to some of the selective (competitive) colleges and universities, you know from the beginning that you will be competing with other students with similar—or even better—credentials. Moreover, you will

THE APPLICATION MAKES ALL THE DIFFERENCE

not be competing against the whole applicant pool, you will be competing within a particular group. When you make the *match* you place yourself in a particular group, then you have to *develop your edge* that enables you to be viewed as better than the other students in your particular admissions groups.

Neither of these two tasks is easy, yet the concepts of *match* and *edge* will help you enormously as you shape your application. Let's say, for instance, that you have a strong academic record: developing the match might consist of mentioning books you have read in your field and courses you enjoyed most and why. Developing the edge might consist of ensuring that you have a strong recommendation from one of your teachers, reminding the readers of your application that you won a history prize, expect to be valedictorian, or did a special research project that won honorable mention at the State Science Fair.

The identification of admission categories was first described by Richard Moll, former Director of Admission at the University of California, Santa Cruz, and now a widely respected consultant to colleges and universities. These categories accurately describe how many admissions officers think about candidates. You may call it pigeon holing, but remember the task of the admissions committee is to put together a class of students each year that is as talented and diverse as they can make it. Therefore they think in broad categories of applicants: scholars, people with special talents, students who have family connections to the institution, special groups who bring diversity to the campus, and "all-arounders" who fill in between the others and balance the class.

Although this theory of admissions categories is more visible in the admissions decisions of selective schools than in the less selective ones, it is very useful for a general understanding of the college admissions process as a whole. The fact is all colleges have their categories; all have groups that they are particularly interested in. The state universities, for instance, have in-state students, out-of-state students, multicultural students, athletes, and scholars. Figuring out what group you are in will help you shape your applications to colleges and universities.

1. Scholar Category

Since the business of higher education is scholarship and research, it logically follows that colleges and universities place a premium on scholarship in selecting students. One indication of the importance of academic strength to colleges is the recent expansion of merit scholarship programs across the country and the more subtle increases in financial aid packages awarded to strong students in the applicant pool. Today well over 60 percent of America's colleges and universities seek to attract talented students by offering them financial inducements.

The scholar category describes different types of excellence. Professors want able, creative, and in some cases, unorthodox minds in their classrooms, so they tell admission directors to deliver scholars. Hypothetically these students have SAT I and II scores averaging over 700 or ACT results of 30 or higher, or they have more modest scores but have three Advanced Placement tests with a score of 5 on each.

If you know one of these candidates, you may not find them very lovable. They may, in fact, be prickly people who seem to know all there is to know about computers or Indians or Shakespeare or cytology. Yet they are the kind of students who will animate college classrooms and labs. They will ask the tough questions of professors. They will spend long hours in the library or laboratory or on the Internet researching a minor point, and they will be elected to Phi Beta Kappa and probably win a traveling fellowship after graduation. They may well go on to a Ph.D. They are the scholars. They will be admitted.

In addition, scholars may not have contributed as much to activities outside their narrow field of interest as other candidates are expected to do. They probably will not root vigorously for the football team or the field hockey team. Their major contribution will be to the intellectual energy of their college or university.

If you feel that you fall into this category of highly able candidates, you should not shrink from identifying yourself as a scholar applicant—in the topic you choose for your essay, in making sure all your prizes and awards are listed, in furnishing examples of your original work, or in the books or ideas that you reference in your application. You want to make sure you are recognized for the scholar that you are.

2. Special Talent Category

Every college and university needs lots of students with special skills. Where would the radio station be without an experienced general manager, the soccer team without a goalie, the football team without depth in its line—three tight ends, eight guards, and a couple of good centers—and the Glee Club without the proper mix of tenors, sopranos, altos, and basses? The

THE APPLICATION MAKES ALL THE DIFFERENCE

list is a long one, happily for you. The admissions office of every college must ensure that all the varied activities of undergraduate life will have students able to sustain them. The smaller the college, the more important this special talent category is apt to be. If Coburn College cannot find three women divers to admit in each freshman class and thereby ensure that the swimming team has at least one good new diver every year, then the whole women's diving program will be threatened and the league championship (which Coburn has won for the last three years) jeopardized. It is not insignificant that the league championship is also reported annually in *Sports Illustrated*.

So if you have a special talent, make sure your counselor knows about it. If you are an athlete, sit down with your coach and make sure he or she knows about your interest in particular schools. Ask "Where can I play?" and listen to what he or she says. When you visit a school, find a way to mention your talent in your interview and visit with coaches, if possible.

A few years ago the author asked the Director of Admission at a small selective college, "What slots have you got to fill this year?" Surprisingly, the director replied directly: "We just have to find a hockey goalie, since our backup goalie has decided to spend his junior year in France. We also need an oboist for our orchestra. Have you got either?"

Applicants with special talents need to realize that there still will be a number of competitors for the particular slot you seek. "Having a special talent is no guarantee," says a first-year student at Princeton and goalie for the women's lacrosse team. "You can have top test scores and a very good high school record, and be in the top tenth of your class, and still not be a shoo in." The college that seeks the oboist may have among its 4,500 applications only three who play that instrument, and all three may play it well. Still, if you think you are a good player, you should shape your application accordingly. Mention your musical awards and experience. Prepare an audiotape, and perhaps a videotape, and send it to the director of the college's orchestra. When you have some positive response from the orchestra director, ask for his or her help in gaining admission.

Similarly, athletes should prepare athletic data sheets, which are easily done on the computer. The times and distances can be updated regularly, and the data sent by e-mail to college coaches. Normally coaches will make their own videotapes, but it does not hurt to ask. Coaches will also be frank about their rankings and what those rankings mean in the admissions process. Sometimes they will even know minimum test and GPA scores that athletes have to obtain. These scores and grade point averages will usually be lower than those in the profile published in *Peterson's Guide to Four-Year Colleges*. If a college is looking for an oboist and a good one applies, the admissions committee will tend to deemphasize a C in mathematics or a 550 score on the SAT II Biology Subject Test. The basketball player who practices 3 hours a day and on weekends is not expected to have quite as high an academic average as other candidates, even though some of them do.

Even though a candidate has a special talent, he or she may not want to *package* his or her candidacy in the same way for all the colleges. Consult your counselor about this strategy. There are two reasons to approach different colleges differently: (1) The competition may be too intense at some schools, and representing yourself as an outstanding member of a particular group may still not be enough to survive the competition. However, if you show your talent, but also express broad interest in the curriculum and other extracurricular activities, then you might be a stronger candidate at that school. (2) You may want to choose the "regular all-round" admission path at a particular school so that you will be able to pursue interests other than your special talent. Some talented high school athletes and musicians and artists want to try new things in college. The basketball player may want to try his hand at sports writing or the oboist at mountain climbing and geology. Take the time to consider what is best for you.

3. Family Category: Legacy or Leverage

An applicant who has family members who are alumni of the school or who has parents or relatives who are in a position to help the school qualifies for this category. Since the alumni of private colleges and universities provide essential financial support, admissions offices are eager to respond to candidates who are the children of alumni. They cannot always admit them, but they do try to treat them in a fair and friendly manner. When a candidate has an uncle, aunt, or grandparent who may have attended the college or university, his or her legacy status is considerably reduced. It is parents who count in the admissions process. Similarly, if a candidate has a sibling or a cousin that attended the school, admissions committees place a slight, positive, weight on that folder. However, if your parents went to the school, your advantage could easily be 2:1 for admission over a person with similar credentials.

Occasionally, the family category can be interpreted to mean families who could help the college or university in some way, usually financial.

THE APPLICATION MAKES ALL THE DIFFERENCE

These cases are sometimes called "Development" cases, because the interest in those candidates comes from the fund-raising office. So, yes, the sons and daughters of the rich and famous sometimes have an edge. And so do the children of influential politicians, whether they are applying to a private college or a public university. Outside funding is important, and Development Officers keep track of such things.

Most applications have questions that will help you establish your family connections to the college or university. They ask where your parents and other family members went to college and usually give space for you to state "other" relationships with the college that your family might have. If one of your parents is a prominent jurist, politician, or businessperson, chances are the college or university will pick up on that and give you "credit" for your good fortune.

Nonetheless, **take care not to rely on your legacy.** Be sure to do the best you can in your classes, on standardized tests, and in the areas where you may have special talent. Make sure your application is as strong as it can be and establishes your match and your edge in one of the other categories described here. As much as possible, you want to gain admission in your own right and not rely on your parents. At some selective schools having a distant connection to the college or university simply will not help. At Wellesley a great-aunt who attended will not make much difference, nor will the fact that your grandfather went to the University of Michigan help you much there. Those schools are just too popular and competitive. On the other hand having a parent who attended one of the Ivy League universities or selective small colleges does help. A 40 percent acceptance rate for legacies at those schools is not uncommon. The normal acceptance rate can run as low as 15 to 20 percent.

In many admissions offices each category is looked at separately after a general review. Your goal should be to gain admission on your own terms, as say a strong student with a special talent as a hockey goalie, who just happens to be the son of the hockey captain of 1981. If your luck holds, you will be admitted on the first round of discussion; if it doesn't, then you hope to gain admission when the alumni "kids" are discussed.

4. Special Groups

From the 1960s until the late 1990s, colleges and universities in the United States responded actively to the social and economic disadvantages of many groups of Americans by admitting qualified candidates from those groups and developing programs to enhance the diversity of their applicant pools. During the same period, colleges and universities responded to the globalization of our economy and communications networks and began to recruit students from around the world. Colleges and universities often recruit students from areas that are of particular interest to them. Sometimes those areas are near the school itself; sometimes they are far away from the home campus. At one prestigious urban school in the East, the admissions office strives to find a small contingent of students from remote rural areas; they call this group their "country kids." When all is said and done, a college may be looking for students from a number of different groups.

Some of the groups that colleges and universities seek are often defined in racial terms: African Americans, Asian Americans, Native Americans, and Hispanic Americans. The recent challenges to affirmative action laws that lay beneath the recruitment of these students has led to a diminution of the efforts of many colleges and universities. However, students falling into those categories should still be true to themselves and indicate their heritage on their applications. They should ask frank questions of the admissions office as to the institution's objectives in attracting minority students. Often there are representatives of American minority groups on the admissions staff, so the answers to these questions are not hard to find out.

International students are a second group sought by colleges and universities, although interest in these students is affected by economic concerns. First, the economy of the home country is a factor because of the exchange rate and the cost of an American college education. The recent collapse of the Asian economy has reduced the number of families who can pay for an education in the United States. Second, because the federal grant and loan programs that underlie the financial aid system do not extend to international students, most colleges and universities cannot afford to extend financial aid to a very large number of international freshmen.

As happens with all special groups, applicants who fall within them have to compete with each other in the admissions process. That is the way the system works. African Americans compete with other African Americans, Asian Americans with Asian Americans, international students with other international students, and so on. Even so, these candidates need to know they do have a competitive advantage because they are sought after by the college. This is especially true at some of the smaller universities and colleges who may not have the budget to recruit nationally and internationally. At very selective colleges, however, the competition within subgroups can be just as intense as among the all-arounders striving for admission.

In applying as a member of a special group, be sure not to exploit your status as a member of a sought-after group. Don't obscure it, either. Think honestly about what your cultural background or other special status (such as being from a Montana farm), has meant to you and what you might learn from being in a much more complex and diverse environment at College X. Think about your potential for contributing to the college as well.

One African-American student handled this quite well in writing his application essay about an academic experience that had deeply influenced him:

> The academic experience that has meant the most to me has been reading the book, *Bury My Heart at Wounded Knee*. This book has broadened my outlook on the meaning of the word oppression. Formerly I thought that African Americans had given that term its meaning in American history. Now I know that Native Americans have experienced their own special form of injustice. Being black myself, I can truly relate to the plight of the American Indians and understand their reactions to their oppressors.
>
> My good fortune in being chosen to attend a special Governor's Summer School in our state brought me in contact with a whole variety of people from different social and economic backgrounds. My contact with Native Americans and others at the summer school has both enhanced and complicated my views on eliminating social injustice in this country. I hope my college experience will help me find some solutions.

5. All-Around Candidate Category

This category is the most difficult to describe, since most people in the world will fall into it. So be it, there is safety in numbers. Colleges need students who can do the work, who are good people, and incidentally, who can pay the bill. They need students with a strong interest in challenging themselves academically; who want to make a contribution to the college community; who will appreciate and value their college experience, the people they meet, and the programs they are offered; and who will become proud and successful graduates. For these reasons admissions deans will admit lots of all-around students. In fact they will tend to overenroll these students. You may be one of them if you focus your application on these points just mentioned: challenge, contribution, appreciation, reaching your career goals, and giving back to the school. You will not necessarily say these things outright, but you will imply them in your essays and choice of activities and examples.

Even if you are not sure of your career goals, be sure to show your intellectual curiosity and desire to explore the university's curriculum. Even if you have no special talent to present, make sure the admissions committee knows that you will take part in some extracurricular activities and that you see the relationship of those activities to a full and interesting college experience. If your high school activities for some reason do not translate into your college plans, then indicate that you are interested in opening a snack bar in your dormitory, or hosting prominent visitors to the school, or even working in the admissions office. Be honest, but be assertive.

Showing your potential for loyalty to the institution and the potential for giving back to it as an alumnus is perhaps a point you can make in your choice of an essay or in an example of someone you admire. College admissions committees want to select people who will perform well at the institution, be grateful for the education they received, and by their success, enthusiasm, and integrity as graduates reflect credit on the college. It is the all-around applicants who most often perform this vital function and ensure institutional prosperity.

Once you have established yourself as an all-around candidate with a solid academic record, desire to contribute, interest in exploring the opportunities in the curriculum and in the extracurricular life at the school, remember to develop your edge, too. To do that, go back to your inventory of interests and talents and try to show that your particular combination of academic interests, extracurricular skills, personality, and understanding of what the school offers makes you that *unique* all-arounder who ought to be accepted.

DEVELOPING AN EDGE

When college candidates determine the group to which they belong and then present their academic, personal, extracurricular, and career interests to the admissions office as a member of that particular group, they have made the match. You may then say, what is left for me to do? Doesn't this approach rob me of my individuality? But there is more to it. As in any

THE APPLICATION MAKES ALL THE DIFFERENCE

marketing process, you need to *refine* your market until you find your niche. In this case, you are trying to articulate your *edge:* that statement, fact, or anecdote that shows you are unique within your category and that you have something to bring to the college or university that no one else has.

Normally candidates develop their edge in their essays, and here it is important for the candidate and the family to be honest in the presentation to the colleges. Admissions officers can smell artificiality. That's their job. Here is a series of comments that reveal failure at developing an edge.

> I remember a moment when, after completing a strong oral recommendation for a boy I knew and respected, being told by a seasoned admission officer that the student's application had sounded a "bit hollow." "It had a false note," he said. His essays, "were contrived and self serving," he continued. "I didn't get the feeling that he believed what he was saying or that he really liked anything." This young man made the mistake of trying to tell the college what he thought it wanted to hear. He probably thought what he had to say might have been trite or uninteresting. So he constructed a false identity, and the perceptive admissions officer saw right through it. He should have let his fine personal qualities and scintillating sense of humor shine through, and he might have gotten into the college he wanted so desperately to attend.

Now let us look at some guidelines for developing your own edge.

1. As an applicant you must not only "know yourself," you need to "be yourself."

This is the first rule to follow in developing an edge. Look at the following statement from a college candidate:

> My goal is to become as educated a person as possible. I plan to become a productive addition to society through my profession as a lawyer, but I believe in the sovereignty of my spirit and its enlightenment is my ultimate goal. Everything is grist for the mill for me: hard-rock guitar with the fine blend of 10,000 Maniacs at a rock concert or the full-voiced choral music of Handel. I enjoy them both. I also enjoy reading Shakespeare, aloud if possible, and Doonesbury, also aloud. I loved going to

the Matisse exhibition at the Museum of Modern Art last year. I like delivering a good cross-check during a competitive hockey game.

The candidate shows himself honestly and forcefully in this passage. He sets himself off from other candidates by his vivid and varied examples and by his honesty about himself. In the end, he represents an intriguing combination of opposites that few admissions committees could resist. Being himself was his edge.

2. Set yourself off from the other members of the group by highlighting your talents.

If, for instance, you fall into the scholar category, tell the college what it meant to you to build your own telescope or put together a clavichord. These are things that intellectuals and creative artists do! When you tell your story, your natural enthusiasm will convey your intellectual interests and illuminate your accomplishments in the process. One boy wrote about a special project he was doing on the poetry of T. S. Eliot:

> Investigating Eliot's early works, the reader sees a growth of Eliot's faith out of the ashes of his self-doubt and questioning. Look at the doubt and uncertainty of *The Hollow Men,* and contrast that with the cogent, assured speeches of Thomas à Becket in *Murder in the Cathedral.* To me this progression of thought is not merely an exercise in intellectual inquiry. It has a parallel in my own life and in countless others. The connection between Eliot's search for his personal definition of God and the meaning of the lives we live is important to me. I too have many questions: Who is God? How does He affect our lives? What is immortality? Eliot has helped me formulate some tentative responses to those questions and to guide my own odyssey.

Now this is a bit overwritten, but you have to hand it to this writer. He makes sense as he discusses a topic that most teenagers—and most adults—find too personal or too complex to tackle.

If you are an excellent swimmer and thus fall into the athlete category, you should describe your accomplishments fully in your application. Tell how you have participated in the local YMCA program and that you have gone to swim camps in the summers so you could compete in the AAU competition—

and you won your event. Mention your times in a few examples to document your case. Then place your swimming in the context of your college education as this young woman did.

> Even though I love swimming immensely and spend 2 hours a day at practice, I do it primarily as a diversion from the arduous course load I am taking in school. Believe it or not they both fit together. From swimming I have learned the value of self-discipline and budgeting my time. I have also learned how to function on a team and to win and lose with graciousness. I have tried to transfer these insights into the pursuit of my chosen career, veterinary medicine. I think I have made a good record at Wheelock High School, both in swimming and in my classes. I want to continue to excel as a swimmer and as a student at Coburn.

3. Show a desire to contribute to the college community.

This rule is especially important for students with family connections, or who are all-arounders, or even members of a special group. In writing his college essay, one son of an alumnus told how he encouraged his music teacher to begin drilling the school marching band so that they could perform better at football games and elicit stronger support for the team. In an essay entitled "The Spirit of 2000," he wrote:

> As the band learned new drills (wheels, turns, figure 8's, etc.) and began to show them off at games, the student body became more enthusiastic about the football team. This past fall they cheered the team on to five consecutive victories. At the last game of the season, nearly every student and faculty member was there! For me the development of school spirit in the student body is the best thing that can happen at a school. It makes for close and friendly relationships among the students. It helps the administration and faculty feel better about the students, and it raises the level of performance in classes as well as in sports. I hope there will be similar opportunities for me in college. I enjoy helping communities with diverse individuals work together toward common goals.

The daughter of another graduate responded to the question on the application asking her to describe the significance of one of her extracurricular activities in high school. She wrote:

> I knew I wanted to take a more active role in the school community. I had taken a personal inventory test in tenth grade and found out that I liked to manage people and could be a leader. So I became actively engaged in my class activities, and this led to student government. As class president, I organized various activities that have raised money to support worthy causes: Greenpeace, relief for victims of famine in flood damaged Central America, funds for the victims of civil wars in Africa, and hot meals to help our local homeless people. I helped organize candy sales, pancake festivals, dances, and a school spirit contest. These and other activities have brought over $4000 into our class treasury; after we have fulfilled our promises to the organizations I mentioned, there will be some money left over to help some of the needy members of my class attend our graduation dance.

A minority woman applying to a large university developed her edge by discussing what participating in a religious activity had meant to her:

> Every Saturday I go to Branch—the young people's group in our church. During the meeting we sing, we pray, we study God's teachings, and we have fun. Sometimes we go swimming or ice skating, or Christmas caroling, or meet with other groups so we can share our faith with non-Christians. I hope there is a group like this at Hanover College. It has meant a lot to me, and I believe that religion can help bring a community together.

4. Present yourself as slightly unconventional within one of the group categories.

Use delicacy and good sense when following this rule. Here is part of an essay that did not work because it presented too rough an edge to the college. The candidate was not admitted:

> People often call me eccentric, and you know what: They're right. I like to be different. I once wore the same sweater for a whole month just to see if any of my teachers would notice. I

THE APPLICATION MAKES ALL THE DIFFERENCE

once did not study at all for a Latin exam. I watched the Bears play the Colts, instead. I wanted to see if I could put it all together on the test. And I got my C! My friend, Bill, studied until 2 a.m., and he told me he only got a B-. My grade was only slightly lower. I didn't do this just to beat the system; I did it to see if I would crumble under the pressure of not having studied for the test.

And another thing I like to do is impress adults in conversation. I know quite a bit about politics and I frequently make political predictions that I know will set adults on edge because they are so outrageous. I get a kick out of this because the adults initially take me seriously, and watching them trying to make a serious response makes me laugh. Then later, some of them see the joke and laugh too.

On the other hand, the following essay enhanced another candidate's chances for admission because it made him different and reasonable.

> Quite frankly, I have encountered some difficulty at Wimset High School because of the restrictions of the school's curriculum and the demands of the coaches. I play football and lacrosse. Sports have cut into my genuine desire to be by myself, to read and to paint. I find myself torn between the school's demands that I achieve success in the traditional ways and the pull of my own interests—which take me beyond the walls of worthy Wimset. This makes me a little eccentric, I guess. But I have been artistic since I was young, and I have not been as productive in this area as I would like to be. I want to change that when I come to college and expand on my interest in art.
>
> Some people regard me as being a little aloof, even pompous. This is because I gave a little speech to our art class one day when the teacher unexpectedly did not show up for class. Everybody was throwing things around or doing nothing, and someone proposed that we go to the corner store for sodas. I told them they could do as they liked, but I did not regard the art class as a creative play-time period. I told them I wanted to finish a painting I was working on. Well, that did it. You should have heard the cat calls, but the painting did take second prize at the art festival at the end of the year. I am not sorry for what I said. I

think one can balance studies, sports, and the creative arts, and I really hope I can find this balance in college.

The maturity and the honesty of this essay gave this candidate a distinctive edge. He was accepted at all the colleges to which he applied. Although he saw himself to be different, he also saw the benefit of integrating his interests into the college environment. Because he is honestly wrestling with the question of balancing his various interests, he is an ideal candidate. Yes, he may be drawn in many directions as he explores college life—he knows that he will have to find a balance among his interests. In the course of exploring and finding this balance among his interests, this young man will touch and influence others. His quest will cause them to change and to grow, and that is what interaction among college students is supposed to be all about. No admissions committee would turn down a person with this kind of *edge*.

Some Details to Remember

When preparing your applications, remember to:

1. Make a copy of your application and complete all the responses in pencil. Erase and make changes as needed. Then neatly print or type your final copy. Have someone proofread your essay before you send it.
2. If the directions permit, compose all your responses on a word processor and attach your essay to the application (make sure to put your name and Social Security number on each page of the essay).
3. For the short answers, it may be just as easy to prepare them on a word processor and tailor them to fit the spaces provided. Print the responses out and cut and paste them on the application. Make sure the directions will permit this.
4. Move from the simple to the complex. Prepare your easiest applications first and then move to the more complex ones.
5. When you are done, photocopy everything, including your check, and send the application off on time.

ELECTRONIC APPLICATIONS

The term electronic application can mean four different things: (1) a hard copy of an application you procure over the Internet and print out on your computer; (2) an application that you procure on a disk, complete on the

THE APPLICATION MAKES ALL THE DIFFERENCE

disk, and send back to the college (In this case, you print out a paper copy for yourself and the college prints out a paper copy for itself when it receives the disk.); (3) a database-enhanced disk (In this case, when you send the completed application back to the college on disk, the disk is read into the college's computer, and an electronic file created. There is now only one paper copy of your application—the one you made before you sent the disk back. The rest of the process is electronic.); and (4) connect to the college via the Internet and complete the application on the college's Web site and then have the application sent directly to the college's computer.

You may want to file an electronic application using one of the private companies that assembles your information and sends it off electronically to the colleges you select. These companies also provide other services such as helping you to identify schools and match yourself to them and procuring financial aid information. They also provide software programs so that you can track your applications at your various college and university choices. For further information contact Peterson's CollegeQuest (http://www.collegequest.com), College Edge (http://www.collegeedge.com), or the Princeton Review (http://www.review.com).

At this stage of technological development, you will find that number 1 is the most common format for filing electronic applications. This is the method employed by the very popular Common Application that many private colleges and universities accept. Students go to http://www.collegequest.com or http://www.commonapp.org, download the application, complete it by hand or by typing in the information, and send the application on to the colleges they want to apply to. The benefit to the Common Application is that it can be photocopied and sent to most of the schools you choose.

A couple of caveats about the Common Application: Remember the advice to establish a match between yourself and each of your colleges. This may necessitate filling out each of your Common Applications differently for your various schools. In addition, schools using the Common Application usually have supplemental forms that they will want you to complete. These will be sent when they receive your application, and the result may be that you will have to make haste to get them back in to the colleges before deadlines. Individual school financial aid forms are an example of a supplementary form.

Electronic applications are available from many of the colleges and universities to which you are applying. Go to their Web sites and find them, or call the toll-free number and ask how a school's particular electronic process works. You can also link to college Web sites through Peterson's CollegeQuest site, the College Board's site, Dow Jones, or America Online.

There are private companies that use electronic applications in a different way. For a fee, you file an electronic application with them—usually printing out a paper copy from their disk. Then the company takes your information and formats it in an application for each of the colleges you choose. The company attaches your essay and any special information a particular college may require and sends off your packet. These companies also gather your recommendations and transcripts and send them off as part of their service.

That is fine, but remember *match* and *edge*. If you use one of these companies, you will have to find a way to preserve those two magic words, and it may not be easy.

Finally, filing an electronic application and filing it early will lead to individualized responses from some of your colleges. For example, if you designate a major in political science and have a high academic profile, you may get an e-mail back from a political science professor. If you are a star athlete, a coach may write to you. This is possible because as your interests are entered into the school's computer, a message can be sent immediately to the coach or the professor. You should consider an electronic format if you don't know the school as well as you would like.

ANSWERING APPLICATION QUESTIONS

Electronic applications are the wave of the future. Until the future arrives you will have to complete some of your applications by hand. Some tips:

- Be legible: Use black or blue-black ink. Strive for maximum legibility. Think about the admissions officer who is reading your application at 2 a.m. Try not to antagonize him or her. If the directions permit, prepare your responses on a word processor and cut and paste them on the application.
- Be consistent. When completing the factual sections of the application where you are asked for personal information, always give your name in the same way—and this should correspond to the way you filled out the SAT or ACT applications, by the way. The same is true for your parents' names and information. If they have titles and use them, you should. Nicknames are off-limits unless asked for. Normally your home is your mailing address unless you are at a boarding school.

THE APPLICATION MAKES ALL THE DIFFERENCE

- Be precise. Give the number, street, apartment number, zip code, and any other details that may be necessary to ensure that communications from the college to you do not go astray. Note that the Post Office has a new, all-capital letters, no punctuation format for addresses. Some schools may require that. In the section that calls for information about your school, you enter the six-digit school code number for the Admissions Testing Program/American College Testing Program. Be sure to use the name of the guidance counselor to whom you are assigned. Find out from him or her your most recent rank in class or percentile, and enter it in the appropriate space. If your school does not rank, then you should write that in the space provided.
- In the section asking you to specify a major, you may be surprised by the number of choices, especially if you do not know what your major will be. If you have some idea of what you want to study, rank your choices on the application, rather than check undecided. (Make sure the directions permit this.) You can also address the topic of your college major in your essay, and thereby make the match between your interests and the curriculum the college offers.
- Be clear. Many students are confused and annoyed by the amount of space given on the application to list extracurricular activities. They struggle with how to say what they do when they are not studying or not at school doing a particular activity. If this space haunts you because you work 15 hours a week, make sure to let colleges know that. There are an increasing number of high school students who are working after school, and they cannot be expected to have as many extracurriculars as those who don't. In being clear, you are making certain that the college sees the real you.

EXTRACURRICULAR ACTIVITIES

Before you begin this portion of the application, list on a sheet of paper those organizations or causes that have meant the most to you and that you have contributed to in your high school years. If you have worked at a job for extensive periods of time, then write down the impact of the job on your outlook and practical experience. Many jobs entail responsibility and management and marketing skills. In either case, job or extracurricular activity, highlight the positions of leadership and responsibility that you have attained.

Samples

Chess Club: 3 hr./wk., three years, played First Board, District Winner (500 players) 1999

Basketball: 12 hr./wk., four years, forward, elected Captain, named *Post Gazette* Player of the week, January 10, 1999.

Sales Clerk: Women's clothing, Saturdays, vacations, and full-time last summer, became Assistant Manager, supervised shipping, display, verification of employee hours, credit returns.

Format:

Position
Amount of time per week devoted to the activity
Skills you acquired
Number of years involved
Special awards, honors, or promotions
Leadership positions and specific duties that define that
   leadership

Now that you have listed these items on your piece of paper, move to the volunteer activities you may have engaged in and place them in the same format. If you are not asked for this information, prepare a supplementary sheet and send it along with your application.

Many students worry that they are not involved in enough activities at school or that they are too young to have had much work experience. Be assured that the job of the college admissions officer reading your folder is to figure out whether you have made good use of your time and have challenged yourself when opportunities arose. Admissions people know that a top student cannot necessarily be involved in seven clubs and three varsity sports. They know also that the young woman who has to work weekends and summers in the clothing store cannot be expected to have a long list of books she has read.

In general, colleges understand that students differ widely in their extracurricular activities. What gives a particular student an edge is the depth of commitment to an activity, even work. The chess player who works after school so she can travel to national championship meets in the Midwest only has one activity to list on her application, but she is a focused and resourceful person. So is the young man from a rural background who has spent a good

THE APPLICATION MAKES ALL THE DIFFERENCE

deal of time raising Rhode Island Red chickens (and has won three regional 4H championships) with his birds. Think about how these two different kinds of students can add diversity of viewpoint and experience to a college class.

Recently a counselor described an unusual combination of extracurricular interests he encountered in a college candidate:

> I recently met a young women in the senior class whose great love, after her pet pigeon, was Russian cooking. She is gifted academically, but she avoids athletics. For several summers she has spent the bulk of her time amassing Russian recipes and cooking for her friends. A year ago her Russian instructor suggested that she publish a cookbook of her favorite recipes in Russian and in English. The young woman managed to accomplish this in the summer between her junior and senior years. She plans to describe this experience thoroughly on her college applications and to submit a copy of her book with each one. Her edge will be this single accomplishment—the only extracurricular activity listed on her application!

Leadership

While extracurricular activities and academics are important, one's leadership ability is often what sets one candidate apart from another in the selective college admissions process. If you think about the task of the college admissions deans at the top schools, it won't take you long to figure out that they want to attract the highest number of the leaders of the next generation to their college or university as possible. "We seek candidates who demonstrate a willingness to take an interest in others," says Harvard/Radcliffe's catalog, "who place themselves in situations that call for personal initiative and leadership."

So you need to review your activities in school, in the community, and during the summer and focus on those in which you have employed your leadership skills. It may sound trite to state that you were a cabin leader in camp or that you led your volleyball team to the regional finals, but it is in situations like these that you develop the skills to manage people and hone your appreciation of the way one operates in an institutional or corporate setting.

When you graduate from college and venture forth into society, you will need not only your well-polished skills as a chemist or policy analyst or mathematician, you will also need to know how to influence people to do things and work with you toward common goals.

A seasoned observer of the college admission process recently observed: "The biggest single mistake that applicants to selective colleges make is thinking that being very active will impress college admission officers. In fact the reverse can happen. A long list of activities may suggest some weakness, indecision, or lack of commitment."[1] So the lesson is: describe your major activities thoroughly, highlight your leadership, and be sure to show that the depth of your commitments is more important than their breadth.

ESSAYS: HOW TO ANSWER THOSE PERENNIAL QUESTIONS

Now that you have dealt with all the questions requiring brief responses, you are ready to go to those that call for longer answers—the essay questions. You will find that most essay questions on applications these days are open-ended: they enable you to formulate your own response. You establish the structure, the examples, and the argument of the essay; the college merely sets the topic. Look at these examples drawn from the Web sites of these schools.

- "Submit a one page personal essay that will help us learn more about you, what is important to you, what you hope to accomplish through your college education. You may emphasize an educational goal or an important milestone in your life. Please do not list your activities or accomplishments in this essay." *College of Literature, Science, and the Arts, University of Michigan*
- "Describe a humorous experience." *Johns Hopkins University*
- "If you were in a position to ask a thought-provoking and revealing question of college applicants, what would it be? (Space for response) Now that you have asked your ideal question, answer it. You may attach additional sheets if necessary." *Dartmouth College*

---

[1]Christopher T. B. Murphy, Associate Director of Admissions, Yale University

THE APPLICATION MAKES ALL THE DIFFERENCE

- "Occasionally students feel that college application forms do not provide a sufficient opportunity to convey important information about themselves or their accomplishments. If there is something you would like us to know, please inform us on a separate sheet. If you wish to include an additional essay, you may do so."

    Possible Topics—
    Unusual circumstances in your life
    Travel or living experiences in other countries
    Books that have affected you the most
    An academic experience (course, project, paper, or research topic) that has meant the most to you
    A list of the books you have read during the past six months
    Harvard/Radcliffe Colleges

- "This personal statement helps us to become acquainted with you as an individual in ways different from courses, grades, test scores and other objective data. Please write an essay (250-350 words) on a topic of your choice or on one of the topics listed below:

    Evaluate a significant experience or achievement that has special meaning to you.
    Discuss some issue of personal, local, national, or international concern and its impression on you.
    Indicate a famous person who has had a significant influence on you, and describe that influence." *The Common Application*

- "In addition to answering one of the three questions on the Common Application, applicants are required to respond to the following:

    Select a short text, formula, or visual image written or created by someone other than yourself. Respond to it. Please write out the text or provide the visual image. Limit yourself to 500 words."
    Amherst College

What Colleges Are Looking For

When you and your fellow seniors respond to these and other essay topics, the college and university admissions officers who read them will be looking for the same things. They will look for evidence of your writing ability, your motivation, your creativity, your self-discipline, your character and personality, and finally, your capacity for growth. Be candid in your essay, because

> ### Make All Optional Essays Mandatory
>
> You can see from these application questions that not all of them are mandatory. In fact, the language encouraging you to write them is quite mild: "to help us understand you better . . . your background and your aspirations."
>
> You may be tempted to skip those essay assignments because of the time it will require and the open-ended nature of some of the responses. Well, don't! The competition won't. The application is the only opportunity you will have to impress the admissions committee. So take it.
>
> At the same time, you do not want to cram your application or write a long essay. Keep in mind that your application will probably receive 20–30 minutes of consideration at a selective college: 15 minutes for the first reader, 10 minutes for the second, and 5 minutes in front of the committee. So don't bore people!

admission officers are really looking for the real you behind all those grades, test scores, and rave reviews in your teacher recommendations. No reasonable admission officer expects an essay to describe the perfect person, brilliant scholar, or champion athlete. They will be suspicious of perfection. They are seeking to know you better and to see how you will fit into the class they are assembling.

This essay in response to the Common Application question about a famous person who has influenced you is very strong. The writer set up a mock interview with Teddy Roosevelt.

> If I had a choice of going to dinner with a historical figure, I would want to dine with Theodore Roosevelt. Of all the people in history whom I have studied, I have the most empathy for Roosevelt and a deep interest in him. I was initially impressed with the fact that, even though he was born to wealth and prominence, Roosevelt had to overcome hardships of his own. His struggle to strengthen his body is well known, but people don't remember that TR's first wife and his mother both died on the same day, and one of his sons was killed in World War I. These experiences strengthened Theodore Roosevelt and gave him compassion for others. I would like to ask Roosevelt's advice

THE APPLICATION MAKES ALL THE DIFFERENCE

on how to express human compassion in the hard and cynical world of today. My generation suffers from a lack of idealism. How would Teddy bring it back?

I would also like to talk to Teddy Roosevelt about how he would address the rising tide of fundamentalism in the Middle East and the nationalism that has convulsed the Balkans and central Africa. How would he use the influence and power of the United States to bring these areas of the world into our global economy?

I would be fascinated to talk with Roosevelt the intellectual. He wrote a history of the War of 1812; he wrote a history of the West; he also loved the natural world and was the first President to pass legislation about conservation. Where would he draw the line between the interests of big business and our need to protect the environment? What would his reaction be to the coal mining companies who want to begin to strip away the surface of those Wyoming hills he loved so well? Would he dam the Penobscot in northern Maine? What about the destruction of the rain forests in South America and in South Asia? We can't use "dollar diplomacy" anymore, or is there a 21st century version?

There are many questions of this sort that I would like to ask Mr. Roosevelt at our dinner, but I would hope he would do some talking on his own. I want to hear that high-pitched voice and that boisterous laugh. I want to check out the stories I have read: that he once walked through the White House lily pond with the Japanese ambassador and that he brought a horse into the White House to amuse his children.

I would also want to find out Mr. Roosevelt's reaction to the famous people of his day: Admiral Mahan, George Washington Carver, Jane Addams, J. P. Morgan, and yes, even Woodrow Wilson.

When I left the dinner with TR, I hope I would have some new ideas of my own about how to achieve change in the American political, social, and economic system. For Teddy Roosevelt did achieve changes in those areas. At the same time he did slowly and reasonably, once you strip away the publicity that he created for himself. He was in the words of one writer, "A Conservative as Liberal." He also had humor and style. Even though he died at the beginning of the century, he is still relevant today as we begin a new century, 90 years later. It would be fascinating to spend an evening with him.

This essay, written by a young man applying to an Ivy League college, is somewhat uneven, but it does show writing ability. It reveals enormous enthusiasm too. This student definitely is a thinker. He has motivation. He has candor. He is creative, too: setting up the dinner scenario. The capacity for growth is clearly displayed here. This applicant is interested in the environment, politics, economics, international relations, and likes to write. Furthermore, the questions he asks are open minded. They are not jabs. The author does not prejudge any of the answers that Roosevelt might give. This objectivity impresses college admissions officers. Students are free to have opinions, but they also need to show a willingness to change them. Otherwise, they won't get much out of those late-night bull sessions in college.

When the admissions officers who read this essay looked back into this young man's folder they found excellent grades in history and a strong recommendation from his history teacher. They noted the young man's social activism in his local community and his leadership in student government. They saw him fitting in very well with the college's history department and contributing to campus political discussions and student government. This essay made the critical difference in his admission to this very competitive school.

Analyzing Two Sample Essays

Here are two more essays selected from applications to two colleges. Each college asked the applicants to respond to the statement: "Describe a significant educational experience in your life." Read through each essay, evaluating each for evidence of writing ability, motivation, creativity, self-discipline, character, and capacity for growth. (Hint: One essay is good, one is deficient.)

A Home Away From Home

The experience that has moved and taught me most was the experience of going on assignment to a shelter for runaways, when I was an intern reporter two summers ago for *Philadelphia* magazine. During my four days there, I came to learn a lot about runaways, why and how they leave home, and how they conceal

THE APPLICATION MAKES ALL THE DIFFERENCE

their identity. I also learned about one of the real values of life, about people taking care of each other. Despite the fact that these were disadvantaged, or maybe because they were disadvantaged, there was a level of camaraderie and genuine concern among them that I had never experienced before. About half the kids at the shelter were black, half were white, but racism did not exist there because the people were bound together by their struggle to survive.

These kids didn't have what so many of us take for granted—love, support, and the security of a warm bed and food every night. Still there was a quality in the way they spoke and acted with each other that I admired and hoped to remember when I left them.

Though I stayed at the shelter for only four days, I came away with both a new sense of the plight of runaway kids and a new sense of hope. "These young people seemed at first like a strong group of oddly matched, but invincible musketeers," I wrote. But in fact, "they were not invincible; they were very vulnerable."

I learned that when a person under eighteen leaves home, even an intolerable home, he becomes a "status offender." He becomes a ward of the state, and is at the mercy of the courts. That is why the "detention" or "incarceration" of these kids has become a common occurrence.

In my short stay at the center I became friends with kids who had been raped or knifed right in the detention centers the courts had placed them in; many had been handcuffed and slept in jails after running away from an insane, alcoholic, sexually abusive or violent parent. Most all had been robbed of their dignity and their self respect, if not their very humanity, by the system designed to protect them.

That is why the network of private, state approved shelters has sprung up. The shelters run by social workers and volunteers and privately funded offer some security and semblance of a home. Some of the luckier runaways are temporarily assigned to shelters before being taken to court for a formal disposition of their particular case.

Early one Thursday morning, I walked with a social worker and Darwin, a boy from the shelter, to the Family Court at

Eighteenth and Vine streets, the court where virtually all of Philadelphia's runaways end up. We sat in the waiting room of Court Room C, then the judge called Darwin in. I had to wait outside, wondering what the decision would be about this vulnerable boy whose parents no longer wanted him. I did not have to wonder long. After a few minutes Darwin was half-pulled, half-led out of the court room by a sheriff, handcuffed to another boy. Although he had done nothing more criminal than run away from a horrible home, Darwin had become a "custody case," another number in the court room files, another kid for the state to file away in a detention center.

In my article I tried to re-create the pain of this experience as well as its wonder and beauty. I tried to communicate not only a sense of my rage, but to elicit from them an outcry of their own. Perhaps they will respond, in powerful numbers, and some small part of this unjust system will change.—*Tania Lewis*

A Pioneer in Space

Long ago I wanted to be a fireman, a policeman, or something equally heroic. I have changed since then, I suppose, and my sights aren't set so high. I would be more than satisfied now, to be a college professor or a lawyer. However, I must still have a trace of my early romanticism because I daydream every now and then of being James Bond or Mark McGwire, hitting his 62nd, or soaring above the earth as an astronaut. I think though if I really could choose a great adventure, I would go into the future and help explore space.

The most exciting possibility for me will be the landing on Mars. I'll be too old before they get around to the rest of the solar system, and I will be dead before mankind is capable of reaching the galaxies. Being the first person to stand on the surface of Mars would be exhilarating to say the least. That would satisfy my desire for adventure for some time—for all time.

If I don't get to Mars, I'd like to be a pioneer of some sort; I'd like to do something or discover some idea or challenge that has never been done before. Because most of the physical frontiers on Earth have been stormed, Mount Everest, the South Pole, the solo Atlantic flight, I am left with the world of space. Though in some ways a second choice, it is the best possible opportunity for me. With the right training and proper contacts both within the space agency, and in the political world, I could reach my goal and satisfy my desire for adventure for some time to come.—*Alton Stoneman*

The Essay With The Edge

These two essays have merit, but in terms of providing insights into the candidate, the first essay has the edge. It gives the student who wrote it an edge, too. This essay not only reveals the candidate's ability to write clearly and even movingly of her experience but it also shows her motivation to confront a social problem with her journalistic skills. There is a degree of creativity here too, not only in the essayist's language, such as the use of "wonder and beauty" in this context, but also in her point-blank admission that she sought to elicit the anger of her readers as she alerted them to this social evil. The author certainly shows a capacity for growth in her desire to see the system change and in her commitment to help that change occur.

It should now be clear why the second essay falls flat. But let us not gang up on the writer. He does show motivation even if it is generalized. He wants to be a "pioneer of some sort," but he is not focused, and at times seems willing to do anything to get into the scientific/space spotlight. Note the comment about the political and scientific contacts he plans on making so that he can be selected for space flight.

Self-discipline, at least in an intellectual sense, does not appear to be this student's strong point, either. He does show an ability to communicate, and he obviously has the intelligence to understand the difficulties of rising to the position of astronaut. He should have probed those challenges more explicitly by talking about the scientific breakthroughs that have to occur before humans can reach Mars. He should have made the connection between the world of study (college) and the achievement of space flight. If only he had said he wanted to explore the curriculum of this fine college and that he liked the idea of being a pioneer who combined different types of training, say as a geologist and a chemist. Instead he says that space is almost a second choice for him and leaves the impression that academic training is somehow unrelated to his goals, whatever they may be. While it is true that the world of ideas and study are very different from the world of action and exploration, there is a relationship. If the writer of the second essay had even glimpsed this connection, and that college could play a key role in his intellectual and emotional growth, then he would have been better off. Little wonder then, that the admissions officers who read the second essay wondered where he would fit. "Nice guy but no edge" was the comment on his folder.

A LIST OF COMMON MISTAKES

Remember these cautionary notes when filling out your application and, in particular, when writing your personal essay.

- Don't seek too much help from your parents, friends, or teachers. It will show—to your detriment.
- Ask friends and parents to suggest topics for open-ended essay questions. Make sure that is as far as it goes. Having a third party correct grammar or suggest imagery is wrong. You must stand on your own in presenting yourself to colleges.
- Do the mechanical work on the application yourself. Word processors make it easy. Electronic applications make it fun. Make sure to produce a paper copy and edit it before sending anything off on the Internet. By no means allow your mother or father's assistant to do any work on your applications.
- Use spell check. Remember if you make a little error, the readers won't hold it against you. On the contrary, a "sanitized" or "professional" looking essay will bring criticism from admission officers.
- Pay careful attention to the instructions on the application. Some colleges want all responses written on the application itself, others will let you paste responses on the application or prepare supplements of your own for extracurricular activities and essays. Do what the colleges and universities say.
- Do not use the same essays from college to college. To do so is to jeopardize your match. Just look at college Web sites—each one is different in look, content, style, and the messages that are put forth. Try to cast your essays and your application so that they resound with the values of the institution to which you are applying. If you have a basic essay that reflects the criteria of ability, motivation, creativity, self-discipline, character, and growth, then you can tailor it to suit the program and the personalities of the various schools to which you apply.
- As you work on your applications, moving, as suggested earlier, from the simple to the complex and from your least to most demanding one, you

THE APPLICATION MAKES ALL THE DIFFERENCE

will subtly improve the sophistication and breadth of your essays in the process. By the time you reach your last and most difficult college, you will be at your best.
- Often colleges will include a supplemental sheet on which you provide additional information and comments. Take care with these sheets, especially if you are filing the Common Application.
- If you feel you have something special to say to a college, something that does not fit on the application or in it, then you should write a special letter to your admissions officer or to the Dean of Admissions.
- Try not to use the phone (or have your parents use the phone) to check if material has arrived at the school. Use e-mail. If you are using one of the service companies, the status of your application will be reported to you. Use the phone to register intense interest in the school, if it is sincere, and use the phone to make sure that supplementary information has been received and is understood. Let us say that over the course of looking at schools in the past year, one university stands out as the place you really want to go. In this case you should consider drafting a short note to the Dean of Admissions telling him or her that Coburn is your number one choice—and why—and that if you are accepted there you will come. You never know what the effect of a positive letter like that might be.

FINAL PARTS OF THE APPLICATION

Now you have finished all the hard parts of the application, but there are still some important tasks to perform. You need to distribute the various parts of the application to the appropriate people.

Secondary School Report Form: Even though many applications are being filed electronically, the link between college and school is generally a "paper" one. You will need to download the Secondary School Report (SSR) Form or take the copy that came in the mail with your application to your guidance counselor. Remember that with this and the other forms, it is your responsibility to fill out the first portion of the form with your name, address, and the school's name and address and the name of your counselor or principal. You also need to put down the ACT or SAT code number for your school. Your guidance counselor will attach his or her recommendation to the form and enclose a transcript with it and send it off to the colleges. Guidance offices have later deadlines than you, but you should still submit the form as early as possible.

Midyear School Report: This form also goes to your guidance counselor, and it too has to be filled out by you beforehand. This form is the last one sent in by the school to the college, normally at the end of January.

Teacher Recommendations: These forms (TRs) go to the teachers you have chosen to write for you. Here again, fill in the top portion of the form first. You also will have to consider waiving your right to see the report once admitted to the college. Unless this waiver deeply bothers you, sign it and give your teachers the maximum opportunity to say what they think. For teacher reports to have credibility, they must be complete and honest. Some teachers, knowing that students will later look at the reports, will be constrained on their recommendations. They may fall back on cliches, or unsupported conclusions, or brevity, none of which is persuasive. Don't take that chance—waive your rights.

Remember to give your teachers stamped envelopes addressed to the colleges. Ask them to keep a copy of their comments in case you decide at the last minute to apply to another school. If you feel your teacher only knows you as a classroom student, you should make up a sheet giving your extracurricular activities, leadership positions, and hobbies so that he or she can have a background to draw on if necessary.

Financial Aid Forms: Have your parents fill out the Financial Aid PROFILE, if it is required by the school, and send it into the College Scholarship Service by February 1. You can apply for this form in the same way that you register for the SAT, either on line from the College Board Web site (http://www.collegeboard.org) or on an application you procure from your guidance office. Also, the Free Application for Federal Student Aid (FAFSA) should be completed if you are applying for financial aid and want to qualify for work-study or if your state has a loan or grant program. The FAFSA is available at http://www.fafsa.ed.gov and can be downloaded and sent in as a paper copy or filed electronically. The reaction time is much faster if you file electronically. (Chapter 7 has more details.)

KEEPING TRACK

By this time, you have a good deal of paper in your room, with all your applications and their various supplements and the like. You need to develop a filing system as well as a tracking system. A manila folder will do for the former, one for each college and one for all the financial aid forms.

THE APPLICATION MAKES ALL THE DIFFERENCE

However, you will have to construct a flow chart for each school, so you can keep track of who received what, when, and in case the college calls and says you are missing something.

After placing all your application materials in chronological order, with a photocopy of the application on top, make a chart like the one below in multiple copies, one for each college, and paste it on the inside of the left-hand side of the manila folder. Make a series of columns from left to right along the long side of the sheet. List the various parts of the application—with spaces between—down the left-hand side, in the first column. Across the top, mark the steps of the process, such as the date you received the application, date you completed and mailed each part, and a column marked "to whom" in which you would write guidance counselor for the SSR, and the name of the teacher for each TR, then another column for a date, when the college notified you that it had received this particular part of your application. Finally, you have a column marked "subsequent action" just in case you need to make a note later on in response to a message you received from the college.

Under the left-hand heading be sure to leave space for any extra letters you are procuring from coaches, prominent alumni, or friends, and for any special letters or projects you are sending in as supplements to your application.

Now comes the most important part—making a photocopy of each part of your application that you filled out. Be sure to photocopy your application fee check as well. If your parents are keeping track of the financial aid information, advise them to do the same for the financial aid applications to the various schools. You will need to refer to at least one of these folders later—the folder of the school you want to attend!

Online Organizers

Students who make use of online college search and application systems may be able to use online application organizers as well. On the Web, http://www.collegequest.com offers a personal organizer that acts like a virtual filing cabinet, monitoring your applications in progress. It helps you build and maintain your list of potential colleges. You can enter personal and academic information into the organizer, and this will be transferred into any online applications that you open on CollegeQuest. This reduces the amount of time you have to spend repeatedly entering information, and it also reduces the risk of errors. Once you have completed your applications,

KEEPING TRACK: State University

Form/Item	Date Received	Date Sent	How	University Acknowledgement of Receipt	Photocopy Made	Subsequent Actions
Application Booklet	15 Sept.	15 Oct.	On line	15 Nov.	Yes	
ACT/SAT Scores	6 June	6 June	CSS*		Yes	
Secondary School Report/High School Transcript	15 Sept.	1 Oct.	M	15 Nov.	No	
Alumnus/a Reference		1 Oct. (Judge Hoffman)	M			
Supplementary Material: Athletic Data Sheet		1 Oct.	Fax		Yes	Coach Allright called State Univ. coach for me on 10 Oct.
Application Fee		1 Oct.	Charged to Credit Card	15 Nov.	Yes	Notification of admission by 1 Feb. or earlier

*College Scholarship Service

you can then print and mail them, or, if the colleges accept electronic applications, you can submit your applications electronically through CollegeQuest's secure connection. An Application Manager helps monitor your applications and gives you a checklist of important steps to complete along the way.

Final Check the Four C's

As you thumb through your applications one last time—after a good night's sleep—make sure that you have met the criteria of the four C's: clarity, candor, completeness, and contribution:

- Have you said everything as *clearly* as possible?
- Have you been *candid* about yourself while emphasizing your strong points?
- Have you been *complete* in your responses to the questions on the application even though some of them may have seemed vague or repetitious?

THE APPLICATION MAKES ALL THE DIFFERENCE

KEEPING TRACK: Coburn College

Form/Item	Date Rec'd	Date Sent	How*	College Acknowledgement Of Receipt	Photocopy Made	Subsequent Actions
Preliminary Application	15 Oct.	20 Oct.	M	15 Nov.	No	
Personal Part of Application	1 Dec.	20 Dec.	D	15 Jan.	Yes	
Secondary School Report/High School Transcript	1 Dec.	15 Jan. (Guidance Office)	M	15 Feb. "No"	No	HS transcript not rec'd; another copy sent 1 Mar.
Teacher Recommendation (I)	1 Dec.	10 Dec. (Mr. Brown)	M	15 Feb.	Yes	
Teacher Recommendation (II)	1 Dec.	1 Dec. (Ms. McPhee)	M	15 Feb. "No"	Yes	Coburn did not receive Ms. McPhee's report; she sent another 17 Feb.
Peer or Other Outside Reference	1 Dec.	1 Dec. (Coach Allright)	E-mail	15 Feb.	Yes	Allright called Coburn track coach for me on 18 Feb.
Supplementary Material: Athletic Data Sheet		28 Dec.	E-mail	15 Feb.	Yes	
Financial Aid Statement	1 Dec.	10 Jan.	On line	15 Feb.	Yes	
Application Fee		20 Dec.	M	15 Feb.	Yes	
Other—Mr. Knowles (Summer Employer)		15 Jan.	M		No	Sent to Wm. Hawkins, VP of Coburn (Knowles' ex-roommate)

*M=Mail; D=Disk supplied by college

- Have you attempted to show that you can make a *contribution* to each of your schools?
- Finally, have you shown a good *match* and a distinctive *edge*?

Simply said, do you feel good about what you have said and the way you have said it? If so, you probably have done well on this, the most difficult part of the college admission process. That is important, because when this process comes to an end, you want to be able to say to yourself that you did the best that you could.

Let us remember one final point about the application process. It has taught you a set of vital skills: you have researched all these colleges and learned to ask analytical questions about them and you have sharpened your organizational and management skills in dealing with all the parts of the application itself and the contacts you have made with teachers, counselors, college admissions officers, college faculty, coaches, and students. In the course of learning these vital skills, you should have learned more about yourself as well.

That should bring you some sense of satisfaction. Rejoice in it and in the confidence that your new skills and self-awareness will serve you well no matter what college or university you ultimately decide to attend.

SIX

Constructing a Powerful Candidacy

The application is truly a "personal statement." It's your chance to reveal something about yourself, your goals, your passions. Admissions committees will notice what you say and how you say it, so prepare your application with care and thought.

Linda Kreamer, Associate Dean of Admissions, Bowdoin College

There is an old saying about fine French cooking: "A lot of the flavor is in the presentation." College candidacies are not different. Taking the time to take a reasonable and challenging high school program and then orchestrating your application, what your recommenders say about you, and what kind of supplementary material you provide—or don't provide—will make a big difference in how you are perceived by a college admissions committee. The key word to keep in mind is how the various elements of your candidacy *fit* together.

Each component of your application folder—grades, scores, and recommendations from teachers, coaches, and guidance counselor—should connect to each other, and the admissions committee ought to be able to see the connections. Although each component will be providing different information, there should be common themes resonating through all of them in order for the application to be truly persuasive. If you have excellent test scores, you must also have equally impressive grades in challenging courses, and you must have testimony from your teachers that asserts you are a very good student. Your guidance counselor will have to confirm what your teachers say.

When the admissions committee keeps hearing the same strong comments again and again, it will begin to be persuaded as to your talents—and that is your goal.

Because there are a lot of strong applicants out there, you will have to make sure of your particular set of impressive talents. For your teachers and counselors to say merely that you have a fine mind and are a good person is not enough to get you into the class at a selective college. There has to be proof in the examples that are cited in your recommendations, and the descriptive language that is used should also enable the committee to draw a line in your favor between you and the other well-qualified candidates who are applying to the college.

As admissions committees construct their next year's freshman class, they are seeking diversity of background, demonstrated academic talent, and a variety of specific skills in sports, the arts, and extracurricular areas. They want a dynamic student body composed of people who are sensitive to each other's differences and who want to build a strong community. They also want students who will be able to have some fun, too. In addition to whatever strengths you are putting forth in your application—academic, artistic, athletic, or extracurricular—remember to show a sensitivity to others, a sense of humor, and, if you can, a hint of your personal integrity.

In order to integrate this last suggestion, reflect a little on the values you identified in the exercises in Chapter 1. Try to integrate those values into your approach to your application and to demonstrate them in your approach to your fellow students and teachers so that it becomes natural for them to be mentioned in your recommendations.

If you work hard because you like academic studies (rather than because good grades impress others and may get you into a good school), then you should convey this fact to your counselors and your recommending teachers. If you have a particular passion, whether for rock music or blank verse, then it is time to let other people know about it. If you feel you might have done better in a particular course had you not spent so much time doing volunteer work, then you should be sure the teacher in that course knows what the facts are. You can present a convincing picture of yourself if your recommendations all speak of hard work and genuine social commitment and the school record shows consistently high, but not always top, performance.

THE STRATEGIC PARAGRAPH
As you plan to build a convincing candidacy, you would be well advised to write a strategic paragraph for each school to which you are applying. In this day of electronic applications, e-mail, and multiple contacts with schools, it is easy to lose your focus. Your strategic paragraph will prevent that and ensure consistency from one communication to the next. The strategic paragraph states how you plan to present yourself to the school and what themes in your candidacy you are going to stress. You should include a series of specific steps that you plan to take with each school, to be sure that your strengths and accomplishments are duly appreciated. When you have written your paragraph, cut it out and paste it on the inside of your folder for each college. Refer to it before you write your essay, make a telephone call to a coach, or ask someone to recommend you.

YOUR HIGH SCHOOL RECORD
The foundation of any college candidacy is the high school record. When admissions officers look at your folder, they are looking for two things:

1. how well you have performed with the talents you have, and
2. how well you have used the educational opportunities available to you.

That sounds simple enough, but it means that the admissions committee will be looking for both breadth and depth in your high school courses. They will be looking for you to have maximum use of your high school's curriculum. If you do not attend a strong or well-equipped high school, that is all right, as long as you have made the most of its offerings. Perhaps you have been able to take some courses at a local college, or perhaps not, because you have had to work after school. Whatever the case, you have challenged yourself as much as you could at your school.

THE STRONG TRANSCRIPT
The model program of Anne Marie Gregory that follows shows a series of course decisions that have been wisely made. No college admissions officer could fail to be impressed by what Anne has done with her time at White Falls High School. She has taken English each year and has shown her ability by scoring well on the Subject Test in writing and the Subject Test in literature. She will take the Advanced Placement English test at the end of her senior year, along with the Math BC level Calculus exam.

THE STRONG TRANSCRIPT

White Falls High School

Name:	Gregory, Anne Marie		
Soc. Sec.:	#001-23-1480		
Sex:	Female		
Parents/Legal Guardian:	William and Carole Gregory		
Address:	14 Mill Crest Road White Falls, Pennsylvania 15820		
E-mail:	amg525@aol.com		
High School Curriculum	**Mark**	**Credit**	
Grade 9			
English (review grammar and expository writing)	A–	1	Class rank: 10/450
Math (algebra II)	B+	1	
Science (biology)	B+	1	**SAT I:**
Language (French I)	C	1	V590–M640 (jr. yr.)
History (modern China and Japan)	B	1	V640–M690 (sr. yr.)
			SAT II Subject Tests: American History—690 English Composition—700 French—690
Physical Education	Pass		Physics—700
Grade 10			
English (themes, poetry, and the novel)	B+	1	
Math (geometry)	B+	1	
Chemistry	A–	1	
Language (French II)	B–	1	
Economics Theory and Practice	B	1	
Music (trombone lessons)	Pass	½	
Physical Education	Pass		
Grade 11			
English (analysis and exposition)	A–	1	Summer term:
Math (functions, precalculus)	A–	1	Typing
Physics*	B	1	Data Processing
Language (French III)	B	1	
			Advanced Placement Test:
U.S. History*	B+	1	
Art (elementary drawing and painting)	Pass	½	U.S. History: 4
*Grade 12***†*			
English (literary analysis)*	A–		
Math (advanced calculus)	A–		
Advanced Physics*	B		
Language (French IV)	B		
Urban Political History	B+		
Music (concert band)	Pass	½	

*Advanced Placement or honors course.
**Marks are for first semester only.
†Advanced Placement tests in English and calculus will be taken in senior year.

CONSTRUCTING A POWERFUL CANDIDACY

Anne's choice of science courses is impressive, too. Beginning with biology, she went on to chemistry and then to physics, in which she has already taken the Subject Test. Science is Anne's favorite subject, and she has managed to take all the upper-level science courses at White Falls High. Anne has slowly built up her command of French, too. Although it is not her best subject, she has taken it every year, and her score on the Subject Test in French (with the listening test) is commendable.

Finally, Anne has taken a solid program in social studies during her four high school years. She has a full year of American history and took the Advanced Placement Test in her junior year. Her score of 4 is very good and will qualify her for placement or credit when she gets to college next fall.

This transcript also shows breadth in that Anne has taken courses in a variety of other areas. She has half-courses in elementary drawing and painting and in concert band. She also has taken summer courses in computing and knows the fundamentals of Microsoft Word and its programs in Power Point and Excel. These skills will help Anne in finding summer jobs, and they will also help her in presenting her work to her college professors. Note also that Anne has not taken full courses in some of these areas, even though the result would have been to boost her grade point average.

Anne's strategy was to build up a solid core of courses in which she could show depth of preparation, then to branch out. Another student with real talent in art would have a transcript that shows full courses in the art field, but then she, too, should pay strong attention to the five core areas: English, math, science, foreign languages, and history. This student might take a computer course or a history elective on a half-course basis to show breadth, rather than computer courses like Anne Marie, but otherwise both young women would cover the same basic areas of preparation.

In planning your course of study for college admission the rule of thumb is to take the core courses just mentioned and go as far as you can in terms of depth. Then branch out. Selective colleges are interested in students with a broad and deep preparation in the liberal arts. Those students who specialize too much in high school are putting themselves at risk in the admissions process.

THE WEAK TRANSCRIPT

Some students pursue the path of least resistance in high school, taking courses in which they are interested but meandering through the five core areas of preparation without achieving sufficient depth. Look at Giselle Ramboult's transcript on page 141. If you take a good look, you will see that she has chosen her courses with an eye to easing her high school workload so she can keep up with her active social life. She is clearly an intelligent person, and it is sad that she made some mistakes that could be easily avoided. With a little planning she could have been a stronger college candidate.

Giselle's transcript gives the impression that she selected easy courses rather than challenging ones. College admissions officers read course descriptions very carefully, and they will form the conclusion that Giselle has not challenged herself. Giselle chose a music or art course in her program each year. Instead of taking substantive courses like history and languages, she dabbles in Drafting, Photography, and Communications Skills. She should have stuck to history and languages and done more with science. She should have gotten in at least three years in a language, two years in history, and three sciences (with two lab courses). While Giselle has made use of the breadth of her high school's curriculum, she did not pursue any of her electives to the next level. She sampled art, drafting, drama, and photography, but she did not study any one in depth. If she were genuinely interested in art, for instance, she could have focused on painting, taking courses that the school offers in watercolors and oils and other media. She could then have prepared a portfolio for examination by the admissions committee or the art departments at the schools to which she applied. If her interests pointed more toward art history, she could have prepared for the Advanced Placement Test in art history. This same argument holds for music or drama.

It is not the courses themselves that have undercut Giselle's chances for admission but the lack of depth in any one field that has hurt her chances for admission to selective colleges. Her transcript has breadth all right, but very little depth. In fact, many of Giselle's courses fall into the category of "gasses" or "guts," admissions committee words for easy or soft.

There is no question that Giselle has done well in the courses she has taken. She ranks fourth in a class of 450 (whereas Anne Gregory, pursuing a more challenging program, ranks tenth.) The admissions committee will note that the ranking system does not take into account the difficulty of Anne's program. They will also note that Giselle has taken no foreign language and has paid little attention to the sciences. The fact that she has no foreign language will automatically disqualify her at many schools. The

CONSTRUCTING A POWERFUL CANDIDACY

THE WEAK TRANSCRIPT

White Falls High School

Name:	Ramboult, Giselle Denise	
Soc. Sec.:	#001-32-5909	
Sex:	Female	
Parents/Legal Guardian:	David and Linda Ramboult	
Address:	15C Town Hill Apartments White Falls, Pennsylvania 15820	
High School Curriculum	Mark	Credit
Grade 9		
English	A	1	Class rank: 4/450
Math (prealgebra)	A	1	
Art	A	1	SAT I:
World Problems	A	1	V550–M600 (jr. yr.)
Speech	A-	1	V600–M650 (sr. yr.)
Wood Shop	A-	1	
			SAT II Subject Tests:
			English Composition—550
Physical Education	Pass		Math Level I—630
Grade 10			
English Composition	B+	1	
Math (statistics)	B+	1	
Language Arts	A-	1	
Drafting	A-	1	
Typing	B	1	
Physical Education	Pass		
Music Lessons	Pass	½	
Grade 11			
English (style)	A-	1	Summer term:
Business Math	A-	1	Elementary Chemistry—B
American History	A-	1	
Geography	A	1	
Drama	B	1	
Music Lessons	Pass	½	
Physical Education	Pass		
Grade 12*			
Communication Skills	A	1	
Cultures of the World	A-	1	
Anatomy	B+	1	
Photography	A	1	
Concert Band	A	1	
Physical Education	Pass		

*Marks are for first semester only.

colleges also want to see broader and deeper preparation in the social sciences. Some will want three Subject Tests, and Giselle has only two, math and writing. In addition, Giselle has not taken any Advanced Placement courses, which, although not required, still have a positive impact on admissions committees.

ACADEMIC PREPARATION

These two transcripts highlight the core courses that all college-bound students should complete in high school. To solidify the point, let's look at the catalogs of two selective universities and two selective colleges and see how they identify those core courses and set up parameters for depth and breadth:

- Four years of English with an *intensive* emphasis on writing
- Four years of mathematics, *preferably including an introduction to calculus*
- Three *or four* years of laboratory science
- Two *or three* years of history or social science, usually including the history of the United States, plus a non-Western history course
- Three or more years of the *same* foreign language
- One year of course work in the fine arts—*recommended*

In addition to covering the academic bases outlined above, "you should read widely on your own and try to become familiar with computers and word processing," says one of the schools. As a college candidate you should realize that the educated mind is continually in the process of expansion and change and does not rest when a course is completed or a paper is done. Colleges and universities are looking for students who are genuinely engaged in the process of assimilating knowledge from a variety of disciplines and experiences and applying it to the challenges they are meeting in the classrooms and the world beyond those classrooms.

COURSE CONTENT

Because college admissions committees and admission officers for a particular region cannot know all of the high schools that candidates attend, you may have to do a little marketing for yourself when it comes to describing the courses you have taken. You cannot assume that the colleges will know you have taken the most demanding curriculum or that they will know how many times the lab meets per week or the types of term papers that are assigned in the tough American history course you took.

Make it a point to ask your guidance counselor for a copy of your high school transcript and any explanatory materials that will be sent along with it to your colleges. Often high schools have a *Profile Sheet* that gives the average performance levels for their college-bound students on such measures as the SAT I, SAT II, and the ACT. Some schools will show the distribution of grades for each upper-level course. If this kind of detail is being provided to the colleges, then the student and family need not worry.

If, however, the eleventh grade Advanced Placement history course is only called U.S. History on the transcript and if the joint English/Theater course for seniors is only shown as English IV, then you need to think about writing a brief course description statement of your own—for your advanced courses—and making sure it is sent to the colleges and included in your folder.

Marketing Your High School Accomplishments

When Anne Marie Gregory found out that her high school did not have a course description sheet, she decided to write her own. She went to a school pamphlet that described the courses offered at White Falls High School and from it developed the following summary.

Anne Marie Gregory
Course Work at White Falls High School

English Program The ninth grade course concentrates on a review of elementary grammar and introduces basic writing skills. The course also deals with the various ways in which people interact in literature, as revealed in dramatic scenes that students write, read, and perform.

In the tenth grade students examine various themes in novels, stories, and poetry and discuss how to develop themes in their own writing.

By the eleventh grade students are ready for a critical analysis of literature. They also prepare a long biographical essay in the spring term, based on direct observation of a person and an in-depth interview.

The study of technique and style occupies students in their senior course in English. Here they discuss the relation of form to idea in literature and explore it in their own writing. A special honors section studies the Advanced Placement reading list and takes the test in May. I will do that.

Mathematics The normal sequence for the college-bound student begins with an introduction to algebra in the ninth grade. Polynomials and linear and fractional equations as well as computation of algebraic expressions are stressed. Exposure to the computer and the language of BASIC are introduced in the spring term.

In the tenth grade the student turns to a combination of algebra and geometry of area and volume and the trigonometry of right and oblique triangles.

Elementary functions, exponents, logarithms, series, limits, and probability are taken up in the eleventh grade, and in the spring some students go on to precalculus (which I did).

In the senior year math students normally take differential and integral calculus, followed by the Advanced Placement syllabus in the spring term (BC Level). I plan to take the BC, too.

Science Biology—plant and animal systems, cell structure and elementary anatomy and physiology—normally begins the science curriculum at White Falls.

Students go on to take chemistry and physics in the next two years, a half year of each in a two-year sequence. The chemistry course covers bonding, energy relationships, chemical reactions, modern theories of molecular structure, and a description of specific chemical families. Able students go on to the Subject Test in Chemistry. (I will probably take it, too.) The physics course begins with the study of the basic laws of conservation and the kinetic theory of gasses. It goes through electromagnetism and field physics with a detailed study of the atomic model. Like Chemistry it prepares students for the SAT II Subject Test in Physics. Next, in the senior year some students go on to advanced physics, which corresponds to a first-year college course.

Foreign Language The foreign language curriculum attempts to develop the basic skills of reading, writing, and speaking a foreign language, as well as some appreciation of the culture it represents. By the end of the second year students have mastered grammatical forms and are able to engage in simple conversation. In the next year, they begin to read the literature in a serious way. This continues intensively into the third year of the language called the "Humanistic Tradition in (French) Literature." In that year we studied Montaigne, Moliere, Voltaire, Gide, and Camus and took the Subject Test.

History The only requirement at White Falls in history is the one-year U.S. History course. However, students can take a social science or history course if they want to. I did both.

The history sequence begins with a history of modern China and Japan in the ninth grade. The China portion of the course begins with an examination of the ancient values of Chinese civilization, then jumps to the impact of Western imperialism on China in the eighteenth and nineteenth centuries. The Japan portion of the course begins with an examination of traditional Japanese society, then moves to a discussion of the impact of industrialization on Japan and her subsequent experiences with totalitarianism, democracy, and world leadership.

The economics course that many tenth graders take explores the classical theories of Smith, Ricardo, and Keynes, then examines three modern industrial models, the U.S., Germany, and Japan. The course also looks at the European Common Market and the impact of NAFTA on American business.

The advanced U.S. History course is designed to prepare students for the Advanced Placement exam. It covers the political, economic, and social history of the U.S. on an intensive basis. It also trains students in conducting effective research in printed and electronic sources in libraries and on the Internet and in proper historical writing.

The senior course in urban history focuses on the development of one European city, Paris, and two American cities, New York and Chicago. The course focuses on how people sought to change their political, social, and economic lives during the period between 1850 and 1970 as they wrestled with the problems of low wages, poor living conditions, and racism and violence.

Art Although White Falls has no art requirement, I took the elementary art course, which focused on line drawings, watercolors, and oils. In the spring term the course introduced color theory, spatial organization, and two of the major styles of historical painting: the Naturalists and the Impressionists. Although it was only a half course, my class was rigorous. When combined with my music lessons and concert band class, I have had several years of study of the arts.

Anne produced this informal course description on her computer. She gave it an attractive layout with her address and Social Security Number at the top and sent a copy to each of the colleges to which she applied.

MARKETING YOUR EXTRACURRICULAR ACTIVITIES

Having written up her curriculum summary, Anne then turned to a brief explanation of her extracurricular and non-school activities. She planned to use the sheet if the space provided on the application was not sufficient. The sheet would also work well on electronic applications, because it could be cut and pasted on the application form. On the short essay portion of her application, Anne expanded on her leadership skills. She also indicated how much time she spent on her activities so that the colleges would know the depth of her commitment to them.

Activity	Length of Involvement	Hours per Week	Offices, Honors, Duties
School Newspaper (*The Clarion*)	3 years	4	Staff, columnist, sports writer, editor
Yearbook (*Pantagraph*)	2 years	2	Staff writer, photo layout
Track Team winter and spring	2 years	6	Two varsity letters High jump, relays
Underground Paper (*The Bell*)	1 year	2-4	Founder, editor
Orchestra	8 years	4	Clarinet, Assistant Bandmaster

Outside School

| Hospital Volunteer | 4 years | 2 | Read, play games with senior citizens at local home |
| Catering Worker | 6 years | 0–4 | Help mother with her business, delivery, setup, and bookkeeping |

SPECIAL TALENTS AND ABILITIES: HOW MUCH TO SAY AND DO

Whether or not to submit supplementary information about your special talents can be a difficult decision. If all candidates for admission to college sent in tapes of their music and poetry, homemade pies, or reconstructed Volkswagens, then the colleges would have to build warehouses to store everything. As part of your strategy for each school, you should be able to figure out what might impress the institution and what might not. If you are a good basketball forward, but not outstanding, then sending a video of your playing is not going to impress the coaches of Division I schools. But Division II schools? That is another matter. Here are some criteria to consider when it comes to submitting extra information or examples of your performance:

- The information or example of my work was not requested in the application or by any admissions officer or coach. *And*
- The piece of information or example of my work will materially add to my appeal to the college, based on my understanding of the college's standards and interest in me. *Or*
- My college counselor or coach or another representative of the college has specifically requested that I submit further information or an example of my work.

When you submit a tape, or information, or a written or visual example of your work, keep in mind a few simple guidelines:

- Keep "it" short, sweet, simple, and to the point. Don't have 20 minutes of audiotape of you playing your clarinet with other members of the orchestra. Concentrate on 5 to 10 minutes of solo material.
- Seek the advice of your coach, teacher, or guidance counselor before sending anything.

- Send evidence, not testimony. That is to say, send examples of your own work, not rave reviews by people who think you are great. Allow the college to evaluate you without being influenced by what others have said.
- Mail your material to the Dean of Admissions or the admissions officer who interviewed you and ask him or her to send the material to the proper person for evaluation.
- Keep copies of everything.

In some cases it may be a good idea to send two copies of your work, one to the admissions office and one to the coach or art department chair. Ask each to communicate with the other. Athletic data sheets can easily be handled in this way.

Whatever you do avoid a public relations campaign, although that is what you are doing! You need to keep it simple and low key. Professionally printed personal brochures with pictures will only put off a college. Use your head. Put yourself in the position of the college admissions officers who have to read hundreds of applications between January and March. Don't give them anything to read that is not worth their time. Submit your best work in as concise a form as possible.

When Anne Gregory's cousin, Rob Rhinehardt, applied to college two years ago, he prepared a data sheet to market his swimming skills and accomplishments to the colleges he was interested in. Because he was at a boarding school, he listed both his home and school addresses at the top of the page and then his e-mail as well. Then he developed two panels, one for his times in different strokes over the short courses and a second panel showing his times and places in the New England Prep School Championships for the past three years. Rob's data sheet is effective for a number of reasons. It presents specific details. It shows the development of his skills over time, so coaches can get some idea of his potential for growth. It also gives the name of his coach, with phone and e-mail, so that the information can be verified and recommendations obtained. The sheet is short, sweet, and to the point.

Preparing Your Own Data Sheet

Not everyone applying to college has the noteworthy swimming record of Rob Rhinehardt or the well-balanced extracuricular activities of his cousin Anne, but candidates can still present their skills convincingly on a single

CONSTRUCTING A POWERFUL CANDIDACY

ROBERT H. RHINEHARDT

Athletic Data Sheet

Home:	37 Dunbarton Drive Ash Forest, Illinois 60333	**School:**	Atlantic Academy Box 566 Mansfield, Connecticut
Phone:	352-882-4605	**Phone:**	223-778-8027
E-mail:	pisces@usanet.com		
Height:	6'2"	**Coach:**	Bill Storms 14 River Street Mansfield, Connecticut 06099
Weight:	180 lb.	**Phone:**	203-772-5487
		E-mail:	storms@highnet.net

I have just begun my tenth year of swimming. The first six were with the Ash Forest YMCA, an AAU team. The last three have been mainly at Atlantic Academy.

Times (all flat start)
Short Course

	50 yd.	100 yd.	200 yd.
Free	22.9	49.2	1:49.9
Back	27.5	59.7	—
Breast	28.5	1:01.8 (New England Prep record)	2:19.0
Fly	25.3	—	—
IM (intermediate medley)	—	—	2:02.0 (school record)

The breaststroke time (1:01.8) placed me fourteenth among prep school swimmers in the nation, and thus I made Prep School All-American. I also anchored a 3:17.9 free relay, which broke the school record, with a split time of 49.2. The relay time missed All-American Honorable Mention by less than two tenths of a second.

Progression of times and places in
New England Prep School Championships

	1997	Place	1998	Place	1999	Place
200 IM	2:07.4	7th	2:05.2	4th	2:02.2	4th
500 Free	5:14.0	9th	—	—	—	—
100 Free (relay)	52.0	4th	—	—	49.2	2nd
50 Back (relay)	—	—	27.8	4th	—	—
100 Breast	—	—	1:04.0	4th	1:02.2*	2nd

*Set New England record in trials.

piece of paper. Rob's and Anne's examples yield several suggestions for the skilled artist or musician who seeks to present his or her unique talents to college admissions officers.

1. Show depth rather than scope. If you are an artist, prepare a portfolio that emphasizes your ability to look at the same object or theme in a variety of ways. Present a series of sketches of the same farmhouse seen from different angles at different times of the day. If you are a musician, you can submit a tape of yourself playing three classical pieces on the piano. Try to show in each instance that you can do one thing well, perhaps better than others, and that you have brought your skills to a high level of perfection.

2. Make variety a subordinate theme. If you have worked in a variety of media, you many want to present one or two paintings or a photograph of one of your experiments with collage or sculpture in addition to your sketches of the farmhouse. As a musician you may want to tape a short jazz piano selection in addition to your three classical pieces. The important point to bear in mind is that you should put your best foot forward. If colleges are going to accept you on the basis of your talent, then you have to convince them that you could, for instance, fill a niche in the music or art program. Every freshman class needs its excellent pianists and its talented pen-and-ink artists. Try not to give the impression that you are a dabbler by presenting too broad an array of evidence of your talent.

3. Explain your work. Write an explanatory set of paragraphs to go along with your sketches. Introduce your musical tape with an explanation of what you are trying to achieve in your performance. Demonstrate to the viewer or listener that you are articulate about what you are doing and that you have a capacity for self-criticism and an awareness of where you are headed with your particular skill. You don't need to brag; just state your case and let the listener or viewer decide how good you are.

Bear in mind, too, that even if you are not as skilled as some other applicant that does not necessarily mean you will be denied admission to the college. All schools need students who are genuinely interested in the arts, even though they may not be gifted as artists. How will colleges be able to fill those courses in music theory or the history of the Renaissance painting if they do not have some of these people in their freshman classes? Schools need athletes who can play jayvee, too. Don't be reluctant to identify a talent you have and your willingness to contribute it.

4. Document your case. A portfolio or a musical tape should be accompanied by a recommendation from your art teacher or music instructor who ideally has heard or seen what you are presenting to the colleges. Encourage your instructor to comment directly on your work. Remind the writer of your recommendation to state his or her own credentials and to suggest how far you can be expected to carry your talents in college and beyond.

Who Gets Your Supplementary Material

To answer this question, e-mail the Admissions Office and ask for the name of the person to whom you should send your data sheet, portfolio, or tape. Many admissions officers like to have a look at these materials first before sending them on for evaluation. If they happen to believe you should be admitted, it helps for them to be familiar with your work. If the material is sent directly to an academic department, be sure to request that the evaluation be sent back to the admissions office and use the name of your interviewer or the person who visited your school as the addressee. Wait a month, and then send that person an e-mail to see if your portfolio has completed the loop.

If this seems a bit painstaking, it is. Most colleges have some system for referring student portfolios and tapes for evaluation, but sometimes it does not work efficiently. Hence the suggestions.

HELP FROM YOUR COUNSELOR

Many high school students fail to appreciate the important role counselors can play in helping the college admissions process work for them. Don't be one of these students. Even if your counselor may always appear to be busy, monitoring attendance, scheduling courses, counseling families, and in some cases teaching and coaching as well as helping students with college and career placement, many will find time for you. Your task is to find a way to cut through the business and gain access to your counselor. As a first step ask the secretary in the counseling office about a good way to get 10 minutes with your counselor. Once you have your counselor's attention, you will find that he or she may know college admissions officers and may have lots of tips on how to make the best use of the "system." To make the most of your time with your counselor, follow these guidelines.

1. When you do go in for a scheduled visit, have your questions written down. An index card will do fine. Refer to the questions in the meeting. The counselor will appreciate the fact that you are not wasting time.

2. Try to ask the secretary the routine questions. Lots of guidance offices have secretaries or even volunteers who can hand you an application for the SAT or the ACT, give you details about the upcoming test on Saturday, or show you a copy of your transcript. Do not undervalue the importance of these people in helping you in any number of ways. Save the analytical questions for your counselor. Use the secretary and the volunteers and even your fellow students for the detail questions.

3. Try to accomplish something in between interviews, e.g., visiting several colleges, investigating several more on the Web, taking more tests, or improving your grade point average. This will advance your college search and give you something to report at the next meeting and a new set of experiences on which to base further questions.

4. Use the interview with the guidance counselor to relate something he or she could not have learned elsewhere. Your meetings with your counselor should not be like private counseling sessions, but they should be informative from the counselor's point of view. If, for instance, you did not make the editorship of the school paper, and everyone thought you would, then tell the counselor the reason why: your viewpoints were too liberal for the conservative student newspaper. Or remember to tell your counselor that you were one of two students picked by your French teacher to attend a national conference and participate in a panel discussion with other French students.

5. Find a way to let your counselor know about any extraordinary challenges you or your family have faced. Your counselor may be interested in your family background but be reluctant to ask. You do not have to reveal every last detail. You should protect your privacy. A general description of anything unusual or difficult, however, will help your counselor understand your unique background and put your accomplishments in perspective.

YOUR SCHOOL RECOMMENDATION

As you speak with your counselor, bear in mind that his or her major obligation to you is to write an original, descriptive essay about you for the colleges. This is the school's recommendation, a document that often runs to 750 words, but could—without sufficient information or knowledge—be much shorter than that. Counselors can also fall back on the check marks on the rating grids and cliches to describe their students if they are not sufficiently informed about those students. Counselors also feel constrained in some instances by families who insist on seeing the recommendation, and they draw back from that specificity of detail and professional judgment that many colleges want to see.

To appreciate what colleges and universities expect from counselors, read the following summaries from the instructions counselors receive.

Academic How would you evaluate the applicant's general academic performance? To what extent has the candidate made use of his or her intellectual potential and of the educational opportunities available at your school and in the community?

Extracurricular What is the quality of the applicant's participation in extracurricular, community, or work activities? Please characterize the applicant's leadership capability.

Personal How would you and others describe the applicant in personal terms, including any special strengths or problems?

Other Are there any special circumstances, background information, or other factors (positive or negative) that may be relevant to this student's candidacy to our college? Would you care to make any additional comments, for example to elaborate on the reasons for your checks on the General Ratings page? Do you wish to compare this applicant with other students from your school who have been admitted to this college?

These questions show you how specific the colleges expect the counselors to be in their reports. Many counselors have too many other responsibilities to begin to provide the level of detail the colleges request. In those instances you will have to lend a hand and help your counselor do his or her job.

Helping Your Counselor With Your School Recommendation

While you are thinking about how to present yourself and your accomplishments and dreams—to your college choices and to your college counselor—remember that the task is to provide positive information, not to rebut negative impressions. Because of the possibility that your records might someday become public, counselors and others tend to communicate in positive terms. Criticisms are omitted and left to the inference of the reader. That fact makes your job easier; it is a matter of fleshing out in detail what the counselor may already have concluded. Think in the following categories:

Academic Make sure the counselor knows the exact level of the courses you are taking and plan to take in the spring term. When discussing your courses with your counselor, refer to them by name, i.e., AP Calculus, not by number, i.e., Math 510. Make sure your counselor knows about any academic work you have done in summer school or in extension courses at the local community college. You should have transcripts for those courses on file in the guidance office. If the counselor seems interested in any particular piece of academic work you have done, offer to give him or her a copy. All your counselor has to say is "no thanks" if that won't be necessary.

Extracurricular Make sure your counselor knows about the leadership positions you have attained inside or outside of school and how much time each week you devote to your extracurricular activities. This is a perfect time to give your counselor a copy of your activities sheet you have prepared for the colleges. This is the time to give your counselor your athletic data sheet as well. If you have to work long hours outside of school time, your activities sheet will show that and your counselor should be told that as well.

Personal All college candidates have to make sure they do not lose their identity as they market themselves to their colleges. You don't want to become a self-styled politician with a sheet on every facet of your being. On the other hand you do not want to underplay or downplay your strengths. Remember, personal qualities are important to colleges and universities, and your activities supposedly demonstrate at least some of your personal qualities.

For example, here are the personal qualities Wesleyan University looks for: "evidence of honesty, fairness, compassion, altruism, leadership . . . young men and women with a genuine sense of responsibility and consideration for others . . . [with] a capacity for commitment to society . . ." If your counselor has some idea of what kind of person you are, he or she can mention your strong traits to your college. Supposedly you are mentioning those traits, too, and so are your other recommenders. The end result is that the admissions committee begins to see a consistency in your candidacy and will respond favorably to it.

Other Sometimes there are special circumstances in your family or in your own life that counselors need to know. You are probably the best judge of whether an incident or situation should be related to the counselor. As you would tell your counselor about any diagnosed learning difficulty, so you should tell him or her about anything that might explain a slump in your high school record, or a period of time away from school, or the lack of extensive extracurricular activities on your record. Once you have discussed any special circumstances with your counselor, he or she can factor the information in the formal school report, or if that is too sensitive, pass the information along orally to the admissions officer who will be reading your file. By no means should you feel that such information would be held against you in the admissions process. Quite the reverse, it usually helps.

ENLISTING HELP FROM TEACHERS

One of the most undervalued documents in an applicant's admissions folder is the recommendation written by a teacher. There are two reasons. Some teachers do not spend enough time filling out the recommendation forms and rely on general comments and the checks on the rating grid. At other times, teachers would like to write more, but the student has not taken enough time with them to recite their accomplishments and plans for study in college.

When picking your teacher references, pick teachers who know their subjects well and who hopefully know you well. They may even know the colleges you are applying to well. Here are some tips so that you can get the most out of a good teacher who would like to write you a strong recommendation.

1. Ask teachers if they would write recommendations for you early, before they are besieged with similar requests from your classmates. If they answer yes, make an appointment to discuss your college plans with them. Before the meeting think about what you feel is important to communicate to them about you the person as well as you the student. Make a list of your values, your strengths, and your accomplishments, then circle those that this particular teacher may be able to highlight in the recommendation. Think about the examples that vividly make your points.

2. When you have filled out the top part of the teacher recommendation forms for the various colleges, prepare a properly addressed envelope to each school for each recommendation. If there is no recommendation form, then prepare the envelope and write your name in pencil inside the flap. Ask your teacher to write just a general letter to that particular school.

3. Make copies of your extracurricular activities and highlight those that are relevant to this particular teacher's recommendation. You can use the activities sheet you prepared for the colleges and make edits in red pen for your teacher to consider.

4. When meeting with the teacher, begin by briefly reviewing your college plans, in particular the subjects you want to study as an undergraduate. You will probably be asking for recommendations from teachers whose subjects you intend to pursue in college, so be sure to get their advice on how to approach their field. Remember not to pick your teachers on the basis of how well you did in their classes. Pick them on the basis of how well you thought they taught their classes and your interest in the subjects they taught.

5. Briefly describe to your teacher what the rest of your life is like at school and at home. You should not go into great detail here, because the teacher is not going to be asked about this by the colleges. However, it is beneficial for the teacher to have some idea of who you are beyond the classroom. To mention that you play two varsity sports or have the time-consuming job of president of the Debating Team helps your teacher to put your accomplishments in his or her course into a broader perspective.

What Colleges Ask Teachers

These questions have been taken from the teachers' sections of actual applications:

- Comment on the quality and nature of the applicant's academic work.
- What intellectual qualities and abilities does this student have?
- What extracurricular contributions has the applicant made to the school and the community?
- Assess the student's talent, dedication, and leadership in areas with which you are familiar.
- Tell us about the applicant's personal qualities, particularly in regard to integrity, values, and relationships with other students.
- What are the first three words that come to mind in describing this applicant? (This is a very frequent question. You might want to think of

the words you would like to have used about you. Keep them in mind as you conduct your conversations with teachers and counselors.)
- Do you have any additional comments that might be relevant? For example, how does this student compare with former students of yours who were accepted by and attended our university?

Following Up With Teachers

After you have met with your teachers and they have written their recommendations, be sure to convey your thanks. Nowadays, you can just send them an e-mail. Also remember that when you are admitted to schools, inform and thank your teachers a second time. Teachers really do care about what happens to you, and you should try to involve them in your application process as much as you can.

ENLISTING HELP FROM COACHES AND SPECIAL INSTRUCTORS

If you have a special talent in an area such as music, art, and sports, you will have read about how we suggest you prepare tapes, portfolios, and athletic data sheets. In addition to working closely with your coach or teacher in preparing these special materials, you should enlist his or her support in the recommendation process. Frequently a coach or a special instructor can make a telephone call to his or her counterpart on the college side and request that a student be considered favorably. A mentor or special instructor can also write a short recommendation to accompany your work explaining its quality and highlighting the unique contribution that you can make to the college's music, art, or athletic program.

You can facilitate this process by asking for an honest assessment of your work from your instructor or coach: "Will I be able to make a contribution to a Division I soccer team? Is it reasonable for me to hope that I can play my clarinet in the Hanover orchestra or sing in the Glee Club at Coburn?" If the answer is yes, then ask what role your coach or instructor can play in helping you to gain admission.

As with your teachers and guidance counselors, provide your special instructors and coaches with some background about your academic ability and other extracurricular interests and accomplishments so these can be mentioned where appropriate. You don't have to be quite as specific or lengthy with these instructors as you may have been with your teacher references or counselor. Just give them a flavor of what you do when you are off the field or not in the studio.

Occasionally in the crush of applications at a college admissions office, tapes, data sheets, and portfolios get momentarily lost. Ask your guidance counselor to check to see that your file including these items is complete. Better yet, put your own acknowledgement card in with your portfolio, with a signature space for the person who received it. If you get the impression from your counselor that your artistic or athletic talents are not coming through in the discussions about your candidacy, then ask your coach or music or art teacher to call on your behalf and plead your case. Usually this will not be necessary, but be prepared nonetheless.

LOBBYING FOR ADMISSION

Once you are satisfied that your counselor, teachers, and coaches and special instructors all know what they are supposed to do, your job of marketing yourself is nearly done. Let us review your strategy. In December your counselor completes the school recommendation, and in January and February colleges are considering your applications. It is during those months that you need to work with your counselor and by yourself to bring subtle pressure on the colleges to accept you. Some possible tactics to employ:

1. Often the counselor can best apply this subtle pressure in the form of a fact-finding phone call to the admissions officer responsible for your high school. The ostensible purpose of this call is to ensure that your folder is complete, to furnish any new information about you (such as grades or teacher comments) that may have come in, and to ascertain how you look in terms of the competition for admission to the college this year. Understand that your counselor cannot call all of your schools for you and maybe not any of them. Some counselors simply have too many duties and counselees. It is still worth finding out whether your counselor will do a little lobbying for you, especially at your top school. If your counselor does call, then you will at least get some assurance that your file is complete and that the college is carefully considering it. Your counselor may know the school well enough to ask what your chances of admission are. Although he or she cannot tell you, he or she can "reflect the tenor of the conversation," so you will have some idea.

CONSTRUCTING A POWERFUL CANDIDACY

2. Another way to enhance your admission to a college you really want to attend is to write that school a first-choice letter. Ask your counselor whether this would be a good idea for your particular choice of school. At the most prestigious and difficult schools, such a letter would be superfluous and even undermine your candidacy. At less selective and perfectly good schools, a first-choice letter could make a marginal difference for you. Colleges are very conscious of their yield statistics, and if you indicate that you will come if accepted, then the school's yield rises. Ask your counselor for advice as to what such a letter should say. Refer to page 40 for a sample letter. By all means avoid writing such a letter unless you mean it. See if the school has a late Early Decision program that you could join. If it does, but the deadline has passed, a first-choice letter is probably not going to be of much help.

3. During the lobbying season, you may want to mobilize some of the special connections you may have developed with a particular college. Discuss such plans with your counselor. If your parents have such plans, then ask them to clear them with your counselor. You want to keep in mind three points when bringing outside influence to bear: (1) coordinate your efforts so all parties (parents, counselor, and the influence bearing party) know what you are doing; (2) avoid overkill—going too far with letter writing, e-mail or phone campaigns; and (3) remember, you only pass this way once. If in doubt about whether to ask someone to help, it is probably a good idea to ask them.

4. Finally, if the news from a given college is not favorable and your counselor all but tells you you are not going to be admitted, you should ask advice about falling back to Plan B. If you have applied over your head, then this means the possibility of starting another application right now. If you are not going to make your top choices, this may mean that you might want to write a first-choice letter to a second-tier school. Or it may mean you do nothing, because your planning has allowed for this contingency, and you are sure that you will be admitted to some schools you will really want to attend.

YOU ARE THE CONCERTMASTER

In many ways your role in the application process is like that of the concertmaster in an orchestra. When the conductor is temporarily called away, the concertmaster, who traditionally plays an instrument in the string section in front, is summoned to the podium to conduct. He or she steps up, raises the baton, and brings it down confidently. The orchestra begins to play. The concertmaster sets the tempo, invokes the various instruments at the right time, and reads ahead in the score to make sure everyone plays his or her part. The concertmaster runs the show, so to speak, and so do you when it comes to marketing your college candidacy.

Like the concertmaster, you are first a musician playing an instrument in the orchestra—filling out those college applications and sending them off on time. Then your role changes, and you have to step to the front and organize your counselor, your teachers, your coaches, your parents, and your influential friends to play their parts on cue at the right time. You need to make sure they work in harmony and use the same words to paint the same picture, so there is consistency in your candidacy. You have to make sure that they come in on cue, when they are needed and not before—and not after, when they cannot be of any use.

If you do all this correctly and smoothly, you will be rewarded, as the concertmaster, with rounds of applause—in the form of well-deserved letters of acceptance.

SEVEN

Financing Your College Education

It is in financial aid awards that you see colleges and universities jockeying for position and trying to attract the best kids. Financial aid changes all the time. So it is important to pay attention and ask questions.
      Robert A. Reddy Jr., Director of Administration and Financial Aid,
      Ottawa University (Kansas)

PLANNING AHEAD FOR COLLEGE COSTS

The birth of a child fills parents and relatives with wonder and amazement. There are so many possibilities for the child, and the parents want to enhance those possibilities in every way they can. Few decisions will be more important to those parents and that child than the one to invest in education.

No parent can be unaware of the price of higher education in this country today. Ever since World War II and the G.I. bill, the federal government has extended its support of student financial aid. An initial commitment of $700 million a year has now risen to $20 billion a year. The price of higher education has leveled off in recent years, but it is still high. The costs of faculty salaries, technology, facilities maintenance, recruiting students, and raising money, not to mention financial aid itself, means that the price of a college education is going to remain high.

Even though the tuition increases of recent years are down from the 8 to 9 percent range of a few years ago, they still hover around 4 percent. This means that tuition will double in twelve years, according to one estimate. A six-year-old child faces a $250,000 four-year tuition bill at a private college twelve years from now; the price today is about $120,000 before incidental expenses. Public universities will cost somewhat less, but given the competing demands for tax dollars in most states, public universities will have to increase tuition and fees in order to make up for the shortfall in state funding. Periodic discussions in Congress about eliminating the subsidy for interest on education loans and recent increases in the funding for Federal Work-Study has added somewhat to public confidence in the commitment of the federal government to present levels of funding. Wise parents, nevertheless, will follow the twin axioms of beginning early and saving regularly for college education.

Benefits of Early Planning

Let's assume that you earn an average annual return of 11 percent in a growth mutual fund; you will need to invest about $11,000 a year for eighteen years to come up with the money you will need for the first year's tuition at a private college. For a state school, an investment of $5,000 a year will yield nearly $30,000 in eighteen years. Assuming an average state school tuition of $8,000 today, that figure should cover approximately two years of tuition. These are formidable figures, but they can be reduced somewhat by investing more adventurously at the beginning of the time period, then tapering back toward more conservative investments as the child nears college. For instance, if you were able to put $10,000 away when your child was born, that money would increase threefold and pay for a second year's tuition. In the table on page 164 we show an average increase of 6 percent in college costs, and we also show somewhat conservative figures for the projected total cost of public and private colleges.

Stocks Versus Bonds

When considering the best vehicle for investing for a child's education, the experts generally agree that investment in stocks is wise even though stocks tend to fluctuate in value. Over the long run, stocks have produced higher rates of return than other investment vehicles. A dollar invested in 1925 would have grown to $727 today, sixty-six times greater than if that dollar had been invested in Treasury Bills.

Income Taxes

In building up an investment for your child's college education, you first ought to be minimizing your income taxes. You might want to transfer some of your assets to your child's name and then reclaim them just before he or she sets off for college. Here is the income tax table for children 14 and over.

Income Tax

$0–$22,000	15 percent
$22,001–$53,500	28 percent
$53,501–$115,000	31 percent
$115,001–$250,000	36 percent
$250,000–over	39.6 percent

For children under the age of 14, the first $1,200 of unearned income is taxed at what is effectively a 7.5 percent rate. Income beyond the $1,200 is taxed at the parent's rate. Therefore, investors will want to have at least $13,200 invested in the child's name. (This amount would yield the first $1,200 of income each year at 11 percent).

At age 14, with college only three or four years away, the child's tax picture changes. Until the age of 14, a child can earn up to $22,000 and be taxed at the 15 percent rate. After that point the child is taxed at the parents' rate. Financial planners advise families in this income category to begin transition from high-growth investments to fixed-income investments when the child reaches age 14. This maneuver will provide a steady and predictable income when paying college bills.

Other Investments

There are other kinds of investment vehicles that have tax advantages for paying for college in the next century. *Individual Retirement Accounts (IRAs)* are one. IRAs can be set up by individuals with after-tax dollars, and those dollars are not taxed by the IRS if they are withdrawn for educational purposes. However, the funds must be put in the IRA before the child is 18, and some banks do charge a fee for withdrawing from the fund. If both parents' combined income exceeds $160,000, then the IRA option is not available. Education withdrawals can be taken from IRA accounts until the student has reached 30 years of age. *Series EE Savings Bonds* are another very conservative investment. These bonds now earn 5.25 percent interest, which is not taxable if the investor has stated that the bonds are to be used for educational purposes. When the bonds come due, they are tax free if they have been maintained in the parents' names and the gross income does

THE INSIDER'S GUIDE TO COLLEGE ADMISSIONS

not exceed $68,250. For incomes between $68,250 and $98,250, the tax is graduated. There are also parameters for single parents, too. *Life insurance* offers another savings vehicle for college. Parents can buy a policy that comes due on the day the child enters college and whose face value is the anticipated cost of the four-year college education. Regular premium payments "enforce" this savings plan, and in the unexpected event in which a parent dies before the child enters college, the policy pays the full amount for his or her education. In addition, earnings on life insurance policies

FUTURE COSTS OF ATTENDING COLLEGE AND SAVINGS NEEDED

Years Until Child Begins College	School Year	Projected Total Costs Public College	Projected Total Costs Private College	Estimated Monthly Savings Public College	Estimated Monthly Savings Private College
1	1998	$ 46,691	$ 99,345	$934	$1,986
2	1999	49,492	105,306	760	1,617
3	2000	52,462	111,624	644	1,371
4	2001	55,610	118,322	562	1,195
5	2002	58,946	125,421	499	1,062
6	2003	62,483	132,946	451	959
7	2004	66,232	140,923	412	876
8	2005	70,206	149,378	380	809
9	2006	74,418	158,341	353	752
10	2007	78,883	167,841	331	703
11	2008	83,616	177,912	311	662
12	2009	88,633	188,587	294	626
13	2010	93,951	199,902	279	594
14	2011	99,588	211,896	266	566
15	2012	105,564	224,610	254	540
16	2013	111,897	238,086	243	518
17	2014	118,611	252,371	234	497
18	2015	125,728	267,514	225	478

ASSUMPTIONS
*The average cost of a public college in 1997–98 was $10,069/year; the average cost of a private college was $21,424/year. (Source: The College Board.)
*Projected Total Costs include tuition, fees, books, and room and board for four years. The hypothetical rate of increase is 6% per year.
*Estimated Monthly Savings assume an 8% annual return on investments up to the fourth year of college. Keep in mind that this rate is only an estimate. The amount you'll need to save depends on the actual rate of return you receive.
*This chart assumes that you have accumulated enough funds to pay for each school year by September of that year. The monthly savings for 1998 assume that they began in September 1997.
TIAA CREF Newsletter, March 1998

normally build up on a tax-deferred basis so that you do not have to face the taxes until you cash in the policy, at which point the parents' income may be lower and the taxes less.

Custodial Accounts

For some parents the thought of setting up a college savings plan that essentially gives all the assets to the child after he or she reaches the age of majority (18 or 21) offers too much risk. In this instance you may want to set up trust accounts to give yourself some control over your child's assets. If you want to utilize the custodial account option, you can open a no-fee custodial account at a bank or brokerage house under the Uniform Transfers to Minors Act (UTMA) or, in some states, the Uniform Gifts to Minors Act (UGMA). These acts allow you to transfer a broad range of property to your child, including cash, securities, life insurance, and real estate. Each parent may give the child up to $10,000 a year. The UTMAs and UGMAs are the arrangements wherein the child is restricted by the trust instrument from spending the funds until he or she reaches the age of majority. Prior to that time the parent controls the composition of the trust and the allocation of its revenues. However, at the age of majority, the assets of the account flow directly to the child. In establishing a custodial arrangement, it is important to appoint a trustworthy and financially astute relative or friend as successor custodian so that if you die, the custodian will be sure to spend the money for the benefit of the child and look out for the welfare of the investments as well. There are distinct tax advantages to custodial accounts, but remember, they are irrevocable. Parents cannot take back any of the assets they give the child, nor can they borrow against the custodial account. Finally, parents who expect to apply for financial aid should steer clear of giving money to their children. The reason is that the federal methodology used in making financial aid offers considers 35 percent of a student's savings as expendable in the first year of college and 35 percent the next year, whereas parents' savings can only be assessed up to 5.6 percent maximum. Imagine a $10,000 savings account in the child's name; it would be liable for $3,500 the first year, whereas an identical account in the parents' names would be assessed only $560. Some difference.

SAVING MONEY WHILE AT COLLEGE

There are several ways to save college expenses.

1. **Cooperative Programs.** Some colleges have what are known as cooperative programs, which enable students to work in paid internships for six-week periods, revert to the classroom, and then return to the workplace. Cooperative programs enable students to practice what they learn and to make sufficient money to defray much of the tuition costs.
2. **Living at Home and Attending a Local College.** This is self-explanatory, and there are variations on the theme as well. Perhaps a student would do this for two years and then transfer to the college of his or her choice. Perhaps a student would choose to attend a less-expensive state school and then transfer to the college or university he or she always wanted to attend.
3. **Shortening the College Experience.** In planning for college expenses, you and your child may want to consider the strategy of shortening the collegiate years from four to three. The most familiar route to follow is to take as many Advanced Placement courses and tests in high school as possible and then find a set of schools with generous policies with respect to advanced standing. These are colleges and universities that will give actual credit for an AP course and not just allow you to proceed to a higher-level course while requiring you to take the same number of courses for your degree. At high schools without a strong AP program, students are frequently given credit for courses taken at a local college. In many instances the colleges to which they are admitted will also give them credit for those courses. The end result is the same—a saving on the number of courses the student needs to complete a degree.

   The *International Baccalaureate (IB)* is another route to advancement in college curricula and a shorter college experience. The IB is a much respected, rigorous curriculum in all of the traditional high school subjects. It is currently offered in 250 high schools across the country. The IB tests that come upon completion of the various subjects are treated in the same way as AP tests by some colleges. Students can achieve advanced standing and complete their degrees in three years.

   The savings of a three-year degree are impressive. At a high-priced school costing $120,000, a family saves $30,000. Say the student goes directly into the workforce and procures a $50,000 job in the first year. Subtracting living expenses of $25,000, the student still makes $25,000, more than peers who don't start working until the next year. Now the family is $55,000 ahead. Likewise, at a state institution costing $80,000 for four years, the initial saving is $20,000. To that we add the first year's income of $25,000 and we have a $45,000 savings, which is more than half what the original price of the education would have been.

As students consider these savings they should be aware of the fact that living at home or pushing hard to graduate in three years will result in a different experience than a four-year stay at the school. However, more families are considering the three-year option, given rising costs and the prospect of graduate or professional school expenses beyond college.

As families plan for college costs, they need to be realistic about the possibility of procuring financial aid. There are several ancient truths about aid that have now become myths.

Myth #1: Money will always be there for able and deserving students. As colleges and universities today have shifted to awarding financial assistance based on need to a mixed system of awarding aid based upon *need* and *merit*, they frequently exhaust or overrun their financial aid budgets. If a student will enhance the school's quality or diversity goals in some particular way, then the financial aid package will be strong in grant aid, but if the student is not deemed to have a special talent or to increase diversity goals, then the financial aid package will favor loans. In some instances, a reasonable candidate who has some funds to pay for the cost of the education could receive a financial aid package that leaves a *gap* between what the college offers in loans and grants, the *Estimated Family Contribution (EFC)*, and the cost of attendance.

Myth #2: Students can work their way through college or go to school on a part-time basis. Studies show that the rising costs of college in the next century as well as the dwindling supply of financial aid make it highly unlikely that students will be able to afford to support themselves as well as pay for their tuition and fees.

Myth #3: The Guaranteed Student Loan (GSL) programs have made it possible for all to afford the cost of expensive higher education. Not so. The GSL programs have raised the indebtedness of many students graduating from expensive colleges to $15,000 to $20,000. This is not a small number. Students today are having an increasingly difficult time paying off their loans before they start families and buy homes. Their college indebtedness is stretching into their middle to late 30s.

Myth #4: "If you just bargain with the colleges, they will give you more financial aid." This myth is quite widespread, and quite wrong. What has happened in the past couple of years is that many colleges have stood by their offers to middle-income families, who promptly sent their children off to less-expensive public institutions.[1]

Tips for Financial Planning

- Keep it simple. Avoid being clever, because you may forget what your strategy was ten years down the road. If you are going to give your child a gift, do so without attaching "strings." Strings lead the IRS to disallow the gift as such and to tax it at your higher rate. If you give your child stock valued at $10,000 and it rises to $50,000 by the time he or she is ready for college, then your child will have to pay capital gains on that increase.
- Familiarize yourself with your state's scholarship programs. Some states have adopted fairly generous scholarship programs for lower- and middle-income families.
- Look for scholarships. Keep your eyes and ears open for changes in collegiate scholarship and financial aid programs. See three good books on scholarships: *The Scholarship Book* (Daniel J. Cassidy, Prentice-Hall, New York), *Scholarships* (Kaplan Books, Simon & Schuster, New York), and *College Money Handbook* (Peterson's, New Jersey). Remember to check the Web for Rotary, Kiwanis, VFW, and state scholarship programs. The most comprehensive Web site for information about scholarships is http://www.fastweb.com. To gain a firm grasp on how the financial aid system works, consult http://www.finaid.org.
- Keep good records. Start now to keep careful records on your income taxes, medical bills, and major repairs to your home or business. An appraisal of the value of your home will be useful to colleges and universities that consider home value as an asset.

---

[1] Sandra Baum, professor of economics at Skidmore, writing in *The Enrollment Management Report* newsletter, vol. 1, issue 6, 1997, p. 12.

- Invest strategically. If you plan to invest on your child's behalf, do so aggressively until the child is 14 and then move toward a more conservative strategy so that there will be a steady flow of income when those college bills roll around.
- Consult with experts. If you do not have the time or experience to develop your own college investment plan, contact a financial planning professional. You can also turn to some of the major banks that advertise themselves as promoting education. Very often they have mutual funds that they recommend for education saving. As parents plan for college, they should think broadly about their retirement planning as well. There should be one plan that encompasses all the family's goals: education, leisure, shelter, retirement, and health.

SOME ENCOURAGING SIGNS

As students and families try to plan for college expenses, they can take some comfort in the sincere commitment of most of the nation's private colleges to try to meet students' financial need. Through innovative loans, grants, support programs, and work-study arrangements, most schools have made it possible for most students to attend. Colleges and universities have also cut costs so that they have more funds to allocate to financial aid. In addition, a number of the high-priced universities and colleges have developed special financial aid packages for middle-income families. Formerly, families with a relatively high annual household income were asked to pay most, if not all, of the student's college costs. Under new policies, colleges now look at the number of children in school or paying tuition at other colleges and the cost of living in a particular area and make their grant and loan offers accordingly. This focus on the hard-pressed middle class has prevented those students from going to cheaper state schools.

State governments have also assisted private colleges and universities through loan-funding programs, tuition prepayment plans, and subsidization of specific programs. In Pennsylvania, students who major in computer science and who take a job inside the state in that field upon graduation are eligible for a substantial reduction of their state loans. Banks have teamed with colleges and universities to offer loans and credit options to families and students. The hard-fought battle over Americorps revealed yet another way to reduce college fees and loans. Students serving in government-approved social service projects garner $4,725 in tuition reimbursement for each year of service, and they can extend the payback time for their loans by as much as ten years if they need to.

On a more general level, the financial success of the American economy in the past decade combined with the collapse of the Asian and Japanese markets has instilled in Americans a sense of resilience. There is renewed confidence in our educational system because that system has enabled us to make the tough decisions and trade-offs that leaders of other nations have not. Americans are beginning to accept the fact that college costs are high because the value is high. College graduates have more choices of career and more flexibility in meeting the challenges of the global economy. Americans understand that attending college means making short-term sacrifices for long-term gains.

While this new realism has led to an ever-intensive quest to gain admission to competitive colleges and universities, it has overlooked the families and students at the lower end of the economic and social spectrum. Those students and families remain at a disadvantage and part of America's unfinished agenda.

THE FINANCIAL AID SYSTEM

The past twenty-five years have seen enormous changes in the nature of financial aid. Federal, state, and private programs have expanded considerably, and more students have been able to qualify for assistance than ever before. However, the process of applying for aid, granting it, and administering it has become more complex and time-consuming. What this means to parents and students is that you will need to consider not only the quality of the college or university's academic and extracurricular program, but also the school's capacity to deliver sufficient financial aid. Furthermore, students and their parents need to understand that the burden of financing the bulk of a student's education has shifted in the past decade from the college and the federal government back to the student and his or her family. When one looks at the balance between loans and grants over the course of the last twenty years, the cost shift is very plain. The graph on the next page shows that at the beginning of the period, grant funds made up 55 percent of a student's package; now that number has fallen to 40 percent. In the meantime, loans have risen from 42 percent of the average package to 59 percent.

FINANCING YOUR COLLEGE EDUCATION

Grants vs. Loans

Grants, which students don't have to pay back, and loans, which they do, make up the biggest part of the typical financial aid package. Their roles have reversed in the past 20 years, with loans comprising an ever-bigger part of financial aid. Here's a look at the trend.

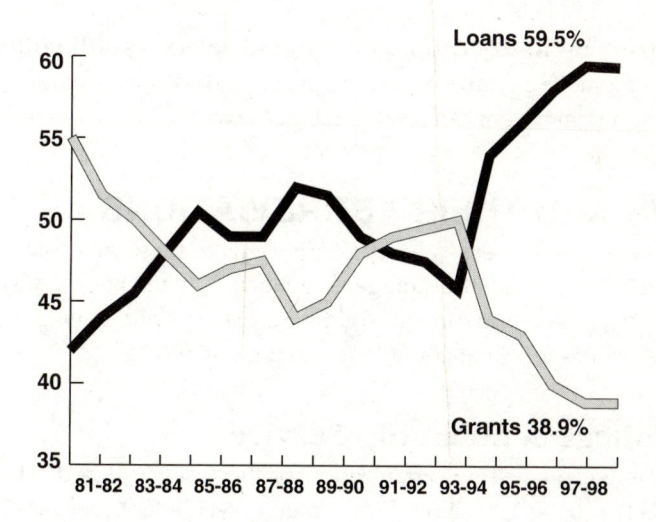

Pittsburgh Post-Gazette October 12, 1998 p. 1. (Source: College Board and Carnegie Mellon University.)

The wise college candidate who needs financial aid should therefore apply to a range of colleges in terms of affordability to ensure that there are financial options as well as admissions options at decision time in April. A sensible college list might include:

- **First choice**—the college or university the candidate most wants to attend regardless of cost.
- **Second choice**—a college that has slightly less difficult entrance requirements and has a good reputation for making—*and sustaining over four years*—reasonable financial aid packages. (You can find this out by reading the college's literature, visiting its Web site to see if there is a commitment to maintain an initial level of funding, and talking to your college counselor.)

- **Third choice**—a college where the candidate's chances of admission are at least fifty-fifty and whose literature states that it attempts to meet the financial need of all admitted candidates.
- **Fourth choice**—a college that offers essentially the same conditions for financial aid as the third, but there is a much better chance of admission, and perhaps a substantial grant in the package.
- **Fifth choice**—in most cases this will be the state university.

Extremely needy candidates should select a sixth college—one that either has a cooperative education program or is near home so that living at home and commuting can reduce college costs.

TERMS AND THEIR ABBREVIATIONS

Before beginning the research necessary to make these financial decisions, familiarize yourself with the strange language of the financial aid world. The simple initials and terms in the following list describe a whole range of programs everyone will encounter at one time or another.

CSS/College Scholarship Service

The CSS is the processing organization of the College Board. The mailing address is Box 6300, Princeton, New Jersey, 08541, telephone: 609-771-7725.

Financial Aid PROFILE

The PROFILE is one of the two basic applications for financial aid (the FAFSA is the other); most students will complete it. Applying for the PROFILE is just like applying for the SAT. Pick up an application form in the early fall at your guidance office. Fill it out, send it in, and you will be sent the PROFILE in a couple of weeks. You can also apply for the PROFILE on line by going to the College Board Web site (http://www.collegeboard.org). The PROFILE can be downloaded and sent in as a paper copy. If you have any questions, you can call toll-free (800-778-6888).

Once you and your family have completed the PROFILE, you send it to CSS, which acts as a clearinghouse for colleges and universities. CSS applies its formulas for parental and student income, assets, and liabilities to your particular set of information, and it makes adjustments for taxes, living costs, unusual expenses, retirement funds, and the support of other children and then sends the results to you and the colleges and universities you have designated. What the schools receive from CSS is an estimated Family Contribution (FC). The FC is the amount of money CSS believes the student and his or her family can be expected to contribute toward the student's college education.

Federal Work-Study (FWS) Program

The Federal Work-Study Program (formerly known as College Work-Study, or CWS) is a federally financed program that provides funds for students who receive financial aid to work on campus or to work for tax-exempt employers nearby. Normally students receive the minimum wage to begin with. The federal government pays for most of the student's wages; the employer pays the balance. An FWS component is part of virtually all financial aid packages in which federal funding is involved. An FWS experience can:

- add breadth and depth to the student's education through the contacts made with other students and the nonacademic challenges that must be figured out and mastered;
- be a valuable asset when looking for a job after college;
- allow the student to meet new people and become involved in the nonacademic part of campus life.

Financial aid awards are often predicated on the student accepting the FWS job and earning a certain amount toward the payment of college fees and expenses. Students should not look on FWS as providing them with discretionary income.

Free Application for Federal Student Aid (FAFSA)

The FAFSA was instituted in 1992 as a way of simplifying the application for all federal grants and loans. *Every family applying for aid must fill out a FAFSA, which becomes available in November in high school guidance offices.* FAFSAs can also be completed on the Web and filed electronically, except for the signature pages. Students and parents should print out a copy of the completed FAFSA for their records. You can go to http://www.fafsa.ed.gov and follow the simple directions. There are two terms that arise from filing the FAFSA. One is the Student Aid Report (SAR). This is sent to you in three or four weeks, sometimes sooner if you apply electronically. It confirms all the information you submitted and refers you to the data release number (DRN) on the upper right-hand corner of the first page of the

SAR. This is the number that you will need to write down in case you want your information sent to additional schools. The other term is Estimated Family Contribution (EFC). This operates in the same way as the FC. Questions can be addressed electronically to the Federal Processor's office, or you can call the toll-free number (800-433-3243).

Grant Aid
This term is used to describe that portion of a student's scholarship that does not have to be paid back. Grants are gift aid. The amount of grant aid you will receive will vary from school to school. Each has a slightly different system of conferring grant aid, so be prepared.

Pell Grants
Some needy students will qualify for this federally supported grant program. Eligibility is established on the FAFSA, and the amount of the grant is currently $3,125 a year. The federal government sets the amount of the Pell Grants each year but recently passed legislation promising to raise the upper limit to $5,800 by the year 2004. When you receive your SAR back from the Federal Processor, it will tell you whether you are eligible for a Pell Grant.

Merit Scholarship
The National Merit Scholarship and the National Achievement Scholarships are based on merit: they are awarded to students on the basis of their performance on standardized tests as confirmed by high school grades. The National Merit Scholarship program is a prestigious one. Students compete on the basis of their PSAT scores in eleventh grade and then confirm their high standing on the basis of subsequent SATs, a strong grade point average, and a strong recommendation from their school. Winners receive a $500 stipend if they do not qualify for aid and $2,000 if they do. A few select winners are chosen for corporate scholarships that may be even higher.

Merit scholarships are awarded by the colleges themselves and are grants that do not have to be repaid. In an era of comparative statistics and rankings, some colleges and universities have used merit awards to attract students who not only will add spark to the classroom but whose high SAT or ACT scores will make the freshman profile look strong.

Need-Blind Admissions
This term is used to describe a college or university admissions system that operates independently of a student's financial need. The student's financial

need is not taken into account in the admissions decision. Need-blind admission was common practice from the late 1960s to the early 1980s because federal dollars were so plentiful. In recent years the withdrawal of federal support for grants to students and the rising costs of high-quality education have forced many colleges to move away from need-blind admissions.

Need-Sensitive Admissions

The policy that many colleges and universities have adopted today is that of considering a student's need in the admissions decision. (This is fully described in Chapter 9.) Need-sensitive admissions can appear in a number of modes:

- A college can be sensitive to the scholarship needs of students on the waiting list and not take those who cannot afford to pay the full bill.
- The college can be sensitive to the financial need of a portion of the applicant pool, usually those near the margin of admission. In this case it will admit only those students with modest credentials who can pay the full fare.
- The university can admit candidates with marginal credentials but not offer them sufficient financial aid. This practice is called *gapping*. The gap expresses the difference between the EFC plus the amount of aid offered and the actual cost of attending the school. Colleges and universities also engage in what is called *gapping for state aid*. In this case, if the student qualifies for state assistance, that amount is not included in the package on the assumption that the student will apply for the money and arrange to have the funds transferred to the college.
- A college or university can decide to make capacity to pay a small, positive factor in the evaluation system. With this system, the college is able to offer full financial aid to all the students it admits, if they use the system shrewdly. (See Chapter 10).

As a rule of thumb, students and parents should make sure to inquire about each institution's financial aid policy in some detail. Ask the financial aid office to explain how students are packaged, and see if the office will give you an indication of the kind of assistance—grants, loans, FWS, etc.—you might receive. Make sure you find out about merit scholarships at each school you apply to.

Preferential Packaging

This is the form of need-sensitive admissions described previously that gives the more desirable students a more favorable ratio of grant to loan and grant to work-study than those who are less desirable.

LOAN PROGRAMS

Perkins Loans

The Perkins Loan is a federal loan for highly needy students. It carries a 5 percent interest rate, but the loan is subsidized while the student is enrolled at least part-time in college. Repayment begins nine months after graduation, and the upper limit on the loan is $4,000 that can be borrowed each year of school.

Subsidized Stafford Loan

This is a low-interest federally sponsored loan issued by local banks. Once a student's need is determined by the numbers on the FAFSA form, the student may borrow up to $2,625 in the first year over a range to $5,500 in the senior year up to a maximum of $23,000 over four years of undergraduate education. Repayment takes place over a ten-year period at a new, low interest rate of under 7 percent. Interest rates cannot rise above 8.25 percent according to new legislation. The Stafford Loan program introduces two new terms: the *origination fee,* which is 3 percent of the amount borrowed that is taken as a fee up front, and the *insurance premium* of 1 percent of the loan, which is billed to the student's term bill. Like the Perkins Loan, the interest while the student is in college and for six months afterward is subsidized by the government. Then repayment begins.

In the present climate of education loans, many banks are competing for customers. Some banks will absorb both the origination and insurance fees. Consult with the financial aid administrator at your school before contracting for a Stafford Loan.

Unsubsidized Stafford Loan

The unsubsidized loan is for students whose need is not great enough to qualify them for a Stafford Loan. The limits of the unsubsidized loan are the same as for the subsidized: $2,625 in the first year and rising to $5,500 in the senior year, with a $23,000 maximum. The interest rates are the same (7.46

percent, not to exceed 8.25 percent); however, the student is responsible for the interest right from the beginning. The student may elect to "capitalize" the interest until he or she graduates. Then, six months after graduation, the student will begin making monthly payments of principal and interest for the ten-year life of the loan.

PLUS Loans

PLUS stands for Parent Loan for Undergraduate Students. These loans are federally sponsored and can rise to the total cost of attendance at the college. There is no upper limit on these loans, but parents must begin repaying them within sixty days of receiving the funds at the rate of 9 percent. They have up to ten years to pay off their PLUS loans.[2]

Additional Unsubsidized Federal Stafford Loans

This loan program is designed for *independent* students. It has slightly higher limits than the other Stafford Loans—$4,000 the first and second years and then up to $5,000 in the third, fourth, and fifth years. The interest payments begin while in school, and principal repayments begin six months after graduation. The interest rates are the same as for the other two Stafford Loan programs.

AID APPLICATION FORMS

Applying for financial aid is much easier than the terminology would suggest, especially with the availability of electronic applications and updating procedures. You should begin no later than November in your senior year of high school by going to your guidance office and procuring applications for the PROFILE and the FAFSA.

These applications can also be procured electronically (addresses mentioned previously), and there are slight price breaks on the PROFILE if you apply electronically. There is certainly a more rapid response time from both CSS and the Federal Processor.

With the PROFILE, you will need to pay a fee of $6 to start and then a $15 charge for each school you want your results sent to. You can list ten schools initially, then pay the fee again, and $15 each for each school beyond the original ten.

---

[2]PLUS Loans and both Stafford Loans have their yearly rate set by Congress. The basis for the interest rate is the Treasury Bill rate plus points for overhead cost.

The FAFSA, of course, is free. Both of these forms should be filed by their respective deadlines. If you are missing a piece of data and the deadline approaches, it is better to estimate the figure and submit the form. You can always amend your form later. Thousands do every year, and the colleges and universities understand this. The importance of meeting the deadlines arises from the fact that some colleges simply will not award aid after the deadline has passed.

Filling out the PROFILE and/or the FAFSA

Students and their families should strive for accuracy when completing these forms. Getting a jump on what information will be asked for by studying the forms on line or in printed form in December will help reduce the haste to complete them in January. Students should be sure to have their Social Security numbers ready for whoever completes the form. International students with permanent resident status can also apply for federal aid and private scholarship funds.

If your parents are divorced, most institutions will require completion of the Divorced or Separated Parent's Statement. These forms can be obtained from your guidance counselor or ordered electronically. Most institutions will ask both parents to contribute to their child's education, even though there has been a divorce. The reason for this statement is that most colleges and universities consider the family as the primary source of college funds. If a parent has remarried after a divorce, then the resources of the new spouse, who is now a member of the student's family, are subject to review when it comes to paying for college. It is often said that students, parents, and the school are the three legs of the financial aid stool, and that the third leg goes on last. In other words, colleges look first to what the student can contribute, then to the family, including stepparents. If there is a gap between that amount and the cost of attendance, then and only then does the college itself contribute grant and loan assistance.

Parents completing the PROFILE and the FAFSA are asked to furnish information about the number of their dependents for the current calendar year and the number of children they are supporting in college. Most of the information requested can be taken from the parents' tax return (Form 1040 or 1040A); however, other information, such as the value of real estate bank deposits and stocks, will have to be gathered separately. Parents will also be asked to project their earnings for the year in which the applicant will enter college. In their responses they should not include any money earned by their son or daughter under any current financial aid program, nor should they project any for the following year. The purpose of these forms is to determine need on an annual basis and to help college officials decide how much aid to offer.

In cases where Social Security benefits are involved, only itemize those benefits that applicants and their parents receive, not other family members. Married students who rely on their parents' support to meet living expenses are required to include amounts received for welfare, child support, or unemployment and any living or housing allowances, whether in cash or in kind. They obviously must also report the earnings of their spouse.

Medical expenses that are not reimbursed by an insurance plan may also be included to offset other income, as can the tuition paid for private elementary or junior high school education of other children in the family. These amounts are then projected for the next calendar year. Finally, there is total income, taxable income, nontaxable income, and federal income tax paid. The end result is a true family income figure.

It is important to remember that each college or university aid office has what is called "professional judgment." That means that each of these expenses will be treated slightly differently by each school. Ask your financial aid administrator for clarification.

The PROFILE goes further than the FAFSA in asking students and parents to provide regular and summer wages, savings and checking account balances, dividend and interest income, trust fund income, and home value.[3] The PROFILE also has a section for institution-specific questions. For example, if you indicate that you want your financial information sent to Coburn, then you will be asked to fill out the few additional questions that the Coburn Financial Aid Office wants to know.

Once each of these forms has been processed and the family has received its copy of the SAR or the estimated Family Contribution, the colleges and universities go to work. In most cases they have computer programs that will run scenarios for them, determining aid following the federal methodology (FAFSA) or their own institutional methodology (PROFILE). They will usually pick the methodology that gives them the smaller need.

---

[3] The PROFILE will ask for the purchase price, actual value, and the amount of the mortgage on the parents' primary residence.

Coburn College
Financial Aid Office
Ivy Hall
Hawthorne, NY 04415

April, 1999

Dear Martha:

Congratulations on your admission to Coburn. We have reviewed your financial aid documents and have prepared this estimate of your eligibility for assistance to help you plan for your college expenses.

This award is based on the information you and your family have submitted thus far. You may need to submit additional information, if previously requested, to finalize this award. Otherwise, you may regard this award as Coburn's offer of financial assistance for the academic year 1999–2000.

Coburn's direct costs for the year 1999–2000 include tuition, fees, room, and board. The total of **$25,746** for tuition and **$6,570** for room and board comes to **$32,316**. We are assuming a double occupancy room and the nineteen meal-a-week plan. You and your family are responsible for the difference between the school's charges and the amount of aid available for direct costs. In addition to these expenses, you should plan for the cost of books, supplies, travel, and other personal expenses. To help you with this calculation, we have included a separate light green sheet. We estimate that books should cost about $675 for the academic year. This will vary depending on the courses you take and the availability of used books.

Financial Aid Available for Direct Costs	Fall	Spring	Total
Dean's Talent Award	$ 2,750	$2,250	$ 5,000
College Scholarship	4,521	3,319	7,840
Federal Perkins Loan	1,581	1,294	2,875
Subsidized Federal Stafford Loan	1,313	1,312	2,625
Total of Aid for Direct Costs	$10,165	$8,175	$18,340
Family Contribution			$13,976
Total Direct Costs			$32,316

FINANCING YOUR COLLEGE EDUCATION

> Students are expected to work during the summer and contribute $1,500 toward their education costs and to have funds available for books, supplies, and personal expenses when they arrive on campus. Students are also eligible for campus employment. Coburn's Student Employment Office will be glad to help you find a position. The initial openings of campus jobs are reserved for scholarship students. You can expect to earn $1,000 each semester.
>
> | | | | |
> |---|---|---|---|
> | **Federal College Work-Study** | $ 1,000 | $ 1,000 | $ 2,000 |
> | Total Financial Aid Award | $11,565 | $ 9,175 | $20,340 |
>
> We have enclosed a number of documents that will help you consider this offer: a sheet that will help you and your parents apportion the Family Contribution, the light green sheet that will help you anticipate your college expenses and budget for them, a sheet explaining how we apply scholarship and loan funds to your term bill, and the schedule of term bill payments. We have also included information about loan options available from the Crest Bank and a description of Coburn's tuition payment plan. It is called our Alternative Financing sheet.
>
> To accept this offer, please sign the acceptance form (pink copy) and return it to us by May 15. The acceptance form does not obligate you to attend the college; it enables us to monitor our financial aid commitments. If you have any questions, please call or e-mail us. We will be glad to help.
>
> Sincerely yours,
>
> Associate Director of Financial Aid

    In anticipating a college's financial aid offer, remember that 35 percent of the student's assets are liable for deployment to meet college expenses in the first year and 35 percent the second, until the assets are nearly used up in year three. At the same time, most colleges look to the parents to contribute between 4 to 5 percent of their assets per year. (The federal cap is 5.6 percent.) Extenuating factors in the case of parents include the age of the parent (the older you are the less you are expected to contribute), the cost of an older child in college, and business or farm losses. Any one of these three can reduce the EFC.

The rest of the PROFILE and the FAFSA is fairly straightforward. Parents will be asked on the PROFILE to project their income for the next year and to provide detailed information about the expenses they bear for the education of their other children. In the case of divorced families, child support, alimony, and the income of the parent with whom the child does not live are requested.

Having done all this, parents then code the FAFSA with the numbers of the schools to which the EFC will be sent and submit it electronically or in paper form to the Federal Processor. The PROFILE gets mailed electronically or by the post office back to CSS, with the fee for the application itself and the processing for each school ($6 plus $15 per school). If you submit the PROFILE electronically, you will need to charge the fees to a credit card.

Make paper copies of everything and save electronic copies on separate disks, one for each form. You may also wish to construct a spreadsheet similar to the one you made for your applications. On it you will enter the dates you received, completed, mailed, edited, and followed up on each form.

EVALUATING YOUR FINANCIAL AID AWARD

When you are finally admitted to college and are deemed eligible for financial aid, you will receive your financial aid package in a letter format. A sample letter is on pages 180–181.

Some Examples from the Alternative Financing Sheet

A number of alternative financing programs are available to assist families with meeting the expenses of a Coburn education. Coburn College does not recommend one program over another. The College only hopes that you will find one of these programs suitable to your needs. The contractual arrangements for these programs are made by the family with the specific vendor.

Payment Plans
Coburn College Budget Payment Plan
- Yearly college charges, paid in twelve equal monthly payments
- Service charge of 1 percent on the outstanding balance
- Payroll deductions and EFT available
- Term bill postings available electronically for parents

Key Resource Group
- Monthly payment plans range from one to four years
- Application form in this packet
- For more information call 800-KEYLEND (539-5363)
- Subsidiary of Keycorp

Tuition Management Systems, Inc.
- Subsidiary of Chemical Bank
- Wide range of payment plans
- For more information call 800-722-4867

Loan Programs
Key Bank
- Achiever Loans for Parents; maximum amount is cost of education
- Three payment options: one year, multiple year, and interest only while the student is in college
- Interest rates based on 91-Day Treasury Bill, currently 8.45 percent, 9 percent, and 9 percent, for above options
- Apply on line: http://www.key.com/education
- Student Alternative Loans: for students, maximum amount is $10,000
- Interest based on 52-Week Treasury Bill is currently 7.63 percent
- Paper application can be downloaded from Web site

Home Equity Loans
- Possible tax advantage
- Interest rates tend to be high, so those in high tax brackets are favored
- Contact bank that holds your mortgage

Option 4 Loan Programs
- Loan amounts from $2,000 to $15,000 per year
- Variable interest rate, Treasury Bill + 3.5 percent
- Repayment period can extend to fifteen years
- Contact United Student Aid Funds at 800-LOANUSA

PLUS Loans
- Maximum loan amount is high, the cost of attendance
- Interest rate is variable. Treasury Bill + 3.10 percent, not to exceed 9 percent. Current rate is near 9 percent
- PLUS loans carry an origination fee of 3 percent and guarantee fee of 1 percent (in a few states)
- Current interest rate is 8.26 percent. Changes quarterly, based on 91-Day Treasury Bill rate
- Contact local bank, credit union, or lending institution

SHARE Educational Loans for Families
- Available to all creditworthy applicants
- Loans begin at $2,000 and rise to total cost of education minus any financial aid
- Two interest rate options: deferred payments of principal while student is in college and monthly payments, including both principal and interest
- Repayment ranges from four to twenty years, depending on amount borrowed
- http://www.nelliemae.org; call 800-634-9308

TERI Supplemental Loans
- Loans begin at $2,000 and can include whole cost of education minus any financial aid
- Loans available to either parents or students
- Current interest rates range from 8 percent to 9 percent
- Credit line option available
- Twenty-five-year repayment period. Three plans: principal plus interest, no principal for four years, and no principal or interest for four years while student is in college
- 5 percent guarantee fee, deducted before disbursement
- http://www.teri.org; call 800-255-TERI

Gate Loan Program
- Parents can borrow up to cost of education at 31-Day Treasury bill rate + 3.10 percent. Current rate is 7.51 percent.
- Fifteen-year repayment schedule
- Can defer payments while student is in college
- http://www.gateloan.com; use loan calculator screen

Evaluating Your Financial Aid Award

When you finally receive your financial aid package, follow this simple guide for interpreting your award. Make two columns. List your direct costs in the left-hand column: tuition, fees, room, and board. In the right-hand column list the sources of the funds that will pay those costs. Now drop down the page and continue the columns. In the left-hand column, list books, incidentals, travel, laundry, phone, and the other basic expenses that you will confront in college. Move to the right-hand column and list the sources of funds that will pay for those expenses. It is in this column that you would list summer earnings, work-study, and any outside scholarship or help from family members you might have received. Hopefully, when you have carried out this exercise, you will find that both you and the college have figured things the same way.

Now you are ready to look at your financial aid offer in comparative terms to see how one college's offer compares with another. To do that you need to look at the way the college plans to fund the difference between your family's contribution and the total cost of education. This is normally done with a combination of grants and loans. As you scrutinize these details, keep in mind the difference between *price* and *cost*. The price is what the institution charges the customer: tuition, fees, room, and board. But you are not paying that. You are paying more. You are paying travel, books, laundry, phone, incidental expenses, and so on. These expenses, plus price, equals the cost.

There are three variables that will make it slightly challenging for you to compare college offers of financial aid:

1. Each college will offer you a slightly different amount of grant aid
2. Each school can have slightly different expectations for you in terms of summer earnings, term-time earnings (FWS), and bookstore expenses
3. Each college will compute your student budget, which consists of your direct costs plus your expenses, in a slightly different way

In your financial aid package your assistance will come in four different forms:

Outright Grant. This is money that does not have to be repaid. Grant money may be based on need, merit, or both. Grants are normally higher for students with higher need or for students who are being offered merit aid. Some very needy students may receive Pell Grants in their packages. Many states also have generous grant programs, in which case an amount for state grant will appear in the grant section of your package.

Federal Loans. Stafford and Perkins Loans have been explained. You should definitely consider the cost of repaying these loans as part of your cost to attend the school.

College or Private Loans. These loans, such as PLUS, SHARE, TERI, and the like, will not be a part of your formal financial aid package, but you may elect to take out one of them later. If you do, their costs become part of your cost to attend a particular college or university.

Summer Earnings/Work-Study. These terms refer to the amount of money you are expected to make during the summer and as a work-study student during the year. Lower expectations from one school may look attractive, but look at the student budget. Is the school expecting you to take out more in loans? Or is the budget for attending that particular school less because it is less expensive or closer to home? These are questions you will need to ask.

Interpreting the Family Contribution

In some cases, students and families are surprised by the size of the family contribution they are expected to make. Here are some possible reasons:

- Families may not have updated their financial information, and therefore the school has made its offer based on earlier information that yields a higher EFC.
- For economic or equity reasons some colleges and universities may increase or decrease the EFC. Recently, a group of selective institutions lowered the EFC for middle-income families so that they could offer them more grant aid.
- In addition, college and university financial aid officers have what is known as professional judgment to interpret some of the financial data that they receive. Parents should understand that although schools may vary in their treatment of expenses, each will be consistent and fair with all its financial aid families. Also, each school will have a published manual for its allocation of financial aid.
- In some cases, a school may come up with an EFC that is greater than that suggested by CSS. In such a case, institutions may respond differently to assets such as savings, stocks and bonds, and rental income property.
- Remember that whatever discretion is used or disparities arise, it is because the colleges and universities are trying to stretch their financial

aid dollars as far as they can go, not because they are singling out an individual family. Some students and families may not receive as much aid as they want, but they should understand that the colleges believe that families should pay as much as they can reasonably afford. If a family has made "other lifestyle choices," such as buying a vacation home or a boat and incurred large debts, that family may not have enough funds to meet the EFC and send their child to the college of his or her choice. This sometimes happens.

Continuing Your Financial Aid in College

As you look over the financial aid awards from your colleges and universities, be on the lookout for strong statements that promise to maintain your level of aid for the upperclass years as a student. Naturally, there will be a qualification about the same level of need, but there should be some assurance that the college will try to maintain the same level of support.

As you proceed through your undergraduate years, realize that some schools may expect the student's contribution from summer earnings to increase as they develop more marketable skills. Federal Work-Study could change slightly. If the student wanted to become more extensively involved in a particular academic or extracurricular project, then FWS would decrease, or if the student wanted to forego $1,000 in loans, then he or she might opt to work more than the estimated number of hours.

In spite of popular belief to the contrary, few schools deliberately reduce financial aid to continuing students. It would not be ethical to do so, nor would it be in the school's interest to reduce aid after the freshman year. In fact, at some schools research on satisfaction with financial aid has convinced officials to increase aid packages slightly, lest students think about leaving. The cost to increase an aid package is far less than the cost to recruit a new student.

As a practical matter, you will have to reapply for financial aid every year you are in college. If you have saved your application from the current year on disk or on paper, it should be easy to update your old application with new data and forward it to the Federal Processor or CSS. What was once a difficult and lengthy process will soon become a relatively quick exercise.

QUESTIONS FREQUENTLY ASKED

What happens to my award after the freshman year?
Each spring the Financial Aid Office will ask families to complete a new PROFILE and a new FAFSA. This process involves updating the previous application with current information and submitting it electronically or on paper. As has been said, if the family's finances have not changed substantially, you can generally expect that the college will meet your need as in the past year. Remember, if you have a merit scholarship as part of your package, you will have to achieve the goals the award stipulated if it is to be renewed.

What if a family's situation changes—is there anything that can be done?
If your family experiences a sudden adverse change, you should report it directly to the Financial Aid Office—even if it happens in the middle of the year. Be prepared to provide a letter or documentation of the change, and be assured that the college will respond accordingly. Schools do budget for these unforeseen events.

When my brother and sister enter college in two years, what happens?
Your family's need will rise, and your school will try to meet it by reducing the FC by one half for each child entering college. If you did not qualify for aid at all, or only loans, when you entered college, perhaps with your brother and sister enrolled, you will qualify for grant assistance.

I may receive a local scholarship when I graduate from high school. Can I "take" that scholarship to my college and use it to reduce my costs?
In recent years, many colleges and universities have abandoned their decades-long practice of applying outside scholarships to the grant portion of students' awards and thereby reducing the amount of the college's funds that went to the particular student. Now it has become common for colleges to allow students to apply outside scholarships to the loan, FWS, and summer earnings portions of their grants. You will need to ask your Financial Aid Office what its policy is.

What happens if for some reason I cannot procure a nonsubsidized Stafford Loan at a local bank?
This is very unlikely. Contact the Financial Aid Office right away. The office will help find you a lender.

Does it make any sense for me to become an independent student to save my parents money?
No. Most financial aid programs are based on the premise that the student is living with his or her parents and that they are providing primary support. In this situation, both the student and the parents have the primary responsibility to pay for educational costs. However, if you are truly independent of your parents, financial aid will be computed differently. To be considered independent, you have to be at least 24 years old, you may not have lived with either of your parents for the past year nor received more that $750 per year from them, and you have not been claimed by them as an income tax exemption for three consecutive years prior to the year for which you are seeking aid. If you are judged to be an independent student, you will be eligible for higher levels of Stafford Loans.

Do I have to accept the work-study job offered to me as a condition for receiving my other scholarship and loan aid?
Absolutely not. If you can make an equivalent amount to FWS during the summer or working off campus at higher wages, or your family can provide the funds to meet your expenses, you do not need to accept the offer of FWS. Some students prefer to work long hours in the summer so they can concentrate solely on their education at college and not work a campus job. That is their privilege. However, it is important to recognize that some work-study jobs, such as those related to Teaching America to Read, are receiving considerable support from the government. Students interested in becoming teachers might want to seek FWS in that area.

What if I need aid and am not awarded any?
You and your family will then have to turn to PLUS Loans and the other loan programs that have been described, i.e., SHARE, TERI, Key Loans, Gate Loans, and Fleet Loans, to name a few. (See the list of Web sites at the end of this chapter.) Financial aid officers will know a good deal about the various loan programs. Most schools will have a relationship with a local bank where you can begin.

SAMPLE FINANCIAL AID PACKAGES

	COLLEGE A	COLLEGE B	COLLEGE C	COLLEGE D
	(Small, selective private college)	(State college, moderate size)	(State university, large)	(Large, selective private university)
Tuition and fees	$24,425	$13,500	$ 8,000	$26,400
Room and board	$ 7,190	$ 5,200	$ 5,000	$ 7,100
Price	$31,615	$18,700	$13,000	$33,500
Miscellaneous (books, supplies, etc.)	$ 1,500	$ 1,500	$ 1,500	$ 1,550
Total budget for attendance	$33,115	$20,200	$14,500	$35,050
Expected family contribution (including student assets)	–$ 5,000*	–$ 5,000	–$ 4,000	–$ 5,500*
Difference to be financed	$28,115	$15,200	$10,500	$29,550
Financial aid package				
Grant (gift money)	$21,465	$ 5,000	$ 2,000†	$22,250
Loans (to be repaid)	$ 4,000	$ 4,000	$ 4,000	$ 4,500
Work-study (campus job)	$ 1,400	$ 1,300	Not promised	$ 1,450
Summer earnings	$ 1,300	$ 1,200	$ 500	$ 1,350
Total financial aid awarded	$28,165	$11,500	$ 6,500**	$29,550
Cost of Attendance (Total budget minus financial aid)	$ 4,950	$ 8,700	$ 4,000	$ 5,500

*Colleges A and D require the PROFILE and FAFSA. Colleges B and C require only the FAFSA.
**Note gap between aid and amount to be financed.
†In-state resident grant.

   The chart above shows the different ways in which colleges and universities package financial aid and the resulting cost of education that the family pays. You should set up a similar chart to compare the financial aid you have been awarded. Remember—after you have made your cost comparisons, you may still want to go to a school that costs more than your lowest-cost school. That is fine, because for good reasons, you see more value in the higher-cost school.

- **Pay careful attention to the relative amounts of aid included in each offer, as well as the bottom line, which is how much families are expected to contribute.** Obviously, high grant figures, even if accompanied by high loans, should command careful attention if the schools are of equal quality and cost. (Colleges A and D are examples.) However, if the school's tuition and fees are high to begin with, high grant and loan figures may have less net impact than a slightly lower grant at a much less expensive school. (Compare A with B.) In the case where one school costs less than another and the grant amounts are about the same, you should consider the less expensive of the two. (See the differences between College C and College D.) When schools of roughly equal quality and cost offer different levels of financial aid, you should strongly consider the school offering the larger financial aid package.

- **Examine the loan structure in detail.** Federally supported loans are less expensive than those from private banks and lending agencies or the university itself. The same holds true for state-sponsored loans. Students and families really need to think about the long-term consequences of the indebtedness they are being asked to assume, whether or not graduate school is in the picture. Furthermore, the federal loan programs will allow you to postpone repayment of undergraduate loans until you are through with full-time graduate school. On the other hand, some of the private colleges and universities have access to private lenders that the public schools do not. So if a family has to borrow, there may be more possibilities at a private school than at a public one. Loans that enable a family to spread out the cost of a college education for ten or fifteen years, such as TERI, can really make a difference.
- **Be wary of financial aid offers with extensive summer earnings and work-study expectations.** Each family will have to decide on its definition of "extensive," but the last thing you want to do is send the student to a college or university where he or she has to work at a job all the time as opposed to participating fully in the educational experience. Parents should avoid stretching their child "too thin." It will defeat the whole purpose.

A WORD ON LOANS

A recent poll of college financial aid officers revealed that many of them think that students are not looking carefully enough at alternatives to long-term loans. They begin by borrowing more than they need because loans are easy to procure. Then they compound their difficulty by extending their payback periods, not realizing that they will be encountering other significant financing costs while still shouldering their college loans. Many students these days are trying to finance their first houses and condominiums while paying off significant college loans. Students and families have to take a hard look at the interest component of the loans that they are offered and make sure that they are comfortable with it.

They might want to recall the Rule of 72, which states that if you divide 72 by an interest rate, you will get the number of years it takes to double the amount borrowed. Assuming a 9 percent interest rate on a $10,000 loan, it will take eight years to make $10,000 in interest. So a student who leaves college with a $10,000 loan and starts a repayment plan at 8 percent ends up paying another $10,000 in interest for an eight-year period. In eight years he or she has paid $20,000 back to the bank. The lesson in this example is that if the family has reasonable resources, it is much easier to take steps so you can pay your costs—or most of them—at the beginning, rather than trying to finance them later. Consider, for example, a savings plan in which a family was able to put away $10,000 eight years before college began in an investment that earned 9 percent. That family would have $17,500 in hand on the day school began. (Capital gains would have taken away $2,500 of the gain.) A totally different situation.

WAYS TO REDUCE COLLEGE EXPENSES

Several ways to reduce college expenses have been mentioned: the three-year degree option, living at home for part or all of the four-year experience, attending a less expensive school than the ones originally considered, and trying to identify schools with strong merit scholarship programs. However, once the final choices of school are in front of you, the range of options narrows. A few choices:

- **Reduce income so the family will qualify for more financial aid in the next cycle.** Owners of small businesses can sometimes do this by buying inventory. Wage earners have a tougher challenge. Sometimes a parent can decide to drop out of the workforce and return to school and in that way decrease the EFC.
- **Investigate college payment plans.** Move to a twelve-month payment plan or an extended plan for four to six years that some schools offer.
- **Increase your payments to your retirement accounts, giving you less disposable income.** If you adopt this strategy, do it while the student is in high school—before the senior year. Otherwise, the allocation will show as income and become part of the family's EFC.

- **Defer income to later years, after the child has graduated from college.** Parents can sometimes do this with trust fund income or with consulting income. In the latter case, consultants and lawyers in small firms can decide not to distribute income in a given year.

With all of these suggestions, the final judgment on what you can and should do should come from your accountant.

FOR MORE INFORMATION

Here is a list of Web sites with information about financing the cost of higher education and the financial aid system that you may find useful:

http://www.petersons.com At this large site, look for CollegeQuest, which is Peterson's full-scale program of college selection, application, and financing.

http://www.collegeboard.org Another large site where you will find useful insights into sources of college funds as well as the PROFILE application and PROFILE form.

http://www.fastweb.com A vendor who provides an application filing service as well as information about completing your financial aid applications and searching for outside funding. It has both a parents' page and a question and answer page with financial aid experts.

http://www.finaid.org This site received national attention a few years ago. It was begun by a Carnegie Mellon student, who has since turned it into one of the most comprehensive sites in the electronic environment.

http://www.collegesavings.org The Web site of the National Association of State Treasurers. Very useful source of information about various state educational savings plans. Details savings trusts run by a handful of states, including Connecticut, New Jersey, and New York. These plans allow parents to put money away tax free for their child's education, and when the money is taken out for tuition purposes, it is taxed at the child's presumably lower tax rate.

http://www.kaploan.com Information on loans for parents and students, descriptions of resources on financial aid, planning for college financing, and a chat room for both parents and students. This site is run by the Kaplan Test Preparation company.

http://www.key.com/education The Key Bank was one of the first to enter the education market, and its extensive site has information on both its Achiever and Alternative Loans and on the process of applying for aid and interpreting financial aid offers. Key Bank also has college financing software (KeyScape) that can be downloaded and studied by parents and students.

http://www.eduloans.pncbank.com PNC has long been active in the education field, and its site describes its loan products as well as gives useful comparative information about the government's loans and qualifications for borrowers. There are instructions on how to fill out forms, what books to investigate, and a link to the Princeton Review site. Has a very useful calculator that lets you put in the present cost of a college you like and the number of years before the child will be ready for that college and gives you the amount of money that would have to be saved to attend that particular school.

http://www.gateloan.com Gate Loans are available at certain colleges and universities at attractive rates. Strong comparative page gives costs of rival products. Calculator function enables a visitor to plug in the amount he or she wants to borrow and see the monthly costs for different repayment periods.

http://www.fafsa.ed.gov Although visitors may think that the only benefit of going to this site is to procure a copy of the FAFSA or to complete one electronically, they will be pleasantly surprised by the information about how the financial aid system works. There is a section for recent changes in procedures, and there are links to various funding sources for scholarships and loans. There is a complete description of all the federal aid programs, including the new Hope Tax Credit that can be claimed during the student's first two years of college.

http://www.nasfaa.org This is the site of the National Association of Student Financial Aid Administrators. Its commentary on the status of appropriations in Congress and actions by the Department of Education is useful if one is planning ahead for financial assistance in college.

http://www.troweprice.com Lots of useful tools to help families plan for college costs and links to other sites. Has calculator so families can figure the costs of college when their children are ready. Can plug in different investment growth factors and see how much money it will take. Has investment planner function that tests the buyer's tolerance for risk. Also has various education fund descriptions and "Insights," an investment newsletter.

EIGHT

For Parents Only—
The Myths and the Magic of the College Search

If you get involved and stay involved, the college admissions process will go well, even if there are a few rejections along the way.
　　C. Joseph Gould, Assistant Headmaster for External Affairs at
　　St. George's School and parent of three college graduates

　　All too often parents approach the college admissions process with confused feelings. Frequently they become prisoners of one or more of the myths that cling to the process of choosing a college. These myths conceal the deeper issues that surround this complex process of searching for a school, such as growing independence, leaving home, and parental acknowledgement that their former children are really young adults.
　　The first myth is that college will confer status on the child and bring the family *prestige*. This myth is best captured in the story of Mary and Abraham Lincoln, who, 140 years ago, sent their son Robert to Phillips Exeter so that he could gain admission to a prestigious college. The Lincolns wanted their son to achieve what his father had been denied in life. Even though the elder Mr. Lincoln was a candidate for the Presidency, he still spoke with a Midwestern twang. "Mr. Chairman" came out "Mr. Cheermun" and "are not" was often expressed as "ain't." Lincoln and his wife hoped that Robert would meet the right people at Exeter and acquire the social patina they lacked and meet the "right" friends who would help him along in life. They were not to be disappointed in the years that followed. Robert, after serving in the army, went on to become a Chicago lawyer, Chairman of the Board of the Pullman Palace Car company, and later a Cabinet officer under President Garfield.
　　But the real question for Robert Lincoln was whether or not his education prepared him for the challenges he was to face in life—the

assassination of his father, the prolonged mental instability of his mother, and the oppressive tactics of George Pullman that sparked one of America's most violent strikes and severely damaged Robert's reputation. At the close of the twentieth century the Lincolns' story has a haunting quality. Like the Lincolns, parents today seem to seek a world of perfection and ease for their children because they themselves have worked so hard and spent so many hours away from their families.

A second myth holds that college is *karma,* a sort of happy interlude between youth and adulthood. Some parents may believe that it does not matter much what goes on during the four years of college because the maturation process will take care of things and that somehow at the end of four years, the young person will learn responsibility and be able to focus on a career. Parents who acquiesce in this myth are apt to let their children chart the course to college, and very often those young people take the path of least resistance. These parents do not set their sights high enough for themselves or for their children. Most students in the course of self-evaluation and thinking about the competitive world of college admissions have moments of self-doubt. Parents who do not recognize these moments and encourage the young person to trust themselves and aim high miss a valuable part of the parenting process.

College as the fulfillment of parents' personal aspirations is yet another myth that traps parents and students working their way through the college admissions process. This myth is sometimes called the *halo* myth because the success of the child rebounds to the benefit and reputation of the parents. Whatever the case, it is more prominent in this decade, where parents seem to be transferring more of their own apprehensions and goals to the college admissions process than ever before.

The most memorable example of the halo myth is the father who insisted his son apply to Harvard—where the boy had no chance of being admitted—because he had not had the chance to go to a famous university. The boy dutifully applied to Harvard and other out-of-reach colleges and was rejected, all because of his father's personal issues. It is significant to add that the father was a psychologist!

One of the most perplexing myths asserts that a college education is a *commodity:* good schools, like good jewelry, cost a lot and are better than those that cost less. In other words, price defines value. Recently, a parent in a wealthy suburb was asked by her daughter's guidance counselor, "Why won't you let Sydney apply to the state university?" The answer came fast. "I am not spending $17,000 a year for my daughter to go to the state university when she can get twice as good an education at an Ivy League school for only 50 percent more."

And there is the equally simplistic flip side to this argument. "Why should I spend $30,000 a year to send my son to a so-called 'prestige' school when for half the price he can have a good time at State U?" Parents espousing the commodity point of view invariably know the price of education but not the value of it. They are asking the wrong questions; they should be thinking about the type of college that best suits their child's talents, aspirations, interests, and personality and that has a culture that truly reflects its stated mission. They should be thinking about the particular features of a school that are going to add value to their child's education and life. Some factors to consider might be the quality of undergraduate teaching, accessibility of the faculty members, facilities for undergraduates, academic and social support programs, overseas and internship opportunities, and a set of traditions and a culture that resonate with the family's experiences and hopes.

HOW TO THINK FOR YOURSELF AND YOUR CHILD ABOUT COLLEGE

In thinking about the right college for your child, first begin by distinguishing your child's needs from yours, lest you both fall victim about whose needs are being fulfilled. Remember that your children want to do the *right* thing. All children do. The psychologist's son applied to all those schools to please his father but in the course of so doing placed his own self-esteem at risk. Moreover, the father's dominance kept the son from making his own plans, taking risks, and experiencing failure and success. Parents need to make sure that the children own the process of applying to college. When they own the process—and it is carefully managed—they can then own the results of the process—the success that flows from it.

Think of the college admissions search as a journey for your child, one that he or she has to plan for and make, and one that leads not only to a particular college but also to the broader goals of independence and a heightened sense of self-worth. Your job as a parent is to teach your child how to plan for that journey and to provide occasional tactical support along the way. Some examples of that support follow:

1. "Know your child." Parents are the people who know their child best. So begin by making a profile of your child.

- What are your child's needs, both personally and academic?
- What are your child's talents, both expressed and still to be realized?
- What kinds of people does your child relate to best?
- How does your child bring out the best in others, and in what kind of settings?
- What is the nature of your child's relationship to you as parents? Independent? Dependent? In between?
- Are there stepparents or noncustodial parents or other significant individuals involved in your child's life? What is their relationship to the child, and how might that relationship impact college choice?

The answers to these questions need to be sought in discussions between parents and stepparents, between custodial parents and noncustodial parents, and finally between parents and their child. The key is to identify the child's interests, talents, and expectations and to make your own thoughts known and set off together on the journey.

2. "The Conversation." Your primary job as a parent of a college-bound student is to precipitate a conversation that hopefully will continue all along the road to the chosen school. Bearing in mind that you know your child better than anyone else, both parents should hold an honest conversation with the child—to understand first his or her real motives for wanting to go to college, and subsequently, how all three of you can work together to get him or her there. The first part of the conversation should explore the child's hopes and fears about the college search and admissions process. Parents should offer their reassurances when they can and be honest about the risks that the family cannot control. Parents will also want to review the career hopes and goals of their children. Suggest to them that they conduct a self-assessment and interest inventory process such as that outlined in Chapter 1, if the student has not already done so.

You should talk frankly with your child about career plans and be especially mindful of those who profess a fixed interest in a particular field. Encourage that child, in particular, to seek practical experience. If your son has a fixed view about the profession he wants to enter, make sure he talks to someone who actually practices that profession. Have him "shadow" that person for a day to see what the career is really like. If your daughter is not sure of her goals just yet but has some ideas, encourage her to explore her thoughts with her guidance counselor. Say she is possibly interested in medicine. Perhaps you could arrange a visit with a friend who has a family practice. Or, if there is time, a child could be encouraged to seek employment or do volunteer work in an area of interest. This is a process that can continue in college until a career path comes into view.

One of the goals of the preliminary conversations that parents and children have about college is *reality,* making sure that your son not only knows what he wants to achieve, but more importantly, that he has a realistic view of himself as he strives to reach that goal. The high school track star who has not set a school record should not aspire to apply to a school with a Division I team. Conversely, a high school field hockey player whose team has twice gone to the New England Championships should not apply to a school with a team below her level of ability.

When it comes to academics, seek the same base of realism. Students who are distinctly scholars—junior Cum Laude, Westinghouse Award Winners, and the like—should be encouraged to strive for the top academic schools. However, those with less success—at least at this point in high school—should be encouraged to apply to colleges and universities where they can do well and not be overshadowed by the precocity of others.

Likewise, when it comes to career choice, parents should make sure that the child understands what the details behind the perceived glamour of a profession are. When you are assured that your child has a realistic view of the chosen profession, offer your support.

Next, explore the question of which schools the student is interested in and why:

- How a particular college meets the specific goals and aspirations of the student—these are academic, extracurricular, and career goals together.
- What kind of students attend the college? Are they people whom your child will want to know the rest of his or her life—or at least, some of them? Is the student population diverse? Sufficiently international to provide a network for the global dimension of the twenty-first century workplace? How do students treat each other at the college? Is there genuine tolerance for diversity and is there a caring community?
- What is the express mission of the college or university, and how well does it carry out that mission? Does the college genuinely care for the quality of undergraduate education—in the classroom, in the dormitories, and in activities and sports?

These questions don't have to be answered completely in the first sitting, but they should be posed, for they are crucial. Finally, in that first conversation parents need to formulate a disclaimer, a statement that clearly defines their interest and their supportive role in the college search process. The parents need to assure the child that they do not intend to control the process. Every family has its own way of transacting its business; sometimes much is accomplished by silence and acquiescence, sometimes humor and teasing serve to transmit messages. In this instance a flat statement disclaiming control and promising support is required.

THE LIBERAL ARTS

In the course of their conversations with their offspring who are bound for college, parents should underscore the importance of the liberal arts as a basis for specialization and entry into a particular field. The liberal arts and sciences have long formed the core of most of America's top colleges and many of its universities. At no time more than the present is a thorough grounding in the traditional liberal arts literature, language, history, politics, economics, philosophy, biology, chemistry, and physics—to name many of the traditional subjects—been more important. It is an understanding of the liberal arts that helps students to see the interrelationships between the various sectors of our lives and that helps students formulate the questions they need to ask about their own behavior and their own particular field of endeavor. A good liberal arts preparation should make students perpetually curious about how others would solve a particular problem. It should incline students always to see the interrelationships between events and to probe for the background causes of particular human behavior. Put simply, a good liberal arts education makes us curious. It makes us lifelong learners.

Students attending college should seek it.

THINKING BENEATH THE SURFACE

Applying to college would not be a subject of so many books like this if it did not entail some complexity. One of the most subtle and interesting elements of the process is that it runs parallel to psychological and structural changes in both the child and the parents. Both parties need to be aware of these changes, particularly parents, so that they can help their children and the family navigate this important transition.

FOR PARENTS ONLY

The Strain on Children

Ask any high school senior in March of the senior year—before college decisions are announced—how he or she is feeling, and some form of the following answer will come back: "I just don't know why, but I am feeling very anxious about all this." This comment stems from a number of sources, broadly defined as separation anxiety. The first source of anxiety is the fact that all seniors know they are going to have to leave high school with all its security of friends, routine, family, and home. Often seniors will fall into "senior slump," a mild form of depression in which they cannot seem to do their work or pay attention in class. Some go even further and engage in behavior that jeopardizes their very graduation. Psychologists tell us that such student antics are really an effort to stop the clock and not face the separation that yawns before them.

The students tell us their questions, too: "Will I get into the college of my choice?" "Will I graduate with honors, as I had hoped?" "Will I be able to separate from my friends, much less make new ones in college?" "Will I be able to leave home and live on my own successfully in college?" And there is the larger question of being able to meet the challenges of the larger world. In the secure world of high school, teachers pick up homework, absences are noted, sports teams and practices are organized, and even social relationships are regulated by parents. What about the world of college, where few of these things are true? "How am I going to behave?" "Will I even get into the schools I want to?" "What if all the plans I have made, my family has made, my guidance counselor has approved, go wrong?" Parents need to be sensitive to these awesome questions of separation anxiety and make sure they communicate the message, "We love you no matter what." The authors of a well-known book on this subject describe the parental role as one of striking a balance between setting expectations and providing support. They call it giving your children "roots and wings."[1]

In helping your child to plan her applications to college and then make her way through her senior year, you need to understand that she is leaving behind the security of high school and the life she has known. There will be unexpected shifts in peer relationships, possibly, as your daughter realizes that in college she will have to get along with a variety of people. This may take the form of cleaving more closely to friends like herself and to

---

[1] Barbara M. Newman and Philip R. Newman, *When Kids go to College: A Parents' Guide to Changing Relationships.* Columbus, Ohio: Ohio State University Press, 1992, p.3.

measuring all friendships by the standards of high school, or perhaps moving toward other, different friends in anticipation of the years to come. This can take the form of an intense relationship with her boyfriend or movement away from a steady and caring boyfriend.

Sometimes, too, separation anxiety causes senseless competition among high school seniors as they worry about gaining admission to the colleges of their choice. One student, worried about his chances of clearing the competitive bars to Stanford, told his guidance counselor that he did not think that Bob, one of his good friends (also an applicant to Stanford), deserved to be admitted. Needless to say, that relationship soured when Bob was admitted and his erstwhile "friend" was not.

As students struggle to define their path to college and weigh the impact of losing friends and their relationships with high school teachers and their home communities, they may well behave differently toward their parents. The most familiar form of behavior is *distancing*, setting themselves apart from their parents literally and figuratively. In the early part of the college search process, distancing may surface as a college choice in California by a boy from rural New Hampshire. When asked why, he may say, "I just have to get out of here." One girl from Connecticut admitted that her choice of college a long way from her parents' home stemmed from the fact that her mother wanted her to study nursing, and she did not. The young woman figured that out in Portland, Oregon, her mother could not do much about her college choice. When distance seems to be more of a consideration than the fit between the student and the college, parents have to probe for the reasons why. Remind the student that she needs to pick a school that is going to help her build on her strengths and interests, not as a reaction to her family's preferences. Reassure her that you are not going to try to control her career or her social life.

Students are also thinking about their families and their friends at this time, and parents may get requests for pictures or anecdotes about relatives long gone or close by. Each family's history is different; it arises from ancestry, race, religion, folklore, legends, and traditions that have been handed down from one generation to the next. Take their requests for talk or for pictures seriously, for these requests and comments are but a part of the larger process of preparation for moving from dependence to autonomy and taking along the right baggage.

As an overall strategy, parents need to keep in mind the importance of not letting separation anxiety contaminate the rational selection of a college.

Try to avoid a power struggle over the various issues that surface, be it a new relationship, a new and apparently frivolous interest, occasional lethargy, or mandatory attendance at a particular family function. Use your diplomatic skills. Stress the positive and points of agreement. Remember roots and wings.

Parental Strains

When I was an admissions dean, I once received a poignant essay from a father whose daughter had been entrusted to my college as a freshman. It was about a bicycle he bought for his wife when they were first married and went biking together. It went on to depict a scene in which he added a child's seat when his daughter was born and the picture he took of her and her mother on the bike. The last memories he had of the bike were polishing and oiling it for his daughter to take to college and putting it on top of his Suburu for the drive to Ohio. He then spoke of his tears as he wrote of his daughter's loss to my college. This poor father had an advanced case of separation anxiety.

Parents need to anticipate the impact of a child going off to college. The event often coincides with an acknowledgment of middle age and a time to revisit the relationship that first brought husband and wife together. The empty house, void of the familiar sounds of the key in the lock, the slam of the refrigerator door, and the bits of conversation that defined your child's busy day, now must be confronted. Parents will have to reacquaint themselves with each other and with, perhaps, new interests and activities that replace the old ones that were centered on their children.

Financial challenges may well sharpen those interests and activities as college costs continue to climb. A smaller house or moving from part-time to full-time work on the part of one spouse may make sense.

Invariably the college admissions process brings parents closer to that day of final separation from their children. As the process unfurls, parents are learning a two-step dance, supporting their child while letting him or her go. "To control less and worry more" is the way one parent put it to me. It is a delicate dance—support, advise, step back, give space for the child to decide and to act, then begin again—support, advise, step back—and so, again.

SOME PRACTICAL STEPS TO HELP YOUR CHILD

Set the Strategy

Before embarking on a costly whirlwind trip to ten colleges, parents and children should think strategically. The goal of this enterprise is to explore a number of options but to end up with some choices! Plan your first trip to some schools where your own analysis and that of your guidance counselor indicates your child will be admitted. Too often the search process for many families begins with their "top" choices, which everyone knows are reach schools, but nonetheless are pursued anyhow. This approach often does not allow for a thorough investigation of the schools where the student can be admitted and, at the end of the process, heightens disappointment when the student is not admitted to one of the top schools. So "concentrate on finding the right less selective college first," to use the words of one seasoned parent.[2]

A second part of your strategy consists in making sure all are agreed upon the criteria for choice of school, that is, size, location, programs, mission, and learning and living environment. Make sure to clarify what the student means by big or small, in a city (what kind of city, how big?), and the environment (fraternities and sororities or not?).

Finally, make sure that your expectations as parents are made clear. If you don't want your child to go to the West Coast or the East Coast because you will have to give up seeing him or her very often, now is the time to say it. Also, if there are financial constraints that have not yet been aired, now is the time for that element of your strategy to be made clear to all parties.

The Campus Visit

The planning for a campus visit to a college presents an opportunity for some real education for children and parents:

- Making the arrangements. Assuming that a family wants to visit five to seven colleges in central Pennsylvania and Ohio, ask the student to plot the outline of the trip and review the driving times and interview and tour times with the parents. Then perhaps the parents can make the motel

---

[2]C. Joseph Gould, *Independent School,* Winter 1998, p.78.

reservations. The student should make the interview and campus tour appointments. Learning to converse on the phone and to make plans with others is a very important skill.

- **Timing.** Try to visit a college when the students are there and classes are being taught. Often this can be done in the spring of the junior year for a preliminary group of schools, even though interviews may not be available at that time. If you have to visit in the summer, don't worry. Often faculty members are available for conversation, and students conduct the tours. You will get some feeling for what life is like. Try to avoid visiting a college when a special event, such as winter carnival or homecoming, is taking place. Such events could distort your view of a school.
- **Plan to conduct your own exploration of the college while your child is visiting.** During the interview you can take the campus tour, or you can inspect the facilities that are of special interest to you. If the college is in session, you can talk to students in a frank, casual way. Sometimes this is more easily done when your own son or daughter is not present. Students can be asked all kinds of questions—about the food, the dormitories, etc.—but the fundamental one is whether they would send their son or daughter to the school. The same holds true for faculty members, if perchance you meet one.
- **Visit a class.** Both parents and students will want to visit a class, and each will have a perspective on the quality of the teaching and the students who are reacting to it. Share these impressions later. Also look for the use of technology in the classroom and in the homework assignments. See if you can make a judgment about the degree of faculty availability to students as individuals. Help sessions, review sessions, and office hours are points of reference. Another question to remember while visiting a class is whether students are encouraged or organized to work in teams. Finally, in a conversation with the professor after the class or in a follow up by e-mail, try to ascertain how successful the college is in placing its students in graduate school.
- **Read campus bulletin boards.** This particular rule of thumb applies to campus bulletins and was given to me by a father who had taken each of his five children on the college tour. "Always look at bulletin boards," he said. "They tell you not only what is going on; they tell you what the issues are; they enable you to assess the vibrancy of the place." Look for bulletin boards in the student center, the visitors' center, and the athletic

complex. If you can't find one, try a conversation with the first student you encounter. Remember the extension of this advice: the college or university Web site. Here again, try to move past the official information on the formal menu and locate the student sector of the site. There you can read the student newspaper, look for chat rooms on campus issues, and review the postings on the campus calendar.

- **Eat in the cafeteria.** Having a meal on campus serves not only to sample the quality and variety of the food but also to study the interaction between students and between students and faculty members. How do these groups relate to one another? Are there cliques of people who sit together and by their behavior seem to exclude others? What is the tone of the room—is it one you resonate to or not?
- **Visit a dormitory.** In the course of your tour of a college, parents should see where students live and how they live. After all, you are paying for these accommodations. The physical condition of dormitories, as defined by lighting, color, noise, security, and spaces for cooking, socializing, study, and computer facilities, will all be important to your child. You will also want to ask about various living options for students, such as theme houses, co-ops, and off-campus living.
- **Financial aid.** If you plan to apply for financial aid, visit the financial aid office and ask any questions you have. Collect information and examples of financial aid awards and try to get a grip on how the financial aid system works.
- **Support systems.** Parents will want to find out where students go if they have an academic, social, or physical problem. Posing a hypothetical question to a student you might encounter, exploring the campus medical facility page, or looking in the catalog under academic support will lead you to important information. Assume your daughter has trouble comprehending a problem in her introductory chemistry course. To whom does she turn? What if your son is driven to distraction by the loud music in the next room in his dormitory? Is there a procedure for settling disputes of this sort? Furthermore, are there study skill sessions for entering freshmen? Are there formal opportunities to talk about homesickness during those early weeks of freshman year? Can someone describe the interface between the advising system and the counseling system? This is a particularly good question to pose.
- **The community environment.** This is an important and elusive concept. How does this college or university operate as a community? Is there

an atmosphere of mutual respect between students and faculty members and particularly among the students? Is there any evidence of intolerance or political correctness on the campus? Do the students seem to be so career-driven as to be callous toward one another? The answers to these questions are generally positive, but they are worth asking, lest the student find out too late that he or she has chosen the wrong school.

- **Mission.** Very often a college's mission is printed on its Web site, and further statements can be found in the course catalog. The importance of the mission lies in how you relate to the institution and feel about it at a gut level. The mission of an institution also offers an insight into how well your child will be prepared through his or her education to meet the challenges of our new century.
- **Background role.** Remember to stay in the background, and let your child go through the interview and touring process and make up his or her own mind about what he or she hears and experiences. Also recognize that the role of parents in helping students make decisions is fully recognized by the colleges. The admissions office will undoubtedly want to help and guide you. The interviewer will probably want to meet you. In a buyers' market, it is important to remember that this does not change your role of helping your child make a good decision.

This list of suggestions need not be applied to all colleges that a family visits. Students and parents may wish to visit some schools just to get a feel for the size or location of a school. Some parents may also want to encourage their children to visit some of their college choices on their own and make up their own minds about a few places. But hopefully both parents and students will be involved in visiting most of the schools under consideration.

The goal of visiting a college campus with your child is to develop your own perspective on the institution. After visiting a small New England college, one mother happily concluded, "There's a chemistry here you can't explain. Whatever happens after this visit, my husband and I will feel that we were involved. We had our eyes and our ears opened, and consequently we know what our son is getting into."

THE APPLICATION

Once your college visits are complete and you have communicated your impressions to your son or daughter, make sure that you do not try too hard to influence the final choice of schools. Rather, focus on the strategy of having a range of choices, from those schools that are sure to accept the student, through intermediate choices of colleges that may well accept the student, to the top choices of schools where gaining admission will be difficult. Try to keep the choices consistent in terms of the quality of the education offered in the student's field of interest.

Once the final selections are made, it is time for the student to work out an application strategy with the college counselor. Here we enter a delicate situation in which parents must avoid giving too much help on the applications while still communicating that they are interested and that they can help out around the edges.

- Schedule. It is perfectly lawful for parents to help their children establish a schedule for obtaining and submitting applications. Scheduling can be done with simple operations of the computer—setting up a spreadsheet that shows the various parts of the application, when they are due, when they were sent, when they were acknowledged, and so on. Having a column on the sheet for financial aid materials will be useful, too.
- Logistical Support. When it comes to the costs of paper, postage, photocopying, fees, and actual mailing, parents can play a helpful role. In an era of electronic applications and correspondence, it is important to keep paper records in case a document is lost.
- The Essay. The application essays invariably challenge applicants. It is important for parents to act as a catalyst for ideas and approaches but not to provide detailed editorial advice or content to their children. Remind the writer that each college is different and may require a different approach (essay). Suggest topics that you feel may be of interest to a particular school. Reassure your child that he or she does not have to take all your ideas. Encourage them to discuss the content of their essays with their teachers and trusted friends. If you are asked to read an essay, do so with caution. Circle mistakes; ask a few questions. Make sure that the essay is the child's own work. Remember that the colleges take their direct relationship with the candidate seriously.

A few years ago, I had just finished what I thought was a fairly eloquent speech on behalf of a candidate to the shrewd dean of admissions at a major Eastern university. By way of response, he picked up a letter from the candidate's file and waved it slowly back and forth in front of my face. "What does it say?" I asked. "It is not what it says; it is who says it," he replied sardonically. "This application is all neatly typed by daddy's secretary on the office word processor, and the boy just signed it." Sure enough, it even bore the father's business address on the envelope. The dean continued, "We are evaluating the kid, not poppa or momma, and we want to hear from the candidate directly!"

By helping your child at the margins of the application with your patience, your resources—perhaps your daughter could print out her application on the office laser printer, rather than her ink jet—and with your encouragement, it is possible to play a very useful role in the application process without taking a direct hand in it. Your job is to see that your child gives it his or her best effort, and leave it at that.

Influence

In his short story "Babylon Revisited," F. Scott Fitzgerald entices readers into his tale with the memorable line: "Let me tell you about the very rich, for they are different from you and me." Fitzgerald goes on to paint a picture of the decadent 1920s in which influence often overwhelmed creativity and justice, and money too often defined human worth. Today we live in a world of much higher public and private accountability, and the inappropriate use of money and influence is constrained by law and public sensitivity. So some parents worry that their child's chances of admission might be jeopardized if they use the connections they might have in the business, political, and academic world to persuade an admissions committee or director to look favorably on their son or daughter.

Here are a few typical questions my colleagues and I have been asked over the years about using influence and some suggestions for appropriate conduct.

Question: Should I write to the director of admissions and tell her that my son definitely wants to go to Coburn as I did twenty-five years ago?

Answer: No, your son should do that.

Question: The other day at lunch, my client Clint Jones begged me to let him put in a good word for my daughter Luanne at Siwash. He said he knows the president from graduate school days. Should I let him do it?

Answer: Probably not. Clint does not know Luanne at all. What new perspective could he shed on her candidacy? It will look like the old boy network trying to force the issue. Thank Clint just the same.

Question: My son came home the other night and said that, out of the blue, his boss on the construction site where he is working this summer offered to write a recommendation letter to his colleges. Should I encourage Bobby to accept the offer?

Answer: Definitely yes, for such a letter will cast a new perspective on Bobby as an employee and as a team member—a perspective the college would not be able to obtain from any other source.

Question: A good friend of mine in college and in graduate school is now president of Hawthorne, where my daughter definitely wants to go to college. My friend and I have drifted apart over the years because we have moved around so much with the Navy. We only exchange cards at Christmas. But I really do think she would want to know if Louisa is applying. What should I do?

Answer: This mother's instinct is correct. She should write a short, informative letter to her friend, the president, so that she at least knows Louisa is applying. Then she can handle it the way she wants. After all, look at it this way. There is not much the president can do if Louisa were to be rejected. So act now.

These questions suggest a few guidelines concerning the use of influence in the college admissions process. Keep them in mind before making a phone call or having a letter written:

- **The person writing the letter should know the candidate well** and be able to cast a different light on the candidate from that available through the usual sources, such as the school guidance counselor, a teacher, an employer, or the application itself.
- **The connection to the college should be strong.** If a recommender is writing because he or she is connected to the college in some way, that connection should be strong. Being a staunch supporter of the school's athletic teams and a regular contributor to the annual giving fund will not suffice. Being a trustee, prominent alumnus in politics or business, or a major donor is another matter.
- **Don't mount a campaign.** Soliciting letters and phone calls from various people may backfire. If you have a strong contact and wish to enlist the person, stop short of suggesting what tactics to use. Merely inform the person that your daughter or son is applying to the school, is qualified, and would very much like to attend. Trust the judgment of the person

whose help you seek to do or not do what he or she thinks best. Some people with great influence maintain it by not involving themselves constantly in the internal workings of the college or university. In such a situation a few simple words will go a long way.

- **Respect the integrity of the institution.** Remember that admissions officers are professionals. They see their responsibility as finding out as much as they can about the candidates who apply. If the candidate's uncle went to the college, the application will contain that information. Your professional status or corporate ties will also be queried in the application or in the interview. Most colleges have an elaborate system for assessing the potential financial and political value of their candidates' parents. The schools keep in mind the possibility that some of the college's future assets may come from the family of a particular candidate. At the end of the evaluation process there may be a dozen or more must-takes or highly desirable candidates as a result of the influence of certain individuals or the research done by the admissions office and the development office of the school itself.

In these connections, parents should know that once the admissions office establishes its rating for a candidate and accepts or rejects him or her, college trustees and presidents seldom interfere or alter the decision. Long ago, presidents and others have learned it is far more equitable to have a thorough and professional admissions staff making final decisions than to tamper with those decisions themselves. Even though they could do so, they seldom interfere once a decision is made. So parents must decide whether to use their influence early in the admissions process and to understand the relative autonomy of admissions offices in controlling the final decisions.

THE GUIDANCE COUNSELOR

At some point in the college choice process parents should make an appointment to meet with their child's guidance counselor. This visit should come after the child has met with and developed a relationship with the counselor and after the parents have read the invariable handouts from the College Guidance Office, attended the high school's College Night, and visited some colleges with their child. The more information the parents can garner about the schools their child is interested in and about financial aid—if needed—the more productive the conference will be.

THE INSIDER'S GUIDE TO COLLEGE ADMISSIONS

Parents also need to be sensitive to the fact that in many schools, guidance counselors have a heavy caseload and are obliged to wear several hats. College guidance is only one of those hats. They also need to realize that despite the folklore they hear about the influence of guidance counselors in the admission of students to particular colleges and universities, they generally do not have much influence.

What, then, is the purpose of seeing the guidance counselor? There are three reasons. First, you want to be sure that the counselor knows your child as a person as well as a student. One memorable conference with a counselor began on a somewhat negative note, then turned out to be extremely illuminating. The conversation went like this:

> "It is too bad that the colleges won't be able to learn how much Susan has overcome. She is too proud to say anything herself," her mother said. The surprised counselor asked, "Would you tell me what you mean by that?" The mother then explained that Susan was born with a hip defect and could not walk until she had corrective surgery when she was four years old. At that point the doctor had recommended that Susan take up swimming to strengthen her lower body and legs. She did this, and in her pursuit of her swim-to-walk therapy developed into a champion intermediate freestyle swimmer. "Not only did she eliminate her limp, she developed the confidence to tackle anything," her mother added, her eyes misting slightly. The counselor made mention of Susan's history and her resolve in his school report to the colleges. The admissions director at one of her top choices—which also had a very competitive swimming program—was heard to say months later, "We'd like to take a chance on Susan; there are heartstrings in her folder."

A second important reason to consult with the guidance counselor is to fine-tune the strategy of applying to college. Make sure you ask the counselor to rank the schools your child is considering, from difficult to moderate to "safe." Also communicate any special contacts you may have at particular schools. Seek the counselor's advice on how your child can make the most of his athletic ability or her dramatic talent in applying to a particular school.

Finally, the opportunity to find out the answers to nagging questions such as how many times to take the SAT I and which SAT II tests to take can be found in the guidance office. Advice on whether to submit supplementary materials to a particular school can be found there, too.

The conversation with the counselor also establishes the fact that you are an interested and supportive player in your child's college search, it develops a relationship with the counselor, and it affirms the desire on your part for open and continuing communication between school and family. This communication will continue over the phone, in the corridors, and even at a chance meeting in the supermarket. The rapport you establish with the guidance counselor will give your child a sense of emotional support. Now she knows she has a team of adults behind her in her search for the right college.

As the admissions process rolls forward, a cordial relationship with the guidance counselor—and sometimes the secretary—can help a family unravel red tape or clarify whether a college has received a document and sometimes to learn how a college is reacting to the candidate's application. In the last instance, sometimes there is an opportunity to shore up a candidacy with an additional recommendation or grade in a particular course or new and better athletic times or videotapes.

On the other hand, guard against overplaying your hand with the guidance counselor. Steadfastly refusing to take advice on:

- limiting the number of applications to the top colleges,
- attempting to go over the counselor's head by enlisting the support of the principal or superintendent,
- secretly relying on an outside source such as a private counselor, or
- leaving the counselor in the dark about tactics the parents are employing on behalf of their child

serve to undercut the counselor's authority, erode goodwill, and, through lack of coordination, jeopardize your child's chances of admission.

INDEPENDENT COUNSELORS

The increased complexity of the college admissions process in recent years has led many parents to seek the services of private counselors. The proliferation of early decision programs and the multiple applications that can now be easily filed electronically are but two of the causes for the unpredictability of admission to selective schools. Private counselors cannot change these factors, but most of them are well versed in the college admissions system and can focus on the needs of a particular student in a way that neither parents nor guidance counselor can. Some indications that a private counselor could help your child are:

- The guidance office of the high school is unable to provide consistent and individualized college counseling
- The child needs special assistance in testing, in values and interests clarification, and in thinking and discussing the college application process that the high school cannot provide
- The family itself is unable to discuss and plan for a coherent college application strategy and needs to be educated by a professional

If you decide to hire a counselor, make sure that he or she is registered with the Independent Educational Consultants Association (http://www.educationalconsulting.org) or a similar professional group. Make sure you interview two or more counselors before deciding on one. Remember, once you find a counselor for your family or your child, you still have an important role to play. So does your child. There is work involved here. Only your child can produce the record and the recommendations to gain admission to college. Private counselors have no special influence, as helpful as they may be.

WHEN TO INTERCEDE

The college search and admissions process is filled with intermediaries. Guidance counselors, private counselors, and admissions officers all come between you and your child and you and the college he or she desperately wants to attend. Moreover, books like this urge parents to stay in the background. They assert that the parent's role is to engage in an ongoing dialog with their son or daughter, to make compromises with them from time to time, and to let them make the occasional "educational" mistake. Parents are told with good reason that just being there for the child is the mainstay of the process. All true.

Sometimes, however, just being there isn't enough. You might find your child in a special situation in which your intercession could make a big difference. Some examples include:

- Your child has a learning or physical disability that is not apparent to the eye. Making sure that the college guidance counselor knows about this is important.

- Your child is not accepted at the top-choice college and has been put on a waiting list instead. You should consult with the guidance counselor or private counselor and consider either bringing influence to bear or writing a letter yourself to the Dean of Admissions.
- You hear that a vital piece of information, such as a recent report on a senior project your child has completed, has not been reported to the colleges. You intercede with the guidance office and ask firmly that the favorable report be sent.

In recommending these tactics, parents need to understand that there are risks. Guidance counselors may be nettled and not put in that "good word" when the time comes. An admissions dean may be suspicious that you are an overbearing parent and "reject" you. Use your good judgment, keeping in mind the following rationale for action of some sort:

- The college admissions process is a once-in-a-lifetime event, and since it will not happen ever again, occasional, extraordinary behavior is acceptable.
- An admissions committee or dean always feels more confident if they have the new and positive information. So if you have any, and there is no other person to send it, do so yourself. (By contrast, admissions committees and deans do not react well to regurgitated information, in this world of spin doctors.)
- "It is your kid." She always will be—and you have certain liberties to break the bounds of convention because you are her parents.

HELPING OUT WHILE LETTING GO

There is absolutely no question that parents have an extremely difficult and delicate role to play in the college decision-making process. There is no acknowledged right way to handle all of the challenges and turns in the road that parents will encounter. There are only some simple words of advice from years of watching families confront this process that may be helpful.

First, separate your own aspirations from those of your children. Your goal is to help your sons and daughters to be the best that they can be—to help them find the institution that will bring out the best that is in them. To achieve that goal, you have to let your child make most, if not all, of the crucial decisions about college. Parents who say, "We are applying to the University of X," should catch themselves and change their rhetoric. Set examples for your children in the college admissions process, support them, and counsel them. Don't direct them, insulate them, or control them.

Second, remind yourself that the college search and application process is a journey from adolescent dependence to adult independence. Your children may not see this point as clearly as you, but you should operate on this premise. Doing so means that you have a dual responsibility: to educate your children about the realities of the admissions process and to inform them about the responsibilities with the immense freedom they will soon enjoy as college freshmen. In this connection, recall the role that separation anxiety will undoubtedly play in your child's behavior, and be prepared. Remember, too, that your child's very mental development is coursing beneath the surface as he or she moves from viewing the world in simple and absolute terms to seeing it as more complex and relative.

Third, remember that, deep down, children do want the advice of their mothers and fathers, and they do want to please their parents. Children will seldom reveal these inner feelings. They are more comfortable with their independent judgments and aspirations. But they will stumble and, at that point, will want and need parental advice and encouragement. The job of parents is to allow their children to make their own judgments and to support them when errors are made. Guiding your child through the college admissions process may be one of the most difficult challenges you will face as a parent during your child's critical years of young adulthood. To allocate time to this enterprise and to try to help your son or daughter attain his or her goals could make this one of the most rewarding experiences of those memorable years.

The difficulty in the end comes down to that of "roots and wings," of balancing the conflicting goals of security, traditions, and home against the aspirations for freedom, exploration, and separation. As you look at the college admissions process ahead, view it as your last major opportunity to educate your child and to reaffirm the values that have shaped your relationship as a family. In the brief time between the summer before the senior year and the colleges' decisions ten months later, you have a chance once again to teach your child the things you value most: family, community, ethics, spirituality, creativity, and vocation—and the importance of a broad education to living a useful life. You can show in this ten-month period, once again, how much you trust your child to fashion his or her own

FOR PARENTS ONLY

responses to the values just mentioned. That those responses will be different from yours, you both know. That you will respect those differences is what needs to be communicated.

Your sons and daughters also need to understand that the education they will receive in college will enable them to act reasonably and humanely in the not-so-reasonable or humane world of the twenty-first century. It will be their education that will help solidify the self-esteem you as parents have made sure to succor. It will be their education that will make permanent the adult relationship between you and the child who is a child no more.

NINE

How Colleges Make Decisions

Each college or university will have a slightly different system for choosing its students, and each one is pretty consistent and fair—if you happen to know how it operates. Few do.
    Thomas C. Hayden, author

A SHORT HISTORY LESSON

The challenge of gaining admission to selective colleges and universities today arises from a number of factors—demographic, political, economic, and cultural. It would take many pages to put the whole story before our readers. Perhaps a brief synopsis will do.

Before World War II, few Americans had the advantage or even the thought of going to college. Like many societies in Europe and Asia today, higher education was for the well-to-do, the very able, and a few others who knocked on the door, were admitted, and got through on scholarships. The war itself changed all that; it showed the need for a well-trained workforce as well as an elite group of scholars who could discover the potential of the atom and put it to military and peacetime use. The G.I. bill, passed in 1945, enabled thousands of veterans of the war to enroll in college, virtually free of charge, and to obtain bachelor's and higher degrees. When these students graduated, they surged into business and the professions and produced the long post–World War II boom that lasted well into the 1960s.

They also started families, and some of them fairly large ones. These children of the World War II veterans became the "Baby Boomers," named for the boom their parents had started. When their time came to go to college, they sought the opportunity as their parents had. In the 1960s they surged into the nation's colleges and universities, lifting the percentage of students who went to college from high school to nearly 50 percent, or about 1.5 million students per year.

Needless to say, colleges and universities had to expand to accommodate these students, and fortunately the government was a willing partner. The G.I. bill was succeeded by National Defense Student Loans. Low-income students received stipends later called Pell Grants, and colleges and universities themselves were able to loan money cheaply to students, backed up by guarantees from the federal government. In addition, the Civil Rights Act and the Higher Education Act in the 1960s enjoined colleges and universities to open their doors wider to admit previously underrepresented Americans, e.g., African Americans, Hispanics, Native Americans, Asian Americans, and women.

As a result of legislation and the increase in the college-bound population, American colleges and universities became larger, more diverse, and more interesting places than ever before. They once again affirmed the long-held American belief that education was the key to social progress. Education was the escalator by which young people could rise to positions of responsibility and influence.

On the practical side, however, the increased number of students applying to schools made competition at the more selective institutions much more intense. More and more good students were turned away because of lack of space. They, in turn, were courted by a group of second-tier institutions that saw an opportunity to recruit good students and to advance themselves in the natural pecking order. So in the early 1970s we began to see the competition among colleges for good students and the beginning of what we now know as the college crunch: a rising level of competition among students for limited places. We also saw the beginning of marketing and recruiting tactics on the part of colleges as they tried to attract and enroll the best students.

Then, two events served as a catalyst that propelled this process of marketing and difficulty of admission to new levels. The first was the oil embargo of the mid-1970s that ended the economic boom of the postwar years, and the second was the inauguration of Ronald Reagan in 1981. President Reagan is famous for what he called "supply side" economics—or letting free markets operate. He was committed to pulling the government back from its very supportive role it played in higher education and drastically cut government aid to students for scholarships and to college and university research programs. Colleges and universities saw their financial aid budgets drop by 20 to 30 percent as federal funding was removed, and they had no choice but to fill that void with their own funds. To make up the difference, they raised their tuition costs and widened their recruitment networks to attract full-pay students and international students who could pay full fees.

Then, a demographic downturn in college-age students loomed on the horizon. High school enrollments fell as members of the post–World War II generation had fewer children than their parents. The number of students graduating from public high school in 1979 was 2.8 million, but by 1992 that number had declined nearly 20 percent to 2.3 million. Demographers forecast that even by 2001 the number will only rise to 2.6 million.[1] Never again will American colleges and universities enjoy the affluence of funding and numbers of students they had in the late 1970s.

The result of the demographic slide sharpened the colleges' desire to recruit more widely, to grant scholarships more carefully, and to compete with each other more vigorously. Most schools built very sophisticated admissions offices run by a new breed of professional manager, they developed modern cost accounting methods to measure all of their activities, and they began to confer on behalf of the government or private banks large loans to students instead of the scholarship grants of an earlier time. And yes, they raised prices constantly over the course of the 1980s and 90s. Recently, the *New York Times* reported that: "since 1980 . . . college prices have been soaring at twice and sometimes three times the Consumer Price Index. Over the 10-year period ending in 1998-99, after adjusting for inflation, the average public tuition and fees went up 53% at public colleges and 35% at private four-year colleges."[2]

One other factor completes the picture of the twenty-first century college and university, and that is the rankings. Over the course of the economic boom in the late 1980s, a new industry begun by *U.S. News & World Report* came into existence. It is called the ranking industry or craze. Fueled by Americans' fascination with statistics and supported by the spiraling costs of a college education, colleges and universities found themselves ranked in books and magazines and by their clientele. To meet

---

[1] WICHE, Report 1993
[2] *New York Times,* "Responding to Middle Class, Some Colleges Trim Tuition," February 3, 1999, C26.

the challenge, collegiate institutions focused intently on building up their applicant pools so that they could lower their *acceptance rates*. They also engaged in elaborate courtship rituals to ensure that their *yield rates* remained high. And they began to use financial aid as a tool to attract students who made their academic and social *profile* stand above their competition.

This history of demographic rise and fall, political support and suspicion, and economic boom and slowdown and boom again has dramatically altered the way colleges make their decisions. Simply said, experience has taught institutions of higher education how to market themselves to students and families, how to predict social and economic trends, and how to stay solvent in a world of rising costs and intense competition. In many ways, colleges and universities today are much like businesses when it comes to marketing themselves to the public, recruiting students, and measuring their success at both. In the old days, the college admissions system was characterized by warmth, informality, candor, and risk-taking when it came to admitting students. The new system is much more sophisticated, rational, equitable, and clinical and less personal than the old. Here is a brief description of how it works.

THE SELECTION SYSTEM

Office Management

In the first place, college admissions offices are well-organized engines for recruitment and evaluation. Generally, each admissions officer is assigned a geographic region that he or she is responsible for. The admissions officer usually travels to the area at least once in the cycle, visiting high schools, hosting receptions, and organizing alumni who assist in the interviewing and recruitment process. The officer is instructed by the Dean of Admissions to try to achieve a target number of applications from the area and ultimately a certain number of accepted students, and most important, enrolled students. The admissions officer is advised to become very familiar with the area and particularly with the quality of its schools. He or she becomes an advocate for good students from the area, and his or her advocacy carries all the way through the admissions cycle.

Admissions officers may also be assigned to look out for a particular target group of applicants as well as an area. In this case, the admissions officer or team of officers might look after all the applications of alumni children, a particular minority group, or the professed athletes in the pool. Very often, applications are read on a regional basis first so that judgments can be made about how well a student has performed in school and in the community. Then, if a student is a member of a targeted group, his or her application will be read again for comparison to other students with the same background. After every reading, a numerical score or letter grade is recorded, as are the written comments of the readers.

Reading the Application

Normally, applications are read at least twice, and sometimes many more times. There are some schools—at least one large Ivy League university, where it is said that the Dean reads every folder of the 18,000 or so that come in. Readers are given precise instructions as to what to look for in the applications, and their reading ability and judgment becomes a part of their job evaluation and promotion. So students should not view the reading and evaluation process in any way as haphazard, even though the results—to the outsider—do not always seem reasonable or consistent.

- The transcript. Readers are instructed first to look at the transcript. Does the school offer AP courses? How many? How many did the student take? What are the grades in those courses? Does the course preparation of the student meet the entry standards for the college, i.e., did the student take 4 years of English, 3 years of the same foreign language, 2 years of lab science, and so on?

    What is the student's GPA? How does the school compute GPA? (Here the GPA will be converted into the college's definition of GPA.) Where does this GPA put the student in the class—top 10 percent, 15 percent, etc? How many of the students in the high school go on to college?

    If the student has transferred from another school, this exercise has to be performed on that transcript. If the student has taken courses at a local college or in a summer program, the level of and performance in those courses has to be factored in. Finally, at the end of this exhaustive look at the transcript, a score is written down on the evaluation sheet in the student's folder. It is the first of several scores.

- Testing. Next the reader looks at the standardized test scores, which are printed on the transcript. These scores are used as a benchmark to the averages for the particular college. They are also viewed with the candidate's transcript. If the candidate's scores are slightly lower than what the transcript would suggest, it is often favorable because it suggests the candidate has worked hard in class. If they are higher, sometimes the opposite conclusion is drawn, and this is detrimental. AP scores are noted too, as are any untimed tests or special testing for students with learning challenges. Usually the testing profile of a student is evaluated with a score on the student's evaluation sheet.

- Recommendations. Next, the reader turns to the student's recommendations. The more selective the college, the more thorough this review will be. At discerning schools, school and teacher recommendations are frequently quoted in committee meetings and writers of exceptional recommendations sometimes publicly thanked by admissions deans. Often the rating grid at the bottom of some recommendations is translated into the college's scoring system. As the reader proceeds on to the next category, he or she is responsible for remembering the quotations made about a student as well as the score.
- The essay. College candidates spend an inordinate amount of time worrying about their essays. They are read carefully by readers and a note made on their topic and clarity of expression. Very often the student's essay helps the reader visualize how the student would fit in at the particular college—that is, if the student has beamed the essay at the college! If not, essays can still be persuasive in their own right. It is fair to say that if all other factors are below the threshold of admission, a good essay cannot get you in. And if you are at the margin, a bad essay might keep you out. Generally though, essays do not make a critical difference in admission to selective colleges.
- Extracurricular activities. The reader next turns to extracurricular activities, and here he or she is interested in quality more than quantity. Readers are especially impressed with long-term commitment to activities such as music lessons or a sport, as well as with leadership, such as organizing clothing donations for the homeless. They also recognize a willingness to take up a new activity, to be a member of a team and be led by others. Representative activities are written down, and a score usually given for personal qualities that are seen to emerge in this category and in the recommendations of the candidate's teachers.
- Special groups. The initial reader also has the responsibility of identifying students who fall into targeted groups and seeing that their applications are passed on to the team assigned to that group. When the Diversity Committee, for instance, receives the folder of a student from an African American, Latino, or Native American family, it might look at a variety of

factors that may have impacted the student's performance, such as family structure, family income, school profile, and other available educational and social opportunities. The Committee on International Students would examine the English writing sample and facility with language, as well as the breadth of secondary school preparation. The Committee on Athletes would confer with the coaching staff about the athletic qualifications of those students. It would also listen to the enthusiasm of a coach for a particular player, and in the end, a score would go down on the evaluation sheet.

After a folder has been read and evaluated by the first reader, it will make its way to a second reader if the total score or rating given by the first reader puts the candidate in the acceptable range. If not, the folder is put aside and might be quickly read again at the end of the process to make sure that the first reader was correct in the evaluation. Students in this early reject category would undoubtedly have scores and grades and recommendations and even an application that fall below the minimum established by the Dean and the Admissions Committee at the beginning of the cycle.

Research

The modern college and university admissions office makes most of its decisions based on research—all kinds of research. First, there is institutional research that, for example, tells the Admissions Director and staff just how well students with certain GPAs and SAT scores perform in the various majors the college offers. Institutional research also looks at graduation rates for different types of candidates; it also reveals how well students from certain high schools perform at the college according to their GPA; it often includes studies of how targeted groups of students perform, such as athletes (in general, by gender, and by sport). Institutional research also provides the admissions staff with various models that enable them to study options for assembling their class. It gives them a historical look back at their actions of previous years and how the students they admitted performed or did not perform.

Most colleges and universities have a fair amount of market research that informs their decisions. They have studies on student and parent attitudes toward the school and toward their competitor schools. They use these studies to craft their admissions literature and their recruiting messages. Moreover, they probably have studied students who have not responded to their overtures or who have come to the college and then left. On a broader scale, colleges and universities keep track of national studies of parent and student attitudes toward education in general and its price in particular. In recent years, concerned about the high tuitions that many schools have to charge, these same schools have been very astute in demonstrating the added value that they offer to their students.

Both market research and institutional research are augmented by the many customer-satisfaction questionnaires that colleges request from families and students. Surveys and market research have enabled schools to fine-tune their approach and to improve communication between family and school.

Research has also enabled colleges and universities to engage in cost-benefit analysis and to make their operations leaner and more effective. It has also formed the basis at many schools for a rational and consistent system for evaluating students. Almost all colleges and universities have some sort of scoring (evaluation) system like the one that follows.

A Scoring System

All colleges have their own unique scoring system that enables them to make consistent decisions and to move toward institutional goals. One can translate the last phrase as meaning improving one's standing in the rankings. The following system is a composite for a good college that has to compete for good students.

Factor	Range	Percent of Maximum Score	True Statistical Weight
GPA	0–18	34%	31%
SAT/ACT	0–12	23%	25%
Target Group	0–9	17%	21%
Application Type	0–4	8%	7%
Personal Rating	1–5	10%	4%
Family Contribution	0–4	8%	12%
Total	52		

Let's assume that the Director of Admissions, in consultation with the research analyst, has put down certain "floors" or minimum levels of performance for both the GPA and SAT. For the GPA, he or she has set a minimum of a C+ average in high school, which translates into 77 on a 100-point scale. For every point above 77, the student is awarded a score point, all the way up to 95, which is an A+ in most high schools. The reader then computes the percent represented by the GPA and then adds to it to obtain the score. An 85 would net a score of 8, a 90, a 12, and a 94, a 17.

With respect to the SATs, the Director establishes a floor of 500 Verbal and 500 Math. (The college is very anxious to improve its score profile.) For every 50 points above 500 on a given test, the candidate receives one score point. So a student with a 550 Verbal and a 600 Math gets a 3, one point for the Verbal increment of 50 and two more points for the two additional 50-point units on the Math side. A candidate with a 700 Verbal and a 650 Math would get a score of 7, 4 for the Verbal and 3 for the Math.

Target groups can be assigned any number up to 9. It may be difficult for the college or university to attract Native American students, so being Native American earns the student a 9. On the other hand, designated athletes may be more plentiful, so the top score an athlete would receive would be 6, according to the guidelines laid down by the Director. Unlike the scoring above, once a person qualifies to be a member of a targeted group, he or she would receive the score for that group. There would be no gradations.

Application type means whether or not the student has applied Early Decision or Early Action. Most colleges and universities value that early expression of interest. Enrolling students under an early program helps colleges boost their yield numbers. Here again, the score is either 0 or 4, depending whether the candidate has applied early. The first reader of the folder notes that fact on the evaluation sheet.

Next is the personal rating, and one might wonder why this rating is rather low in terms of its percentage of the maximum score and statistical weight. The answer is experience. The experience of many colleges is that when the personal factor is given too much weight, it can swing the decision in favor of the candidate but it reduces the other indicia of class quality, such as GPA and SAT profile in the process. Personal scores are determined by looking at a student's recommendations and any personal information he or she submitted about himself or herself.

A top score of 5 would indicate remarkable achievements in school or extraordinary personal obstacles that may have been overcome, and in general ample evidence of true leadership. A 4 would recognize some examples of leadership, evidence of strength of character, and willingness to take responsibility. It is a good rating. A 3 rating shows achievement of what one might expect of an average candidate for admission—good work habits, involvement in school life, favorable recommendations, and perhaps some potential for leadership in college.

On the other hand, a 2 indicates some lack of commitment and involvement in high school and some question as to whether the candidate has the maturity requisite for a strong college performance. The lowest rating, a 1, indicates that the reader has reason to have serious reservations about character and willingness to become involved in college life. This type of student, no matter how high his overall score, would undoubtedly be discussed by the admissions committee.

Finally, there is the matter of a family's capacity to pay for the cost of the university or college's education. On this scale, if the family can pay the full bill, the student receives 4 "bonus" points; if the family can pay three fourths of the bill in the estimation of the Financial Aid Office, then 3 points, and so on. If the family is total need, there are no points assigned. It is important to note that this is a hypothetical rating system. Not all schools need to take account of ability to pay, but an increasing number do. For those schools, family resources make a difference in admission.

Next Steps

Prior to the reading of folders, the Director of Admissions establishes certain score parameters for the incoming class. Based on the statistics for previous classes, the Director sets a score at the top end of the scale for automatic admissions. Using the scale here, he or she might say that all students who obtain 38 and above will be automatically admitted. The folders of these students are then set aside, their admission letters typed, and often special strategies employed to attract them to the school. Mailing the letters early is one such strategy.

Similarly, the Director establishes a low number, near the bottom of the scale, below which no one will be admitted. These folders go into the automatic reject pile, where they may be re-read by the Director to ensure that justice has been done.

The rest of the application folders, with their scores attached, now proceed to the Admissions Committee. In our hypothetical college, that might be 50 percent of the total number of applications received. Before the committee can meet, however, all the scores are entered into the database along with recent test scores and other last-minute information. Then printouts are produced for every member of the committee, with a two- or three-line entry for each applicant—each line packed with numbers and abbreviations undecipherable to anyone but a member of that particular admissions staff.

The Committee

Admissions Committees meet regularly during February and March, and the Director normally chairs the discussion. Often, the Committee will proceed by area and region, and the first reader who is in charge of that area will present each case to the committee. The area person is the candidate's advocate. If the candidate is reasonably qualified, the area person will make a case for him or her, and colleagues on the committee will either agree or disagree. Often, comparisons are made between the case being discussed and a previous case or one that is coming up, and that is encouraged because the committee—the college or university itself—is striving for consistency in its decision making. Again and again, admissions officers will be asked by their colleagues or the Director:

"What kind of a high school is this? How good is it?"

"Do you think that the candidate has made the most of the educational resources he had at this high school and in his community?"

"How do you know he is a 5 personal? Is he as good as the kid I presented the other day (reads from the print-out)?"

"If we take this kid who is in the 2nd decile of his class, what will the guidance counselor think of our supposedly high standards? Will the counselor flood us with weaker kids next year?"

"I think you are reading too much into this candidate's essay. She is not strange; she is just a little eccentric. What do the rest of you think?"

The Director is often the final judge of these conversations and will try to proceed by consensus whenever possible. When the Director senses that the committee agrees on a candidate, he or she will signal the recording member of the group to put an 'A' for admit beside the name. When the opposite occurs, he or she will instruct the recorder to place an 'R' (rejected) beside the candidate's name. If there is not a clear consensus for admit or reject, when the discussion has run its course, the Director will say: "let's put Sarah on the Waiting List." With no objections, the next case is called.

When emotions flare over the imminent decision on a case, the Director may table the case and bring it up later. When the committee's questions don't produce ready answers from the area person/advocate, the Director instructs that person to call the candidate's school and ferret out the missing information.

If a candidate has a *hook*—is a member of a targeted group—but comes up at the margin of admission in the committee's discussions, the Director will postpone the case to a later time when all candidates from that group who did not make it in on the first round will be considered. At the later stages of the selection cycle, the Admissions Committee will hold special sessions for international students, minority students, athletes, and alumni children. At some schools there is a category for development cases—those students whose parents are influential economically or politically and whose resources could benefit the school. These cases will not be resolved by the Committee but in a discussion among the Director of Development and the Admissions Director, and sometimes, the President.

All along the way, the Director will remind the committee of the target number of students the college wants to admit and to reject. He or she will keep a box score on the admit rate to date. If the committee consistently admits too many students, its members know that there will have to be a lop session at the end of the committee process. At that point, the Director will tell each area person that he or she will have to move a number of their accepted candidates to the Waiting List. This is often painful because advocates naturally grow fond of their candidates. The Director, however, is ever mindful of the college's overall selection rate and being consistent from one area to another and from one group to another. The Director's goal is to keep the selection rate as low as possible and still bring in the class.

Once all the candidates have been considered and decided upon, the committee disbands for a time. Admissions officers turn back to the challenge of persuading accepted students to come. They plan visitation days to the campus. They write personal notes at the bottom of the acceptance letters. They prepare themselves for the questions from students and parents about the Waiting List and whether a rejected student could attend a local community college and hope to transfer to their school next year.

Financial Aid Leveraging

As those recruitment plans are being made and before the letters are sent out, the Director and perhaps a few of the senior associates meet with the Financial Aid Director. Their purpose is to ensure that the admissions rating system is translated into the financial aid offers made to the families of accepted students. This group has met many times before and has set the school's packaging parameters. Their decisions will determine how the college or university leverages or deploys its financial aid. Simply put, students with scores at the top end of the admissions rating scale will receive a high percentage of grant or gift aid in their financial aid packages, and those at the bottom of the admissions scale will receive a much lower percentage of grant aid and a higher percentage of loan aid. The object is to attract as many top students as possible. This practice is called *differential packaging*.

Pursuant to the college's leveraging policy, the Directors of Admission and Financial Aid or Vice President for Enrollment may decide not to give full aid packages to students at the margin of admission. This is a practice called *gapping* or deliberately leaving a gap between what is offered to the student and what it costs to attend the college. The gamble on the college side is that the student will, in the absence of other options, find the funds to attend the college. "Why not give him the funds to attend?" "Because he will not add to the profile."

Universities and colleges sometimes will engage in a third financial aid practice, called awarding *merit* scholarships to students at the top end of the admissions rating scale, even though they did not apply for a scholarship. This award is an outright bid or price discount to encourage outstanding students to come to the college and, of course, to enliven its undergraduate body—and increase the profile.

Taken together, these three policies—differential packaging, gapping, and merit scholarships—define the financial aid landscape in this era of American higher education.

Waiting Lists

The politics and the procedures for dealing with the Waiting List will be discussed in the next chapter. The point here is to indicate how waiting lists are put together by admissions committees.

As the Admissions Director guides the committee's deliberations, many students will be put on the Waiting List—30 percent of the applicant pool is not uncommon. After all, if the Director misjudges the yield and fewer students accept the college's offer than estimated, the Waiting List will have to be used. So students who are put on the Waiting List by a competitive college with a relatively low yield, say 30 percent or so, will probably have a chance to gain admission from the Waiting List. Conversely, students who are wait listed by a very selective school with a yield above 60 percent will have much less of a chance of admission.

Most private colleges and universities will try to fill their class with their first mailing of admission letters, with accompanying financial aid awards. If the strategy is to offer all the institution's financial aid to the first round of admits, the college will have to wait until their offers to needy students are declined before they can offer aid to any student who is an aid recipient on the Waiting List. This is a lengthy process, lasting two to three weeks, and colleges want to fill their classes. So, very often, they construct two Waiting Lists, one for financial aid candidates and one for students whose families can pay the full cost of the college. Non-need students therefore have a distinct advantage in being admitted from the Waiting List. This is one of the sharper realities of the college admissions process. The first offers of Waiting List places often go to these full-pay students.

If the college or university is true to its scoring system, it will take students from the Waiting List according to their rank on the scoring scale. They may, however, have to bend their standards if extreme pressure is brought by the student's family and the family's "friends in high places."

Applicants to public universities can expect a slightly different experience with the Waiting List. Often public universities have rolling admissions; in this case, when the university fills, students may be rejected or put on a waiting list. As the cycle advances and some of the accepted students decide not to enroll, the university moves to its waiting list. The availability of housing is sometimes the rationale for putting students on waiting lists. Applications filed after deadlines is often another. Financial aid is more cut and dry. Usually there is less aid and a lower price than private institutions, and when the aid runs out, students have to rely on loans and work-study and their own resources.

NAVIGATION POINTERS

It would be a futile exercise, indeed, for students or parents to try to discover the precise system a given college or university uses to select students. It is far more fruitful to continue to focus on matching yourself with the school in

HOW COLLEGES MAKE DECISIONS

your application, in your essay, in your interview, and in any subsequent correspondence or conversations you may have with the Admissions Office.

- Try to look for what the institution says is important, all the way from the mission statement to the order in which questions are asked on the application.
- Listen carefully to oral presentations by admissions officers at receptions, in group sessions, and in interviews. Write down the key words used, and use them yourself if you agree with their meaning.
- Look at the college's video, explore its Web site, and yes, the pictures in the viewbook. Can you see a consistent image that is being projected? Write it down. Check it out with your guidance counselor and with your friends who are applying. Then ask yourself how comfortable you are with the image and feeling you get about a school.

Remember that the college admissions system at the turn of the new century has much to recommend it. It is research based. It is rational and consistent, even though it may not look that way from the outside. And, for the most part it is fair—fairer than the old system, where students who were favored by counselors, coaches, and alumni often had the upper hand. And last, remember those demographics; they are increasing very slowly. That means that your chances of admission are not going to decrease very much, if at all, in the years to come.

TEN

Acceptance, Rejection, or Wait List: What to Do Now

With all the splendid college options within American higher education, it is important to realize that there are many good matches. Students need to maintain a healthy perspective.

Parker J. Beveridge, Dean of Admissions, Colby College

There is a swirl of emotion that surrounds the college acceptance, rejection, and wait list process. If your application to the college of your choice results in acceptance, you are ecstatic—if not, you are apt to be tearful. If you get put on a waiting list, there is the frustration of not knowing and wondering whether the wait list will ever move. Amidst all this emotion, students are apt to lose sight of the fundamental question: Which college is really the best match for me?

ACCEPTANCE

When you are accepted by a college, you will naturally feel a sense of relief that you have gained admission, but you should not take the position that your acceptance has validated every feature of your scholastic record and your moral character. The admissions process is an imperfect one; it relies mainly on information prepared by students, counselors, and teachers. Occasionally students look better on paper or on a computer screen than they do in fact. This is especially true for students who test well. College admissions officers are all too frequently influenced only by high test scores, high GPAs, and high recommendations.

So if you consider yourself a winner in the college admissions sweepstakes, walk humbly and share your joy by extending a friendly hand to those who are not as fortunate, keeping in mind these words of Ecclesiastes:

> I returned and saw under the sun that the race is not to the swift, nor the battle to the strong, neither yet bread to the wise, nor yet riches to men of understanding, nor yet favor to men of skill, but time and chance happeneth to them all.

WHICH COLLEGE TO CHOOSE

For some students, this is an irrelevant question. They are the ones who are admitted to State U. or Coburn or a school where they have always wanted to go. They give a whoop of joy when they get their letter and send back their deposit right away. For other students the choice is more difficult. If you have followed the strategy of this book, you have at least three acceptances to consider. Now you return to the criteria you established when you put your final list of colleges together—academic programs, location, size, availability of extracurricular activities, and last but not least, cost. Remember that difficulty of admission is no longer the issue. The college you may choose is not necessarily the one that was the most difficult to get into. Rather, you need to discover where you would be the happiest and the most productive. That is going to be a place where you are the most likely to succeed and not struggle.

Let's revise the original selection criteria somewhat and use them to pick the right school:

1. Curriculum and course requirements
2. Student-faculty relationships both inside and outside the classroom
3. Student life and special programs that you want to participate in—athletic, extracurricular, overseas, internships
4. Cost and affordability over the next four years

How to gather the additional information you need to choose the right school:

Campus Visit

Plan to return to the campuses of the schools that have accepted you and examine them once again. Usually admissions offices will host campus visit days for accepted students or, if you can't attend on one of those days, help you plan a visit of your own. When you return to the campus, plan to spend a night in a dormitory, attend classes, take meals with students, and explore the areas in which you would be participating—the school newspaper, the swimming pool, and the like. Talk to faculty members again. If finances are a consideration, go to the financial aid office and ask for a projection of your costs over the next four years.

If a campus visit is impossible, use the phone and e-mail. The admissions office usually asks students to take calls from prospective students; the financial aid office is glad to take questions, too. You can e-mail faculty members and coaches whom you may have met on your visit in the summer. Remember, colleges are always updating their Web sites. Visit the site, read the student newspaper, look at the faculty publications section, and look for student chat rooms to visit.

Your Guidance Counselor

Guidance counselors can be extremely helpful at this stage. Very often they have a supply of college catalogs—the ones with the courses in them. You can review the curriculum in these catalogs and use the other information in your guidance office (videos, viewbooks, and college search programs) to confirm and deepen your original impressions of the school. Then there is the counselor. He or she may know you better than you think and be able to offer advice as to how well you would fit into the various colleges that have accepted you. After all, he or she has the experience of seeing other students from your school attend the colleges you are considering.

Friends and Peers

Peers, with all due respect, are the third and least valuable source of information. It is best to talk with friends who are already in college and then turn to peers who have been accepted at the same schools as you. Be wary not to go to a college just to be with friends from high school. You will find, once in college, that you and your friends will change and possibly grow apart. That separation will provide an additional stress you don't need as you adjust to college life. Your best source of information is ultimately your friends who actually attend the colleges you are considering. Ask them questions about your four criteria.

REVISITING THE ORIGINAL SELECTION CRITERIA

At this point in your selection process, revisit some of the selection criteria presented in Chapter 2 with a slightly more critical eye. Compare each of your schools closely with one another. Make up a chart for each of these criteria and leave space to add an additional criterion. Call the fifth column "Experience" and use it for your conclusions about each school. What is your best prediction of your experience over the four years at University X?

Are the curriculum and the course requirements right for you and your goals? Look in the catalog and examine the curriculum more closely than you may have done earlier. Is there sufficient depth? Let's say you want to focus on computer engineering. Are there sufficient courses in this field for you to develop this specialty? You will need courses in electrical engineering as well as in computers themselves. Is computer engineering a department or just a major? It could make a difference.

Turn next to the distribution requirements. Here you have a dilemma because you want to have sufficient breadth to take courses related to your major, such as organizational behavior, but you also want to continue with your Spanish. The question is whether the distribution requirements make that difficult to do. The only way to really answer the course requirements question is to make a mock four-year schedule for yourself and see if everything you want to do fits in.

As you create your schedule of classes, remember that distribution requirements may not be as restrictive as they look, if the college has a trimester system (three quarters a year) or it allows multiple courses to satisfy the distribution requirements. Chapter 11 offers further suggestions in planning your course of study in college.

The point of looking so closely at the curriculum is to ensure that at the end of four years you will be well trained in a particular area and well versed in the liberal arts. Your particular expertise coupled with a capacity for independent thinking and broad awareness of other disciplines besides your own will make your education truly valuable.

What is the quality of the teaching?

Apart from examining catalogs and course descriptions, you really want to know about the quality of the teaching of those courses you will take. Statistics about class size can tell you something; attendance at classes will tell you more; talking with professors, even more. Your real interest here is to ensure that the teaching is good and that the learning is effective. The learning part is you. Will professors spend time with students outside of class and office hours? Do they run review sessions? Are they available by e-mail and phone if you need them? This is what you want to know. On some campuses there is a confidential guide to courses and instructors that is put out by students. The frank appraisals of various classes will tell you what to expect in the way of learning, evaluation, workload, and grades.

Will the college give you course credit?

Some colleges and universities will give you credit for work done at other colleges as a high school senior or for Advanced Placement (AP) courses and tests. You will need to ask your schools what credit, if any, they give for exceptional high school preparation such as AP work. If you find out they do, you may be able to register for the AP tests in May, if you have not already done so. Some colleges will not grant any credit for AP courses, and you therefore must stay there the full four years. Others will grant full credit, so you may be able to omit a required course and shorten your college stay or take another course instead. Still others will grant placement in higher-level courses, which means that you complete the four years of college, but you reach a higher level of proficiency in your AP areas than do other undergraduates.

The discussion of AP courses and credit should lead you to examine more closely any accelerated degree or advanced-standing programs offered by your schools. Students with definite college and career goals who are looking to shorten their college stay and move directly into the workforce or on to graduate school could save themselves considerable expense at certain schools. Working out your proposed course of study and discussing it with professors and department heads during your campus visit is the best way to ensure you make the right choice.

Are there good student-faculty relationships?

A positive answer to this question is important because the teaching and learning experience at your college will be crucial to your success. Yes, you may have a wonderful social life and great friends, but if the classroom experience is not fulfilling, your college experience will be compromised. Talk to both faculty members and students directly. Ask faculty members how much time they spend with students outside the classroom, in the lab or on field trips. How much social time do they share with students? In other words, do they take their out-of-class commitments seriously? Ask faculty members open-ended questions to see if they will tell you what you want to know without pressing too hard and making them feel uncomfortable.

Ask students similar questions. You want to know how serious they are about their academic work. Do they feel they have access to faculty members? Are office hours adequate? Does access to faculty members via e-mail really work? How satisfied are students with the quality of corrections they receive on homework and on papers they prepare? Finally, how would they characterize their classes? Are they animated? Do students get a chance to speak? Do students feel that they are getting good value for their tuition dollar in the classroom?

Do you resonate to the campus atmosphere?

The term *campus atmosphere* is vague, but it is meant to encompass the college's mission as well as the reality of its campus environment. Prospective students should try to form a judgment about the genuine openness of a college campus—the tolerance for divergent points of view. They should try to get a feeling for whether the college really cares about enriching students' lives and helping them reach their goals. Some things to look for might include whether professors begrudge spending time with students outside the classroom, whether there is a system for evaluating courses, whether there is a concern for how the school's graduates perform in the larger world, and whether there is a cloud of political correctness that hangs over the school. Many students reassure themselves about a school by asking, "Are my friends going there?" and "Will I be happy there?" You need to go deeper.

What is the quality of student life?

There are at least two parts to this question: the way students look on education at the college, and the way they interact with one another.

The first question drives at the seriousness of the students—why they are at college and how much they believe that a good education can improve their lives. The second question can be answered by observation. After going to the campus and talking with students and observing them, perhaps in the cafeteria or other gathering places, you will be able to make an accurate assessment of the quality of student life.

Is there help when you need it?
Try to get a feeling for how the school's advising system works, right from the resident advisers and up the chain to the Dean of Students. Ask students how well the system works and to give examples. Also inquire about programs for learning disabled students, international students, and multicultural students. Are there programs that help them become assimilated into the mainstream? Try to get an understanding for how the psychological and social counseling program works at the college. Then inquire about the academic advising system, both in terms of course selection and concentration in your major and in terms of assisting students with academic difficulties of one kind or another. Is there a Learning Center to help with study skills and writing, for example? Does the Learning Center help students who are a little bit behind on learning how to use the computer? Where do students go when they feel stressed beyond their limits? What is the role of the campus ministry in student life?

What are student priorities?
Previous questions have touched on student priorities. They are important. Try to ask students the first words that come to mind when describing their school. Listen carefully. "Too much work." "Great parties." "Great teaching." "Good Career Office." "Girls have it tough." "Winters are awful." "As long as you fit in, you're fine." Each of these responses need to be weighed against your own needs and preferences before you make the decision to enroll.

As you go from college to college and ask these same questions, your own judgment will become sharper, and as you think about these responses, you will come up with ways you can cope with the negatives aspects of a particular school.

Do the students show respect for each other?
The way in which students treat each other in a college environment could have significant ramifications for your own experience. You need to discover whether students respect the differences between one another. Are they sensitive or insensitive? Take a close look at the dormitory situation at night. Do stereos blare? Is there trash lying around? Are there people constantly coming and going from each other's rooms? Could you get any studying done there? What happens to students who are not particularly

social and like to have some private time? Are they respected by their more social roommates? Try to stay on the campus on a Saturday night to see if the social life is to your liking. You may be shocked at how some students who have never been away from home before interpret their newfound freedom. Throughout your stay, focus on the relationships among the students. Is there mutual respect? Could you meet some fine people and find friends at the school? Could you also have genuine fun? If the answers are positive, you are all set.

What about the facilities?

You will need to check out the library when you visit. Can students who want to study find a refuge here? Are the rights of users respected, or is there a lot of socializing going on? Are the library hours convenient? What about computing facilities if you don't have your own computer? Do the dormitories have them, departments, the library? Is there a computing center? What are the rental facilities for computers? Now the gym. Is it open for recreation at reasonable hours? How about practice rooms, if you are a musician?

Are there special program opportunities for you? It is also a good idea to explore in greater depth the extracurricular activities that attracted you to the particular college or university. Promising swimmers should talk with the coach about their prospects for making the freshman squad. Musicians will want to know if they can join the orchestra, and radio announcers will want to see if they can have their own show in the first year. As you explore your extracurricular activity, look carefully at the competition. It may be that you will not make the freshman squad or that you will have to sit out a year before joining the band. These situations may lead you to another school with a greater opportunity. Be straightforward with the questions you ask coaches, teachers, and college admissions officers. They will give you honest answers. They know that some students want to contribute on the athletic fields or in the studios and that if they can't, they may go elsewhere.

How strong is the career planning program?

In your efforts to distinguish among the schools that have accepted you, one special service deserves particular attention: the career planning program. Though it might have been of secondary interest to you when you were applying, now it is of primary importance. This is true even if you don't know what career path you want to pursue. A good Career Office is perhaps

WHAT TO DO NOW

more important to those students. It can be of great value to you as you seek to clarify your objectives and crystallize your career plans during your undergraduate years.

Visit the Career Office, and ask how the office sees its role. Does it begin its program with contacts with freshmen? How does the sequence of services unroll over the four years? What databases of job requirements, job openings, and alumni and other contacts exist in the office itself? What is the nature of the recruitment of students by companies, on campus and off campus? Is there a network for young graduates just entering the job market to keep in touch with each other and interested undergraduates? Are there some success stories that the career officers like to relate?

The Career Office of the college or university should be able to tell you how many graduates went into various fields last year and what the average number of job applications per student was. Some offices may have statistics on the "satisfaction rates" of the students it served. Others may direct you to their alumni job directory and invite you to see where last year's graduates were placed.

While you are visiting the Career Office, make a special point to ask whether the office has a testing program that enables students to discover the areas in which they might have a special talent. Does the office offer a course or individual advice on decision making and career preparation for first- and second-year students? Are there skill and personality inventories available electronically in the office so that undergraduates trying to determine what they might be good at can assess their skills and investigate the job market?

Finally, you want to ask about the internships for undergraduates that are sponsored by the Career Office. Here again, ask to see the current listings for internships and for summer employment that is job related. All of this will help you arrive at a judgment about the vitality and efficiency of the Career Office and how well it can serve you.

Counseling for graduate school

How about graduate school counseling? Does the Career Office or the Dean of Students' office offer a program of instruction in completing applications, assembling recommendations, and assessing graduate school programs? How well is the college or university regarded by the graduate schools? That means the faculty members and the quality of the students they prepare.

What will it cost?

Finally, there is the question of the cost of your four years at a particular college or university. Assessing your financial aid offers has been discussed in some detail in Chapter 7. If you are at the margin of need or merit aid from the college, you still should ask the financial aid office about the student employment situation for your freshman year and whether or not you might qualify for aid in the sophomore year on the basis of your grade point average or a change in your status of need. Today many colleges have become concerned about the retention of good students, especially those who are financially stressed. Some are looking at ways to change financial aid packaging for upperclass students so that they will remain at the school and not go to a cheaper institution.

Even if you are not a financial aid recipient, you may still have to plan carefully to meet college expenses. When college bills are due becomes important, as does the availability of college-supported loans or loans from cooperating banks. You will also want to know about supplemental fees for health insurance, parking, room deposits, laboratory fees, and student activity fees. Your parents will want to know about payment plans. Some families like to pay by the month; others take out extended payment plans and pay over a six- to eight-year period. Campus jobs are another point of interest. Are scholarship students favored over non-scholarship students? Are there enough jobs on campus for both groups? If you cannot visit the campus and the financial aid office, you can phone or e-mail them and get the answers to these very important questions.

Comparing financial aid packages

In Chapter 7 there is a detailed discussion on how to go about this exercise. Be assured that the colleges do not want you or your families to miscalculate. They will be more than happy to explain their offers and even to interpret the offers of their competitor schools. Once you have formed a judgment as to which school you want to attend, try not to make cost the overriding factor. If two schools are $2,000 apart and you prefer the more expensive one, enroll there. You and your family will be spending close to $150,000 over the course of the next four years, and a $2,000 price difference is only 5 percent. The added value of your happiness at a particular place is worth the cost.

Final Decisions

If your schools are beginning to blur during this final analysis, don't be alarmed. Your original choice of colleges and universities was supposed to be based on similarities to begin with. Remember academic program, location, size, cost, and quality of student life. They should blur somewhat. This is a natural occurrence. As you look back over all your notes, reexamine your criteria, consult that "experience" column on your comparison chart, and talk to your family once again. Don't be afraid to decide on your gut feelings. If you see yourself as happiest at one particular school, you should attend that school. If one college among all the others seems to have a good sense of itself, its students like it, and its atmosphere and environment are what you like, that probably is the one.

In the end, even if you think you are making a visceral judgment, you really are not. You have followed a very exhaustive and objective process, and you are just using your gut to tip the balance toward the one school where you will be happy and productive. You have made the right decision.

IF YOU ARE PUT ON A WAITING LIST

Because students apply to so many colleges and can only go to one, colleges admit more students than they can accommodate and try to guess how many of their acceptances will actually enroll. To cover their bets, if they guess that fewer will enroll than actually do, they construct waiting lists to which they turn if there is a shortfall. Although the waiting list is sometimes difficult for students, it helps the college accomplish four objectives: (1) to fill the class right up to the last bed that will be occupied, and for day students, the last parking place allocated; (2) to have an opportunity to review appealing candidates who were not quite strong enough to make it in the first round; (3) to respond to political pressure from alumni, coaches, guidance counselors, and students and parents themselves and elicit their gratitude; and (4) to control their financial aid budgets by admitting only full pay or nearly full pay students from the waiting list.

Knowing these factors, students put on a waiting list may be there for:

- **Academic reasons.** Your grades and scores were simply not as strong as others, but they were close. If some of the accepted students with a slightly higher academic profile decide not to come, you could make it in.

> **Not Making Your First-Choice School**
>
> If you were rejected by your first-choice college, try not to indulge your disappointment. Excessive worry about the meaning of admissions committee decisions can undermine the self-confidence you've worked so hard to build up. Families and guidance counselors frequently advise students to reach for a top college as a way of ensuring that candidates set high goals for themselves and put in the maximum effort. Even if you do not achieve a specific college as an objective, you've still gained something important. In your striving, you have found new reserves of energy and strength, and you have also developed a range of new skills.
>
> The kind of emotional and intellectual growth that you have experienced cannot be measured, but it is very real and should not be forgotten just because a selective college has sent you a rejection letter. As you and your fellow seniors rush home to find out how colleges have decided your fate, please ponder these ultimate truths:
>
> True education is not to be found in a particular college or university. True education is a process of self-discovery informed by learning from particular academic subjects that are being studied. It is a process in which individuals pursue their own interests and perfect their own abilities under the discerning and compassionate eye of interested and able teachers. The truly intelligent person is one who is able to make the most of the college experience, to discover opportunities for learning and living and growing in the classroom, in the dormitories, in extracurricular activities, on the athletic fields, and everywhere. Acceptance or rejection at a particular school is ultimately of little consequence as you learn and become an educated person and contributing member of our society.

- **Political factors.** Sorry to say this, but your profile did not match that of the accepted class, but you have friends in high places, and the admissions office knows it. The college can't take everyone like you off the wait list, but frankly, if you bring even more pressure to bear, you could make it in.
- **Financial reasons.** In the recent era of enrollment management, ability to pay has become an even stronger factor in the admission of certain students to college. Some colleges and universities will be frank with you

and say that you are on a financial aid waiting list. In that event, when someone with a financial aid package equal to yours turns the college down, you should be moved up to the accept category. The more aid you need, the less this is apt to happen. Look at it this way. Say the school costs $27,000 a year, and you have awards totaling $18,000; it is very tempting for the college to admit two students who each have $9,000 awards to the school instead of you. Why? Because in those cases, each of those students brings $18,000 in loans and his or her own funds to the college. Two students actually bring $36,000, whereas you only bring $9,000.

Action Plan for the Wait List

Being placed on a wait list is in some ways more agonizing than an outright rejection letter. You should prepare yourself for this ambiguous response and react as quickly as possible:

1. Secure your place at one of the institutions that accepted you. You generally will have two weeks to review the colleges that have accepted you. Follow the advice mentioned about comparing them and then send your reply card to the one you like best. Also send in your deposit, which will be forfeited if you do not attend. Look on your deposit as reimbursement to the college for its expenses of carrying you as an enrolled student before you withdraw and attend the wait list school that has finally accepted you.

2. Find out what your status on the wait list means. Are you there because there is absolutely no hope, because of your financial need, or because you were very close to admission? Ask your counselor to interpret your status. If you know one of the admissions officers at the college well enough, e-mail and ask directly. Be diplomatic when asking these questions.

3. Rally your support. Make an ally of your guidance counselor. He or she can serve as your intermediary with the college and give you much-needed advice. Next, mount a campaign to gain admission. Enlist others—coaches, teachers, and perhaps people such as your neighbor who offered to write as an alumnus and who you turned down. You need not behave like you did when you were a regular applicant. Now all bets are off, so to speak. Remember to show commitment as well as interest. Be prepared to go to the college if it accepts you—and that includes accepting its financial aid offer.

Get a letter of support from a teacher who knows you well but who did not write for you the first time. Get your neighbor's letter sent in. Call anyone at the college who took a special interest in you, such as a coach or faculty member, and see if they are disposed to help.

4. Write a letter to the Dean of Admission or the person in the admissions office whom you know best. In that letter reiterate your interest in coming to the school. Make it clear that you will come if accepted. Address your deficiency, such as a weak sophomore year, and point to your steady improvement since then and your recent A in calculus. Affirm your interest in contributing to the life of the college as well as its classrooms. Mention your special talent, whether academic, artistic, athletic, or extracurricular. And mean it.

5. Send in your recent grades and any documents that show your recent accomplishments. Perhaps the document is a newspaper article on your athletic awards, perhaps it is a short paper on Tolstoy, with a grade from the teacher. Use your good judgment.

6. Make sure your financial aid application is complete. If your family was not able to provide all the tax information for last year by February 1, make sure the college has it now. If you are accepted from the wait list, you certainly want to receive a reasonable financial aid package. Otherwise your acceptance is a hollow victory.

7. Develop a schedule for your various actions, as you did with the application. Prepare a grid showing each item you submit and when it was submitted. Also show your e-mail and phone messages and their responses.

Call the Wait List School

After you and your supporters have submitted all your material, wait a week and then ask your guidance counselor to telephone the college again to reiterate your interest. Or you can call yourself. Find out if the wait list is beginning to move. Ask if you are still a viable candidate. (If the college has gone to the wait list once and not included you, your chances are sharply reduced.) You may learn that the college still has questions about a couple of points that you can now address. Perhaps you got Most Valuable Player or won National Merit Finalist status.

As the conversation proceeds, here are some other questions that you may need to have answered:

- What new information would you like concerning me? Another teacher recommendation, new sprint times, a tape of a recent recital?

WHAT TO DO NOW

- Would it help me to write a letter to the Dean of Admissions restating my sincere desire to come? Now you have done this already, but the purpose of asking again is to reaffirm your intention to attend the college. The last thing admissions officers want to do is to take people from the wait list who then don't come. This reduces *yield,* a term discussed in the previous chapter, and a sensitive number for many, many colleges.

Normally the waiting list process takes a month to six weeks following May 1, which is the reply date for many schools. Financial aid concerns prolong the process. You may have to make several calls to the admissions office to check on your status.

Risk Being a Pest

Being placed on a waiting list allows you to take stock of your own feelings about a school. If you are not passionate about attending a college that has wait listed you, do not play the waiting list game. Let others who really want to go there stay on the list. Make sure you don't get caught up in something that is really not that important to you. Remember, you may get two wait list decisions—or even more.

Most colleges do not rank people on their waiting lists because they know they are going to have to respond to various pressures. Admissions directors are besieged by coaches whose best-laid plans have gone awry and there are no basketball centers, by development officers who have just discovered that one candidate's father made a fortune a month ago when he sold his company for $40 million, or by the president of the college, who writes a letter for another boy whose father sits on the powerful budget committee in the state legislature. Even guidance counselors get into the act, saying, "The whole school simply does not understand why you did not accept Jenny White and put her on your waiting list."

In this somewhat chaotic situation, you should realize that your own chances may be slim because of the many institutional priorities that have to be met. Whether you like it or not, the swimming coach cannot field a team without any divers, nor the basketball coach a team without a strong center, nor the admissions director who needs a good relationship with a guidance counselor who sends her fifty candidates a year. Nonetheless, the candidate who is not afraid to take a few risks and overstep a few of the conventions often has a chance.

Parental Role

Only as a second line of defense should parents become involved in wait list activity. Parents often have difficulty understanding the fact that colleges and universities really want to deal with students. Most of these students are 18 years old and eligible to vote, but sometimes parents forget that. By all means, consult with your parents, but take most of the actions yourself. Recognize, too, that neither you nor your parents are entitled to know everything that goes on in the decision-making process. Sometimes the coaches who make virtual promises to students in their enthusiasm to have them enroll are turned down by the admissions committee. Sometimes weak alumni children are put on the waiting list to soften the blow of rejection. Sometimes students from the same high school group are put on the wait list for the same reason—so as not to offend the guidance counselor and the principal.

Still, this admonition that parents stay removed from waiting list activity has its exceptions just like any other. Occasionally parents can summon the perspective and the eloquence to breathe new life into an ordinary candidacy. The letter on the following page is one such example.

The sample letter was written by the father of a young man seeking admission to a prestigious university with high admissions standards. After checking with his son's counselor, the father wrote his letter on plain stationery that did not call attention to his status as a prominent diplomat. The letter has both style and substance, and the tone is properly deferential. Mr. Foss sympathizes with the pressures Mr. Thomas and his committee are under. While he does reiterate his son's talents, which Mr. Thomas already knows, he does so in the context of a life lived in a foreign country, so that the committee will realize that Dan is not only an American, he is an international student as well. Mr. Foss mentions the Student Council position Dan has attained—a point that will not be lost on a selective school seeking to identify the leaders of the next generation.

In addition, Mr. Foss makes the point that Dan is mature and thoughtful. If admitted, he is not going to squander this opportunity by spending a semester or two to grow up. Finally, Mr. Foss shows his understanding of what kind of institution Hanover is, what it stands for academically, and what kind of students it wants to attract: intelligent, serious, ethical, and reasonable human beings who know what they are about. And the letter is not overly long!

WHAT TO DO NOW

Rua Marie Satzke 144
Buenos Aires 04664
Argentina

Mr. Dwight A. Thomas
Director of Admissions
Hanover University
Middlemarch, Connecticut 06590

Dear Mr. Thomas:

My son Daniel A. Foss is currently on the waiting list for admission to the class of 2005 at Hanover. Since it is his most fervent wish to attend Hanover and be a member of one of the first classes in the new century, I ask your permission to say a few words on his behalf.

From Dan's application you know that he has lived in Buenos Aires for the past five years of his life and attended the Argentina-English Academy here for four of those years. Then last fall, he went to the United States and attended St. James Academy. St. James has been an ideal decompression chamber for Dan's reentry into the academic and social world of the U.S. His schooling here was mainly conducted in Spanish, and the Argentina-English Academy is quite a conservative place.

Dan made a good transition to St. James, achieving high honors for the first as well as the current marking period. He entered into the theatrical life of the school, had parts in two plays, and still found time to practice his beloved trombone an hour a day and play in the St. James Jazz Band. He was elected as his dormitory representative to the Student Council as well. Dan's mother and I are very proud of his accomplishments, and I know the school is too.

My plea for Dan is based on the fact that Hanover magically combines all the criteria that he set in selecting his ideal college. We wanted a school with a tradition, a school that had maintained its academic integrity over the years, that still supported and respected individual accomplishment, and paid attention to civility in its community.

> Perhaps because of his experience in Europe as a child and now here in Buenos Aires, Dan insisted on an urban school. He likes those wide boulevards and the museums and coffeehouses of Buenos Aires. He also wants a school that is fairly large and able to attract a genuinely diverse student body. He wants a strong Latin American Studies Department, which Hanover has. But more than that, Dan detected in Hanover an ambiance that seemed to him more cosmopolitan and less stylized than universities of comparable standing.
>
> Dan is very interested in international relations. He wants to major in government and do field studies in Latin America. His strong preparation at the hands of his Spanish teachers in the International Baccalaureate curriculum has trained him well.
>
> I sincerely believe that Dan would prove to be a responsible if not prominent person on the Hanover campus, making a solid contribution to the community as he learned in it. I hope that Dan's references show that he is a thoroughly enjoyable, warm, and kind young man. He is also a mature and thoughtful 18-year-old with a great deal of self-reliance and initiative. He is happy in himself and enjoys his moments of relaxation and solitude.
>
> Recognizing that you and the admissions committee have many wonderful young people to choose from, I earnestly hope that you will review Dan's case and deem him a worthy gamble. You won't be disappointed.
>
> Yours sincerely,
>
> George A. Foss Jr.

NO ACCEPTANCES?

Time and chance do play an occasional role in the admissions process, and if you are one of those people who end up rejected or wait listed everywhere, there are steps you should take. First, make haste to your guidance counselor's office and ask your counselor to diagnose your

WHAT TO DO NOW

situation. He or she may say flatly that you applied "over your head," in which case it is time to listen to the advice offered. Or your counselor may be as surprised as you are; in that case ask him or her to call what you thought were your mid-range schools and see if he or she can find out what went wrong.

Try not to indulge in a litany of "if onlys." If only I had been a better athlete . . . if only I had applied to my mother's alma mater, which I didn't like . . . if only I had lived in Alaska . . . Focus instead on what went wrong and in getting back on track.

1. Work on remedying your deficiencies. If your testing was weak, perhaps there is still time to take the tests again in June. If your transcript was too weak, perhaps there is extra work you can do in a course and improve your grade. Maybe there are summer school courses you can take to strengthen your transcript.

2. Work closely with your college counselor. Trust your counselor to call the colleges that rejected you and ask the embarrassing questions as to what went wrong. He or she may say, "You applied over your head." Well, it's time now to listen to him or her. Or your counselor may be surprised and want to help. Follow his or her advice as to what steps you could take at a particular school where you might have been close to getting in. Should you apply next year or apply at midyear? Apply at midyear after taking and doing well in some courses at the local community college? What makes sense?

3. Find another school and apply to it. Assuming you want to proceed with your education in the fall, it will be important to find another school to which you can be admitted. The National Association for College Admission Counseling puts out a list every May with the names of schools with vacancies. Your counselor may have it. Also, state and regional associations of colleges and universities sometimes do the same thing. (The New England Board of Higher Education, 45 Temple Place, Boston, Massachusetts 02111, is one.) Furthermore, some state schools with many branch campuses will publish the names of the campuses with openings in the newspaper. Also check their Web sites. Another option is the large state schools that have conditional admission, i.e., they will accept you for fall enrollment, but you must achieve a certain GPA by the end of the semester in order to be admitted to regular standing.

4. Seek advice from one of the colleges to which you applied. Few people take advantage of this option—calling the admissions office and requesting an appointment to review your application and gather suggestions as to appropriate next steps. This step can be very useful, especially if taken at your first-choice college. It sends the message that you are serious about attending the school, and if you take all the steps that the college recommends, how could they turn you down next time around?

APPLYING TO A NEW COLLEGE

In addition to the suggestions above for finding a new college or university, you might want to consult your "fan mail" from colleges last fall. Perhaps there is a school in that box that looks a little bit more interesting now. Alternatively you could approach some of the lesser-known private liberal arts colleges. It would be to your advantage if you could pay a good deal of the tuition at these schools. Ask them if they would consider a late application, and if they will not, which school might. Be prepared to discuss your credentials over the phone with admissions officers. Your guidance counselor may be able to suggest some schools.

Private Liberal Arts School. Let's assume that you have selected a private liberal arts college, and you call the Director of Admissions. After confirming that there "might" be an opening for a qualified candidate, tell the director what has happened to you. Offer to fax him or her your transcript and scores, and perhaps a recommendation if you have one. In that packet, include a letter from yourself indicating that if you were to be accepted by that school, and the finances could be worked out, you would definitely enroll in the fall.

When the director has had a chance to look over your information and to have talked with your counselor, make an appointment to come to the college to visit or to speak with the director again on the phone. At that point, after hearing the director's reaction to your credentials, make sure that this is the *only* college you are applying to. You want to be sure and so does the college that if there is agreement to accept you, you will come. While speaking with the director, mention the fact that you are or are not a candidate for financial aid. At this point, late in the year, the director will have his or her eye on the financial aid budget.

Public College or University. You can approach public institutions in one of two ways, either for admission in September or for admission in the middle of the year (January). Because many state schools are very large, they might have room for just one more student, especially if you are willing to give up housing and financial aid. State colleges sometimes have specific programs that are under enrolled, where you could begin and later transfer. You need to watch the regulations here because sometimes it is easy to transfer out of a department, but not as easy to transfer into another department. Some state universities also agree to enroll students who are able to begin in the summer. Ask about this option. Ask about January. Ask about beginning at a branch campus and then transferring to the main campus.

Perhaps a state school sounded uninteresting last fall, but now you may see your opportunities to get a good education, become independent, and pay less for your education than you had planned as advantages worth considering. Finally, going to a state school for two years and then transferring to a smaller private college at the end of two years is not out of the question, either.

REAPPLYING TO A COLLEGE

Should you choose to reapply to a college that has rejected you, you will need to make a visit to that school and find out why you were rejected. You need to take careful notes on your conversation with the Dean of Admissions so that you can remedy your defects and make a much stronger case when you apply for admission again. Some suggestions for the reapplication process:

1. Let some time elapse before you apply again. At least a year is advisable. Give the admissions office time to put this year's class together, and don't go to the school for a visit until late June or early July.

2. Seek a face-to-face interview at the college with the Dean of Admissions or Associate Dean.

3. When you do bring up the subject of applying again, you should not be timid or embarrassed. The admissions process is not perfect. Decisions are close, and occasionally an injustice is done. You will know that soon enough because you will be invited to reapply. If your chances are not going to be good the second time around, you will be encouraged to consider other schools. And you should take this advice.

4. Emphasize the learning experience you have derived from the college application process and stress your seriousness about your

education. Acknowledge your weaknesses, but don't be overly apologetic. Show flexibility in your response when it may be suggested that you do something you never thought of before, like take an extension course or reconsider your choice of major. Remember that the more advice that is followed, the more likely you are to be admitted.

5. Confirm the advice you receive with another college visit or with your counselor.

Whatever you do, make sure that you have some fun and relaxation during the period between your rejection and your reapplication. Restore your spirit and your energy. Build your confidence in an activity that you are good at. This is a period for growth that perhaps has not taken place earlier. Make the most of it.

TAKING A YEAR OFF

If you are one of those students whose applications were rejected by all your schools, or you are not satisfied with any of your college options, you may well decide to take the year off and apply for admission the following September. Like students who are going to make another run at some schools, you should make a pilgrimage to the college or university that you most want to attend and discuss your plans with the Dean of Admissions.

As you prepare for this meeting, consult your guidance counselor and reflect on your own. You don't want to be in the position of asking the admissions dean to do all of your educational planning for you. Once you have the reactions of the dean and your counselor, make sure you follow their advice. Chances are both will suggest some kind of academic work to improve your record for your second application. Your counselor may suggest reviewing your personality and preference information and offer to administer the Kuhlman Anderson Preference Test and the Strong Campbell Interest Inventory Test. Take your counselor up on the offer and ask about freeware on the Internet that would help you to clarify the match between you and a particular school.

As you go through this review, be ready for some criticism if you have been nonchalant about the application process or frivolous when you should have been serious. If these criticisms are patterns, think about an experience that will provide you with confidence in your abilities. Being open to criticism will help you deal with your own imperfections and put them behind you.

The Year-Off Experience

The phrase "year off" is really misleading. It is an American term. The Germans have the word "Wanderesjahr," meaning a wandering, exploratory year. That is more accurate. If you have been told that you projected a bit of immaturity in your application essay and that you seemed indifferent to the opportunities of college life, you may want to use your year off to sharpen your sense of self-worth. Outward Bound is a highly regarded wilderness program that puts students on their own with each other. The National Outdoor Leadership School is another program that focuses on self-reliance in the wilderness. There are also urban semester programs and social service programs that put students on their own and hold them accountable. Of course, there are jobs that provide this opportunity, too. If you are fortunate enough to be able to take a semester or a year to study abroad, Peterson's book *Study Abroad* should be consulted. Visit Peterson's Web site (http://www.petersons.com/stdyabrd/) to find a wealth of information about programs of study and travel.

Every student will have a different plan for a year off. Your plans will evolve naturally from a discussion with your parents, counselors, and colleges and self-reflection on your own values and goals. Inevitably you will emerge from your adversity as a stronger person. When you do secure college admission the following year, your acceptance will be a lot less important to you than the educational and personal growth you have gained in the interim.

ELEVEN

Making the Most of the Freshman Year

The freshman year begins a four-year period of unlimited freedom, the greatest you will ever have, but also a period of exciting responsibility. The trick is to balance the two effectively.

B. Ann Wright, Vice President for Enrollment, Rice University

When Barbara Crowley decided to accept the offer from Hanover College, she knew she had to keep moving with her college planning process. She had reached the end of the important chapter of selecting a school, but now she had to turn the page and make sure she made the most of the freshman year. In this new phase of the college admission process—the entry phase—Barbara knew she would have to make intelligent and informed decisions about a number of items she had received in her admission packet.

The first decisions would concern the courses she would take in the fall. Barbara promptly sat down with her registration card and the Hanover catalog and began by reviewing the requirements that she would need to meet in order to obtain her degree in four years. Once she understood the requirements, she could construct her academic road map or course of study. Her father called it her strategic plan.

CHARTING THE ACADEMIC PATH

Barbara perused the course catalog and made a note of the requirements for the degree on a separate piece of paper. Then she looked long and hard at the Economics Department's offerings. She knew she wanted to major in economics and enter the business world when she graduated. She also knew she wanted to take a broad range of courses while in college and to avoid overspecialization. That could wait until graduate school. She also wanted to be sure she had a mix of practical as well as theoretical learning and decided to include her summer work opportunities as well as an early internship in business in a plan for her first two years at Hanover.

The Hanover catalog states that you need to take eight courses in a given department and four more courses in related fields (total: twelve) in order to establish a major in economics. In addition, the university-wide requirements for a degree required that each student had to take two courses each in social sciences, the humanities, and the sciences (total: six). However, students received credit for the field in which they were majoring, so the final number of additional courses was only four. The remaining requirement at Hanover was called the multicultural requirement. This was a loosely defined requirement that students take three courses in non-Western cultures.

Hanover had two other requirements for the degree, but these did not necessarily involve specific courses. These were a quantitative reasoning requirement that ensured a moderate level of mathematics proficiency (Barbara would learn later that her 680 on the SAT II Math 1C Subject Test qualified her already) and a writing proficiency requirement. Barbara noted that courses marked with a dagger qualified for the writing requirement, and she resolved to take one of those in economics in her first year.

Barbara now made three shrewd decisions so that she could reach her broad educational objectives. First she decided to begin work on her major right away so that she could attain an advanced level of study in her junior year and qualify for some special seminars in her senior year. Second, she decided to meet her distribution requirements as soon as possible so she could benefit, sooner rather than later, from the breadth of the subjects she would study. Getting the distribution requirements out of the way would keep her options open for new areas of exploration in the junior and senior years.

Then Barbara made a third shrewd decision: to overlap her courses where possible so that she could benefit from, say, studying the same period from two different perspectives. This would give her the opportunity to transfer her knowledge of one subject area to another. Since she was interested in economics, Barbara would focus on the economic dimension of the courses in literature, philosophy, and history that she would take in fields related to her major.

Counsel from the Campus

Having set her strategy in place, Barbara decided to gather more information from two important sources: the campus itself, via the Internet, and from a

Hanover student. Barbara went on to the Hanover campus network and looked at the Economics Department offerings. She also looked at the biographies of the faculty members who were teaching the courses and noted their comments on their particular fields of interest, projects that they worked on with students, and articles they had recently written. She looked especially for the connections of individual faculty members with companies and research organizations where she might do an internship.

Then Barbara picked up the phone and called Ron Barrow, a Hanover undergraduate who lived in the next town. Ron was studying economics at the college and was just completing his junior year. The admissions office had suggested his name when Barbara was trying to decide between Hanover and Coburn a month ago. The conversation with Ron yielded two interesting insights. First, he suggested that Barbara take the course in research and methods that the Economics Department offered (Economics 90), even though it was not required by the department. Ron said it would be of inestimable value to Barbara when it came time to write her senior thesis.

Ron Barrow also suggested that Barbara study the economy of one particular region intensively, and since this advice coincided with that of her father, who was a corporate executive with some international experience, Barbara decided to follow it. She chose Latin America as her region.

Ron also reminded Barbara to consult the *Confidential Guide to Courses and Instructors at Hanover.* The guide was an annual publication prepared by resourceful students anxious to give an objective opinion on each course in the catalog. The guide gave the name of each teacher of each course, the number of students in the class, the average number of pages assigned each week, the quality of the homework and research assignments, the number of papers and exams and the relative difficulty of each, and the quality of the lectures and discussions. The guide was an invaluable tool in ultimately choosing which courses to take when and in learning about the quality of teaching and student-faculty relations in and around the classroom.

The guide's analysis of Political Science 35—The Political Economy of the U.S. went like this:

> **Political Science 35.** Political Economy of the U.S.: Money and Power—Prof. Peter Fowles. Two lectures and one seminar a week.

Although this is one of the toughest courses at Hanover, it is a must. Fowles is inimitable as a lecturer; he has a broad command of his subject, gained from eleven years of perfecting this course, a real compassion for students, and considerable practical experience in the field as a consultant to two government committees. (He is currently advising the Ethics Committee of the House on guidelines for conversations and relations between House members and Washington lobbyists.)

You will have to do virtually all 200 pages of reading each week because Fowles has a way of referring to it on exams. Fortunately most of it is included in his inexpensive text, available at the bookstore.

Fowles and his two assistants expect you to ask questions in the seminars. If you don't, they will. So do the reading on the schedule and don't leave it to the end of the course. Fowles is not above stopping his lecture from time to time to ask a student if he or she has understood what has just been said. Who else would bother?

There are two short papers—one a description of how a particular institution operates politically and economically, the other an analysis of a policy question, e.g., "The Proper Role of the Federal Reserve Board in the Global Economy." There is also a stiffly graded hour exam and a final. However, the range of the questions on the final exam allows students to bring their particular area of interest into play. It is not just another test. Fowles is going on leave the year after next, so this is the year to take this course, one of Hanover's crown jewels.

Internship Experience

After Barbara had digested the contents of the guide, she turned to the internship section of the catalog, under Career Counseling. There she learned that students could use the long Christmas vacation that stretched through most of January as an opportunity to seek an internship. You needed to sign up with the Career Office, have your faculty adviser's signature, and a written commitment from your employer. Barbara decided to investigate working at the World Bank in Washington, D.C., for six weeks in the middle of her second year at Hanover.

DRAWING UP A PLAN OF STUDY

Barbara then proceeded to draw up a Plan of Study Sheet (see next page). She made a series of vertical columns: one for the fall semester, one for January (even though the school was on vacation), and one for the spring semester. Then she added three columns in which she could keep a running total of the major and distribution requirements she had met and the number of credits she had taken. She did not fill out the entire sheet but filled in what she knew. Even though she could have done this entirely on the computer, she chose to put the format on the computer and leave the spaces for specific courses blank. She later filled them in in pencil. If her plans changed, she could erase the pencil entries easily and alter her plan.

The First Year: "Casting a Wide Net"

On her sheet Barbara wrote in some of the courses she wanted to take for the fall and winter, based on her study of the catalog, the economics Web site, the guide, and the conversation with Ron Barrow. Since she wanted eventually to enter the world of business, Barbara decided that for her first summer vacation she would seek a job that would acquaint her with the inside operations of a major business. She wrote in "banking" and thought tentatively of applying to her local bank for a job as a teller, messenger, or credit coordinator of some sort. Barbara thought it would be a good idea to pencil in courses in mathematics and computer science in her freshman year. She put in a course in probability and statistics, followed by a calculus course (Math 35) in the spring term. Both of these would meet the distribution requirements for science, and both are clearly related to economics. After writing these courses down on her Plan of Study, Barbara put a "C" beside the ones that satisfied her concentration for the major and a "D" beside the ones that satisfied the distribution requirement. Then she entered the totals for each in the appropriate columns.

Barbara also made sure that she followed the principle of overlap. She chose History 11 to go with her introductory course in economic theory. For her fourth and final course in the fall semester . . . she paused and then decided to take a plunge into the broad lake of the liberal arts. She chose Music Theory and Harmony (Music 30). Barbara had always felt deprived of music in her home. Neither her parents nor her older brother took an interest in things musical. On the other hand, Barbara had made several friends at school who loved to talk about and play music. So Barbara decided to investigate this unknown area. Here again, the guide was helpful.

Barbara Crowley's Plan of Study Sheet

Fall Semester	January	Spring Semester	Total Courses Fall	Jan.	Spring	Total Concentration (C)	Total Distribution (D)	Summer
Freshman Year Economics 11. Foundations of Economic Theory (C) History 11. Western Tradition: The Greeks to the Enlightenment Math 35. Calculus (C) Music 30. Theory and Harmony (D) Freshman Writing Course (no credit)	Ski break at Christmas Work in department store	Economics 12. Applied Economics: Money and Banking (C) Political Science 35. Political Economy of the U.S. (C) Math 37. Probability and Statistics (D) Art History 10. The Art of the U.S. (D)	4		4			Bank teller, messenger, credit coordinator (work experience within the business world)
			8			4	3	
Sophomore Year Economics 41. Corporate Management (C) History 33. Imperialism in the Nineteenth and Twentieth Centuries (C) Math 41. Computer Programming (C) English 29. The Literature of the Victorians (D)	Ethics of Investment: U.S. and South Africa—A Case Study	Economics 42. Corporate Finance (C) Economics 90. Research Methods in Economics (C) Biology 37. Ecology and Progress (D) Psychology 15. Organizational Behavior (D)	4	1	4			Camp counselor, social service job National Forest Service (work experience outside the business world)
			9			5	3	
			17			9	6	

C = A course required for concentration. At Hanover College the minimum requirement for a concentration in economics is eight courses within the Economics Department plus four from related departments (total: twelve courses minimum).

D = Distribution courses. Each student must take six courses to meet this requirement: two in different departments of the social sciences, two in different departments of the humanities, and two in different departments of the sciences.

Music 30 was taught by a wonderful German couple named Kleberg. They were famous for being interested in students who were just passing through—meeting the humanities requirement—as well as the avowed music majors. Music 30 represented the breadth that all liberal arts students should strive for.

When it came to her first long vacation, from Christmas through January, Barbara had no problems making her decision. She decided to go skiing. She would return to the campus refreshed from her break. Barbara's spring schedule would include a course in applied economics (Economics 12)—the second course in the introductory sequence—and Professor Fowles's political science course. Barbara hoped that the overlapping study of economic and political systems (Political Science 35) would enhance her perspective in both areas. She also chose probability and statistics (Math 37), a course that she hoped would help brighten up her resume as she sought summer employment.

Barbara's last choice was an art history course, The Art of the United States (Art History 10), which would meet her third distribution requirement for her first year, and more important, satisfy her long-standing craving for some knowledge about the work of American painters. Barbara traced her interest in American art back to a visit she had made to the U.S. Customs House in New York. She had only been a little girl at the time, but she vividly recalled her sense of wonder at the beautiful murals there. One of the reasons she had decided to attend Hanover was the strong reputation of its Art History Department.

The Second Year: "Gaining a World View"

As Barbara thought about her second year at Hanover, she reaffirmed her decision to focus on her major early on in her college career. She decided to take the course in corporate management (Economics 41), described in the guide as a "heavy course, for majors only." She also decided to take a course in imperialism in the late nineteenth and early twentieth centuries (History 33). Barbara knew that the interface of literature and imperialism in the nineteenth century would be an interesting one, so she opted to take English 29, a literary analysis of the prominent Victorian writers of that period.

Barbara also decided to complete her foray into mathematics by taking an intensive course in computer programming (Math 41). She knew that this was a very useful course in terms of the jobs she would be seeking. She also thought about taking an off-campus reading course via distance learning, called the "Ethics of Investment," during the January vacation period in the sophomore year. This course had received an excellent report from Ron Barrow.

In the spring of her sophomore year, Barbara would capitalize on her study of imperialism and the ethics of investment and attempt a course in corporate finance (Economics 42). She also thought it would make good sense to enroll in Organizational Behavior (Psychology 15) at the same time, since it was a distant cousin of corporate management (Economics 41). She then tentatively chose a course in research methods in economics (Economics 90). Finally, she would complete her distribution requirements in the spring with Biology 37, Ecology and Progress. The Biology Department designed this course for nonmajors, and it was reputed to be "reasonable" in terms of difficulty. Barbara had three tough courses already and did not want a fourth one. Following up on her idea of gaining a broad perspective in her chosen field, Barbara decided to seek a summer experience outside the field of business following her sophomore year.

Junior and Senior Years: "Focus and Breadth Together"

Barbara had planned a sensible and challenging course of study for her first two years—one that enabled her to sample a broad range of subjects while getting a good start on her major. She realized that some changes might be made if her interests shifted, or if her academic adviser convinced her of the wisdom of following a slightly different path. However, careful planning would achieve her goal of allowing quite a bit of flexibility in her final two years of study.

During that time, Barbara decided to continue with her study of a foreign language, Spanish, and to pursue a special concentration in Latin American economics within her major. Barbara's parents and high school teachers had convinced her of the importance of knowing a second language and, through it, becoming conversant with another culture. "Knowledge of another culture is the fundamental premise of our global economy," her high school history teacher had asserted.

Even though the junior year would be one of increasing focus, Barbara wanted to explore courses beyond the social sciences. She planned to return to music, art, and literature in her final two years. These and other courses in psychology, philosophy, and history would enable her to communicate with and learn from others who shared an interest in them. Equally important, these courses represent different modes of thought and a different set of questions asked of the material than an economist would ask. Barbara would learn how people in other disciplines thought about their material, and she would be able to communicate with them when they met again in the workplace years from now. She would be more aware of the wider world beyond her chosen specialty of economics than others who chose a narrower and safer route. That breadth of knowledge would help put her own life and work in perspective; at the same time, it would inform and enlighten the decisions she would make as a business manager later on.

Having carefully considered both the benefit of a broad liberal arts experience and the practical benefit of strong preparation in her major, Barbara Crowley was able to achieve both goals. She made the most of her opportunity to attend Hanover and eventually to find success in the complex world of business beyond.

WHAT COURSES SHOULD I CHOOSE?

Signing up for your courses and meeting your faculty adviser is going to vary from college to college and from university to university. Some schools will encourage you to sign up for your courses on line after a conversation with your faculty adviser. The conversation with your adviser will probably take place when you go to the campus in the late summer for orientation. But it could take place earlier by phone and be followed by online registration in the early summer. In that case, you would know your classes and instructors when you got to campus. Whatever system you encounter, try to draw up a study plan of your own, as Barbara Crowley did. This will enable you to ask intelligent questions of your faculty adviser and others who will be helping you register for classes. Planning your schedule will also enable you to get a fix on just how many required courses your school wants you to take in the first semester and how much freedom you will have to branch out on your own.

When you meet with your faculty adviser, remember that there may be differences between the way he or she sees your study plan and the way you look at it. Hear out your adviser. Most advisers are faculty members; they are individuals; they have their opinions; and they know the institution a lot better than you do. Give them a chance—assume they want to help, assume they have a keen interest in your case, and make sure they know what your goals are. If you do not get along with your adviser, you can usually change to another faculty member. Before doing that, remember to examine your reasons. If you are changing because you don't like the advice given rather than the personality, then you probably ought to stay with your original adviser. Remember that at most schools, your adviser will change once you have entered your major, at which point you will be assigned an adviser from the department in which you are majoring. Often, these advising relationships between students and faculty members lead to close friendships that last well beyond the college years.

Once you have your adviser's approval of your course of study, you can move ahead with registering for the actual courses (or you may do it together on line). As you go through this process, be sure you have the catalog nearby because if a course is filled, you will need to select an alternate right away. Your adviser can always be consulted again if you run into trouble while registering. Your adviser will know what the exceptions to various rules are, where the shortcuts are, and what the contingency plans are if a course fills up. So stay in touch with your adviser until you are completely registered for your courses. Your adviser is your academic guide.

WHERE WILL I LIVE AND WITH WHOM?

As Barbara put the finishing touches on her plan of study, her mind had already moved ahead to the social relationships she hoped to form on the Hanover campus during the next four years. Would she be radicalized by the politics on campus? Would she fall in love? Would she learn to ski? Would she feel lonely and miss her family? The answers to all of these questions were probably "Yes, at least for a few minutes."

Barbara decided to focus her attention on the most important dimension of her nonacademic Hanover experience—her housing arrangements. In her acceptance packet, she read that the college offered single, double, and triple rooms and that you could also elect to live in one of the smaller, theme houses. "Theme" meant that the house was organized around a particular language or culture or was focused on a particular goal, such as the environment, poverty, or international affairs. Whether you picked a theme house or a large dormitory, you were asked to fill out an elaborate questionnaire indicating your choice of major, your extracurricular interests, musical and artistic tastes, political views, hobbies, and your own preferences for a roommate. The Housing Office then pores over these questionnaires and tries to find compatible combinations.

Barbara Crowley chose a dormitory, not a theme house—those could come later—and a double room. She asked for one roommate, a nonsmoker.

MAKING THE MOST OF THE FRESHMAN YEAR

She thought that two roommates might be harder to manage and wrote a short paragraph asking for one—a roommate who was quiet and serious about pursuing her academic studies and had an interest in the arts.

The Housing Office agreed to Barbara's request a few weeks later and sent her the name of her roommate for the fall. Following a suggestion from the Housing Office, Barbara wrote her roommate a friendly letter of introduction. This overture led to an exchange of letters, and by the time the fall term began Barbara and her roommate had gotten to know each other pretty well. They had divided the responsibilities for furnishing the room, thus saving a good deal of duplication of wall hangings, appliances, and even general reference books. More important, they had established a tradition of discussing their needs and aspirations first, before acting on them! This tradition would help them deal with the few controversies that might arise later.

On a larger scale, Barbara and her roommate, without being conscious of it, had come to terms with one of the biggest anxieties facing college freshmen—the loss of high school friends whom they had known all their lives. Now they both realized that there would be new and different kinds of relationships to look forward to in college—relationships that could be actively created and not just be the result of living on a particular street in a particular community.

Barbara and her roommate succeeded in placing their relationship on a solid basis from the outset and in maximizing the chances that a strong friendship could grow from it. They had, by their exchange of letters and phone calls, prepared themselves to handle some of the unusual challenges that college undergraduates face: how to make decisions about socializing and study in their room, how to respect each other's right to privacy, and how to share their possessions equitably. Barbara and her roommate were thus able to avoid the shock experienced by one undergraduate woman at an Ivy League school who, in the first week of school, returned to her room to find that her roommate was entertaining a young man. Because the young woman had to study, she sought refuge in the bathroom until 2 a.m., then returned to her room to find her roommate and the young man in bed together. This became a nightly practice, forcing the roommate to retreat to the common-room couch with her sleeping bag. Eventually she became so exhausted by the routine that her grades plummeted, and she had to go to the infirmary for a good night's sleep.

Guidelines for Getting Along with Your Roommates

This incident suggests a few simple rules that will help you establish a good relationship with your roommate and continue in that mode:

- **Communication.** Make a pledge with your roommate to talk early and often about potential trouble spots. Make sure that the first time your roommate entertains a visitor late into the evening, beyond the time that both of you normally go to bed or at a time when both of you have agreed to study, you need to take it up with your roommate the very next day. "I think that something went wrong last night. My recollection of our understanding was . . . What was yours?"
- **Space.** Try to reach a clear understanding with your roommate as to what part of the room is your space, what part is his or hers, and what part is common to both.
- **Borrowing.** Having a discussion with your roommate about borrowing things is essential, and the sooner the better. If you have a car, you probably don't want others to drive it. The same holds true for your computer. But you have to bring those matters up and reach an agreement. Perhaps there are things you will willingly lend, such as athletic equipment and books. Make those items part of your understanding, too.
- **Shared Responsibilities.** You and your roommate need to share in the responsibility for keeping your room or apartment clean. When does that happen? You may have refrigerator and food supplies and laundry soap that are shared and occasionally need to be replenished. Work out some orderly arrangement for that during your first days together. Remember nothing is too small to be discussed.
- **Sensitivity.** Living away from home is not always easy. Coping with the stress of new relationships in college as well as new classes and a new environment is not always fun. Occasionally your roommate (and even you) will feel low and in need of encouragement. Try to provide that for your roommate and be considerate of his or her needs for quiet, for consolation, and for diversion. In thinking about others, you will increase the likelihood that they will think about you and that together you will both be able to overcome most of the setbacks of the freshman year.

If you and your roommate cannot get along, you should use the counseling system described as follows to try to understand your predicament as best you can and take steps to rectify the situation. If you cannot repair the situation, there is always next year. In the meantime there are lots of interesting people to meet and get to know and to plan to room with next year.

DEANS, COUNSELORS, AND RESIDENT ADVISERS

When Barbara read through her housing information packet, she discovered that Hanover had fine advising and counseling services for its students. The first line of defense was the resident adviser (RA) system. RAs were upperclass students who lived in dormitories and advised and supervised dorm residents and acted as the social chairperson for various dormitory receptions, parties, and intramural athletics. Barbara found the RAs to be concerned and careful counselors who were able to keep their conversations with advisees confidential and to provide a good deal of leadership in the dorm community.

Beyond the Resident Advisers lay the health/psychological services, the counseling center, academic advising, study skills, and the Dean of Students Office, with its clutch of tireless and concerned deans who dealt with all matters of student concerns, from the laundry service and all the way to students who were severely depressed and had to leave school for treatment at home.

Students at many colleges often seem unaware of the capability of these various offices to render immediate and useful advice and counsel. At the University of Chicago, twenty counselors operating from the dean's office, most of them full-time, oversee the relatively small undergraduate population of 3,000 students. These counselors frequently give both academic and personal advice and follow the progress of their advisees throughout their four-year stay at the university.

Every college or university will have a counseling center or a counseling system for dealing with the difficulties that arise with roommates, homesickness, test anxiety, or problems with friends or family. Don't be hesitant, or worried that the problem you have may be too "academic" for someone in the counseling center. Get the advice you need. Here is a good rule of thumb: *If you are thinking about seeking advice and counseling, chances are you should see someone.* Counseling can help people in a variety of ways: to learn to make better decisions, to become aware of their feelings and needs, to improve interpersonal skills, to manage stress and anxiety, to improve communication skills, and to cope more effectively with life. Look at it this way. These services are there for you. Not to use them could undermine your progress.

Also think about the university or campus ministry as you adjust to college life. For some students, the ministry center on campus can act as a strong stabilizing influence because there is a connection perhaps between their past association with a church at home and their present "home" on campus.

As Barbara Crowley drove with her family to Hanover in the fall, she was only dimly aware of how much her educational experience in the next four years would hinge on her ability to develop personal relationships with others and to understand fully her own needs and aspirations. She had done all that she could up to this point. She had read all the material she had been sent. She had familiarized herself with the various ways she could get help—academically, socially, spiritually, and health-wise. She had resolved to extend herself to other people and to try to forge new relationships without being too judgmental. Her efforts would help to offset the loneliness of being away from her home and friends for the first time. This openness to new relationships and new experiences would ensure Barbara her education in the broadest sense and reduce the vulnerability and uncertainty that many college freshmen experience.

THE TRANSITION TO COLLEGE LIFE

If you were to visit any college campus during the first beautiful days of September and ask passing freshmen to describe in a word the experience of their first few weeks of college life, their response would undoubtedly be "freedom." This is the only accurate and natural response you could possibly expect. Students will define that freedom differently—freedom from home, from family, from day-to-day assignments, from required sports, from required group activities, from a code of behavior that earns favor with teachers, neighbors, and family. In each case, though, students will define their freedom as freedom "from," rather than freedom "to."

Psychologists know that the transition that a freshman has to make during the first weeks of college is an extremely difficult one. In many cases going to college involves a complete break with the past and hence a real discontinuity in a student's life, especially if they have not been away from home before. The structure and routine of family life are left behind, the numerous ties to community groups, peer groups, and school groups are severed, and, most important, the regular nourishment of self-esteem that came from family and peers and school has ended. A new life has to be kindled in college, new challenges divined, new relationships begun, and new outlets for your talents discovered. It is not easy. A book like this can only scratch the surface of the freshman-year experience and offer some kind words of counsel. It can set before the prospective freshman a sort of informal agenda to consider during the summer before college begins.

For sound advice on the freshman-year experience, look at *The Ultimate College Survival Guide* by Janet Farrar Worthington and Ronald T. Farrar (Peterson's, 1998). It covers a range of topics we can only allude to here.

A Little Fish in the Big Pond

This phrase refers to the feelings of the typical freshman upon first encountering his or her classmates at orientation. For the first time, perhaps, the freshman encounters a mass of other students who are as intelligent, as resourceful, as funny, as good looking, as athletically or musically gifted as he or she is. Often students become depressed when they realize that they are no longer the big fish in the little pond, but rather a little fish in the big pond. Here is some help in dealing with that pond:

- **Acknowledge the legitimacy of your own feelings of loss.** After all, the stability, security, and success that you have left behind cannot be expected to be permanent features of your life. We live in a world of flux and change. College is our introduction to it. Feelings of loss are a natural part of the process of coming to college. Accepting these feelings helps us to move ahead: to choose, to explore, to take risks, and to create a new reality for ourselves.
- **Communicate your feelings of frustration and loss**—and of elation and joy—to others, be they roommates, resident advisers, deans, professors, or chaplains. When seeking advice, remember to search for the new questions rather than answers.
- **Try to make your college your new home.** Establish a routine, form relationships, begin activities, and figure out the support systems. Avoid cultivating a fierce independence or a separateness. Make sure you spend some time decorating your room, and make sure to bring those photographs to remind you of the good things you want to remember—and to which you will return at Thanksgiving!

- **Redefine your conception of success.** Lower those standards you simply cannot meet in this new environment. Set new standards that you can meet. Move around the limits imposed by grades or social relationships or athletic competition, and look for new areas of challenge. In doing so, try to avoid the feeling that you are betraying yourself. Who knows, you may discover that there are myriad ways of proving yourself, and in fact, you may be better than your fellow students at some things.
- **Remember that frustration and a sense of loss are cyclical.** For most people, excitement and progress follow periods of disillusionment and frustration. If you encounter a low point, realize that it may be caused by exhaustion. The shift of responsibility from your high school counselor, friends, and family telling you what to do and how to plan your life, to you taking the responsibility for all of your activities, is enormous. If nothing else, it is tiring. So relax, rest, and remember that temporary frustration and shifts in mood are a natural part of the healthy process of transition.

Making the Campus Work for You

Some practical tips to help you orient yourself and find direction amidst all that freedom of the first few weeks of college:

1. **Stay loose.** Do not seek out a single small group of friends and cling only to them during those first weeks. It will be tempting to do that, especially if a group of you are from the same high school. Social groups of various sorts will coalesce during the first few weeks, and you will naturally want to be a part of one of them. Fine, but try to avoid loyalty to just one group, for it may eventually fall apart and leave you stranded. By definition a group has to exclude someone, and that excluded person may be of interest to you. So loose affiliations are much to be preferred over group solidarity during the first weeks of school. If you find that you are going to the dining hall with only one group of friends and you are socializing with this same group, break away somewhat. Try to go to the dining hall with someone new, or even alone, once or twice a week so that you will create for yourself the opportunity to meet different people from different backgrounds.
2. **Join at least one, preferably two, extracurricular activities during the first week of your freshman year.** Join something on a whim. Too often college students defer this type of decision. They say to

themselves, "First I've got to get my courses taken care of, then I've got to get to know the people in the dormitory, and then I will go out for the orchestra." Avoid this kind of thinking; enter extracurricular activities right away. As one Harvard freshman told his adviser, "You know when I came here from high school, I knew no one. The first thing I did was to join the orchestra, and suddenly I found a bunch of friends." This may sound calculated, but a little planning of this sort will ensure that you develop different bases of friendship in college: your classes, your dormitory, your extracurricular activities, and so on.

3. **Avoid adopting a particular personal style, lest you become known only as a campus character or a member of a particular group.** This is particularly hard for some minority and international students, whose culture shock on coming to college is sometimes greater than for other students. In their momentary disorientation, it is natural for these students to gravitate toward one another. Even so, try to balance the reassurance of group acceptance with the need for individual identity and creating your own relationships.

4. **Try to get acquainted with at least one person or family that has no ties to the academic life of the college.** Often an older family will be anxious to meet students and glad to give a little informal advice. The natural places to meet people who are not directly connected to the institution are in church, in a social service situation, or in a part-time job.

5. **Try to make friends with an older student, preferably a senior, during the first weeks of school, and get to know this student.** These "elder statesmen" can give all sorts of practical advice—where to shop, which courses to take, how to avoid bottlenecks in registration or in purchasing books, or how to deal with the job market, if you are seeking college work-study. A senior friend will give you a perspective on all that is going on around you and happening to you.

6. **Read a newspaper unconnected with the college at least twice a week.** You may want to buy the local newspaper to find out how the college fits into the broader community and to learn about what events are occurring outside the college in the world. A local paper will also tell you what events are occurring nearby that have nothing to do with the college but may be of interest to you. The local apple harvest festival or traveling circus may strike your fancy. Or you might want to attend the local crafts festival. It is up to you. Reading the local newspaper will also

help you relate to the townspeople you meet. Some students want to subscribe to their local hometown newspapers to keep up with people and events they have left behind. Some students want to read a national newspaper. Fine. It may well help them compare what they are learning and seeing to the broader landscape of national and international political events.

7. **If you are a member of a church or synagogue in your home community, by all means retain that membership while in college.** Apart from the spiritual sustenance that religion provides, the opportunity to meet people outside the college and to have contact with the lives and hopes of people from the real world helps you put your own life in perspective. If you don't belong to a church, nor care to join one, plan to participate in the college's lecture series and expose yourself to the larger issues that surround your college experience.

8. **Get to know your advisers.** The first person to become familiar with is the resident adviser in the dormitory. RAs know the system, and they are familiar with the anxieties and the joys of freshmen. They want to help. Seek them out. Your faculty adviser is the next person to get to know. He or she is assigned by the dean of the college to look out for your academic success and to make sure your adjustment is a smooth one. However, your adviser will be remote from you, as a faculty member, and you will have to exercise some initiative to contact him or her and keep him or her apprised of your work. The type of contact you have with your faculty adviser will vary. You may have to make appointments to see him or her in their office, if your adviser is a very busy person. Or you may be invited to correspond by e-mail in between meetings. At smaller schools students see their faculty advisers quite regularly and informally. Once a social relationship develops, faculty advisers can expand on their roles as academic counselors and be very helpful regarding the various challenges that freshmen confront.

9. **Set up a schedule.** The most important task for you to accomplish in your first several days at college is to prepare a schedule for your use of time. Set up your life. Write down the times of your classes, your study times, sports times, campus job, and social activities. You can do this neatly on the calendar program of your computer. The purpose of doing this exercise is to make sure you manage that one big new commodity you have discovered in college—freedom—carefully. Far too many freshman students waste far too much time because they have never had

the luxury of having had so much time before. Try not to become one of them. Set up your schedule. Learn to discipline yourself so that you can manage your seemingly endless free time effectively, and you will have a successful freshman year.

Keeping a Healthy Perspective

To say that college is properly a time for risk taking, experimentation, and testing your limits and then to suggest that freshmen should be mindful of their health is almost a contradiction. Perhaps, but pursuing a healthy diet, getting regular exercise, and not stretching the limits of your endurance at every available opportunity is what we have in mind. The fact is that unless students have a regular schedule and keep in mind the importance of physical health, they may develop habits that plague them the rest of their lives. Not eating breakfast is one bad habit that college life encourages. Going to bed late and rising late is another. As innocent as these two habits are, they can make adjustment to the workforce difficult. And low blood sugar in the morning at important meetings can impair your performance. So think about sensibly managing your health in college, even though many of your peers won't bother.

Try to maintain your perspective, too. What is perspective? It is the capacity to see beyond yourself and remember that everyone else is new, too. Everyone else to some degree feels that he or she is no longer the big fish but rather the small minnow in the pond. In maintaining your perspective, you will be able to build a structure for your life (a schedule) that will make your college your new home. That structure will consist of your multiple ties to various members of the college community—the town, the people, your fellow students, your faculty adviser, members of the clergy—or the extracurricular activities that you have joined. It will also rest on your awareness of the more distant world of your home, the nation, and the international community, through which you maintain contact through newspapers, magazines, and visitors who come to speak on campus.

By taking the initiative to establish these ties and by making use of your schedule, you will be able to create a college life that has meaning, continuity, and joy.

MAINTAIN TIES WITH YOUR FAMILY

The pressures of new roommates, new friends, and new freedoms and the enormous amount of free time have an impact on your parents as well as you. "Freshmanitis" is a communicable disease, and your parents may become upset by your confusion and complaints. So in communicating with your parents, try to balance the good with the not so good. Remember that as you go off to college and during the college years, the relationship you have with your parents will undergo a dramatic transformation. Both you and your parents will need to work out your roles as mature, independent men and women. That, of course, will take different forms for each of you. Parents, for instance, may make the early error of trying to protect you from your mistakes, but they will soon recognize that they cannot do this with you away at school. You, on the other hand, may think that your parents will always be there to bail you out, but that isn't going to happen anymore, either. Now they are but listeners and counselors, and you are on your own.

This transformation underscores the need for a frequent and healthy dialog between you and your parents. How to shape that dialog:

1. **Students: keep the lines of communication open.** Being away from home, perhaps for the first time, should not mean that you drop all contact with your family under the guise of your new-found independence. A weekly call or letter or e-mail will keep your parents informed about your activities and your state of mind. Show that you still care about them and your other family members at home. Scan in a photo of you and your roommates, and send it home by e-mail or in an envelope.
2. **Students: plan to show your parents some examples of your college work.** Let your parents know you have a bit part in a play or maybe will get to play in the upcoming field hockey game or have written an article on the freshman experience for the school newspaper. Send your parents a short paper you wrote. Seek their advice occasionally. Remember, your parents are paying for much of your college education, and they are entitled to see some of the results of their efforts and yours.
3. **Parents: realize that colleges are shifting the burden of education from the institution to the individual and that this a totally new experience for your child.** Colleges often speak of acting *in loco parentis,* but they have a different definition of the phrase than you do. Colleges give young people much more freedom than they ever had at home and that they may ever have in their lives. Students who have been used to parental direction (and protection) up to this point in their lives now feel exposed and frightened at having to make decisions for

themselves. Parents should emphasize with this fear. They should try to help their children formulate the questions they should be asking of professors, advisers, and peers and use the college's Dean of Students Office, counseling department, and faculty adviser to find answers for themselves. Try to help the student understand the support system and use it to help himself or herself.
4. **Parents: don't nag.** Understand that constantly exhorting your son or daughter to get to work or do better will probably not achieve the desired result. Take the position, rather, as the attentive listener who can help your child discover the sources of assistance that are available and the options that present themselves. Let your children hear the "echo" of their own words.
5. **Parents: send care packages.** Remember to include the hometown newspaper and any recent family photos that may have been taken.
6. **Finally, both parents and students: realize that the trials and tribulations of the freshman year are short-lived.** Parents should temper their reactions to problems with the understanding that most crises are probably transitory and that some crises are necessary. Matriculation statistics show that more than 90 percent of freshmen move on with their class to become sophomores and three years later to graduate with their class. An even higher percentage of students obtain degrees within five or six years after entering college.

DEALING WITH DIFFERENCES

There are many forms of differences that you will encounter in college and university life in the beginning of our new century: differences of race, of class, of outlook, of background, of religion, of place of birth, of gender, of sexual orientation, of even a simple approach to a simple problem. These differences have always characterized American life and today are more pressing because of our entry into a global society and because of the change in our commitment to affirmative action. Ever since the 1960s, Americans have taken seriously the commitment to open opportunities to women and minorities, and nowhere has this commitment been more dynamically expressed than in admissions policies of the nation's colleges and universities.

In the late 1990s, Supreme Court and lower court cases have cast doubt on the legality of affirmative action practices in admissions, employment, and in government contracts. Once again, educational institutions have become the place where the debate on how to make our society more democratic and open is being actively joined.

Most college and university communities today are quite diverse. Amidst the majority community of white students, the minority communities of African American, Latino, Native American, and Asian American are very visible. There are also a variety of other minority groups in broadly representative college communities today: women, gay people, ethnic Americans, international students, and mixed-race students. Such variety is bound to produce tensions on occasion, and it requires the sensitizing of all young people who will be moving from simpler, more homogeneous communities into the complex environment of a college or university.

Students will have to be mindful that the biggest deterrent to successful integration of diverse viewpoints and diverse people is ignorance. They will need to take upon themselves some degree of responsibility of learning about the differences that they may find separating themselves from another student. They cannot take for granted that the differences will eventually blend together thanks to the general goodwill of the community. Unfortunately, residual prejudice may still exist in spite of the good intentions of students, teachers, and administrators.

All students need to be aware that minority students may not find the role models or the tolerance of their viewpoints that they were accustomed to at home. There may not be a large African American Studies Department, for instance, or there may not be a large Southeast Asian Language and History Area Studies Program. At the same time, majority students may find that there are some very ethnocentric courses in the curriculum at the expense of broader courses that they were expecting to find.

In discovering these situations, students need to recognize that colleges and universities today are reflective of the struggle of our national culture and our society to define the fair and just society that we aspire to be. However, that struggle is a lengthy and difficult one. As a society, we are not sure how we want to deal with race, gender, sexual orientation, and class. These are issues we are working out in our national culture, in our literature, in our drama, in our music, in our politics, in our law, and yes, on our college campuses. As you seek to explore your particular area of interest, remember to talk with your adviser and other faculty members who can help you find answers to your particular questions. As you go through the process of your exploration and your education and find something that is insensitive or unjust, you owe it to yourself and your college to try to change it.

Learning and Living Together

Majority students who have little previous experience with minority students in high school will find that the collegiate environment is very different. In general, more than 20 percent of their college class will be composed of people of African American, Asian, Latino, and Native American descent, not to mention other students of color and varying ethnicity from countries around the world. Moreover, all these groups, majority and minority, now have to live together on a 24-hour-a-day basis. In high school, different groups lived in different neighborhoods; now everyone is thrown together in a 300-person dormitory. You have to make the most of this situation. Examine your own feelings about race, and make your own exploration of relationships with diverse groups an integral part of your college education.

Members of the majority and minority communities will approach questions of race relations and conduct differently. Majority students may wonder at the need for an exclusively race-based membership in the African American Students Organization or the Native American Students Organization. They may take exception at being excluded from some social affairs put on by minority groups or from eating with them in the dining hall. African American students may counter that they often congregate at meals and form exclusive clubs so they can build relationships with other members of their group and support each other strongly. Like the white students, they are far from the neighborhoods where they are in the majority, and they need to recreate the support system they are missing. White students are still in the majority, they argue.

Minority students often contend that they have no antipathy for the majority community with whom they have daily and frequent contact in classes, in sports, and around campus but that they just need to be with each other. Asian students will add that their desire to be with one another is a privacy issue. They believe that public behavior should be restrained and reasonable and do not wish to offend anyone with their occasional desire for separateness.

There are no magic solutions to the tensions that sometimes arise between groups. The point for everyone is to realize that individual and group behavior, no matter how mild or short-lived, does have an impact on the community and on others.

Ways to Avoid Tension Caused by Differences

You may find the following bits of advice useful:

1. **Avoid stereotyping.** Thinking in stereotypes about members of your own racial community or about members of other communities leads nowhere. People are just too complicated. Take each of your classmates on his or her own merits as you find them. Avoid plugging people into preconceived categories. To think someone said or did something because of his or her racial background is to rely on a mental stereotype. This is unkind, simplistic, and unintelligent. It runs counter to the purpose of the education you have come to college to obtain.

2. **Be yourself.** Avoid assuming a pose just because you think it will help you win friends and simplify the complex questions of racial and group interaction. If you are a farm person from middle America, be proud of it and make no secret of it. At the same time, listen carefully and see what you can learn from others. Don't make yourself out to be a cattle baron. If you are the well-educated daughter of a Mexican-American dentist, avoid presenting yourself as an impoverished Latino from the barrio. This posturing complicates the challenge of meeting your brothers and sisters honestly and helping them to relate to members of the white middle-class community with which you are quite familiar.

3. **Avoid separatism.** Exclusive behavior only reinforces prejudice and decreases the chance for communication. If you are moving only with members of your own racial group to classes, to meals, and to various social activities, you are succumbing to peer pressure and accepting social barriers they have erected. Break out and meet people from other groups as soon as possible.

    Observers have noticed that separatism along racial lines is occasionally a subtle way in which minority college students force others of their race to conform to their will. The ultimate result of this kind of peer pressure is to restrict your circle of friends. If all your friends at college come from one particular racial group, you have failed to realize an important goal of your college education—to understand various and different kinds of people and to make some of them your friends.

4. **Be wary of humor at someone else's expense; look at the history.** Steer away from facile attempts to harmonize race relations, such as employing humor, even if the jokes come from a member of the target

group. Jokes can be taken the wrong way and can perpetuate stereotyping. Leave such humor to the professional comics, lest it unintentionally fracture the delicate bond among the races at your college. When trying to understand another culture, read its history and learn where its customs come from. Ask a friend from that culture to recommend a book that reveals the culture fairly and fully.

5. **Know your college's grievance policy.** Acquaint yourself with the institution's grievance procedure for racial difficulties. Even more important, find out how to react to questionable remarks by a professor or the suitability of a paper topic. To whom do you turn? You owe yourself an understanding of how the procedure works—if you harbor resentment because of a slight or a misunderstanding, you are giving in to your own prejudice. You need to trust in the good intentions and real commitment of university officials who want to see inequities, however slight, be corrected and see justice done.

6. **Study the multicultural world.** At Hanover there is a requirement that students take two courses that satisfy a multicultural requirement. All students should do this anyway, because the goal of your college education is to gain a greater understanding of yourself in relation to the world at large. It is both logical and necessary to take a course that explores the ways in which people of different racial groups relate to each other. No one should complete a college education in America today without seriously contemplating the racial and ethnic diversity within our society. Your leadership in the workforce of tomorrow will depend on your understanding of the complexity of our national and global society.

GRADE FRENZY

One does not have to be attending college as a freshman today to recognize that there is an intense concern about career preparation and getting good grades on many campuses. This has led to a virtual fixation on making good grades in order to gain admission to graduate and professional schools and to top jobs with the leading corporations. Grade frenzy touches every college freshman in one form or another, but students need to strive to avoid it if they can.

First, arrange to discuss the courses that will lead toward your chosen career with your adviser. Find out what role in gaining admission to graduate school the grades in your courses will play. Check what you hear from your adviser with testimony from the Career Office. Then, when it comes time to take a particularly hard course, balance it with some other choices that are reputedly easier. Try to preserve breadth in your course of study. Don't avoid breadth because you fear failure. Some schools will even let you take courses on a pass/fail basis. The further a course lies from your chosen path of study, the more logical it is to take it on a pass/fail basis. Medical school committees are not going to be alarmed if you took a course in music theory on a pass/fail basis or that you got a C in art history. Finally, try to do your experimenting in the first two years of college so that if you happen to do worse on a course than you wanted, you will have two years of strong grades to demonstrate your ability in your chosen field.

Frenzy: Danger Signs

Beware of these red flags:

- If you find yourself working on successive Saturday nights, it probably means that you are succumbing to grade frenzy. If you think it is because you have so much work to do, you should discuss the situation with your academic adviser soon. Either you are not planning your work effectively, or you are too concerned about your grades.
- If you are beginning to lose your friends because you say you have to study and cannot join them for meals or socializing, it is time to reassess your study situation. Making friends and socializing and pursuing your extracurricular interests are integral functions of your college experience. You are harming yourself socially as well as educationally if you can't keep your old friends and make new ones and still get your work done.
- If you are tempted to do something that you know is academically dishonest—such as copying another student's results or taking information from the Internet or a written source and not crediting the author or cheating directly on an exam—you are already in the clutches of grade frenzy. Discuss this situation with your adviser. Go to the counseling center. Try to relax and find your friends again.
- If you reach the point where you are unable to carry on a major outside activity because of the urgency of academic studies, you know you have arrived at the edges of grade frenzy. The varsity oars woman who can't make practice because of her reading assignments or the champion chess player who can't make the weekend match because he is behind in lab need to reassess. Outside activities, remember, are there to provide an outlet, a diversion. Look at it this way—your outside activity should serve

MAKING THE MOST OF THE FRESHMAN YEAR

as a check on your tendency to spend too much time on your studies. If it fails to do that, you need to look at your study habits and your priorities.
- Think carefully about the system of grading itself. Excessive emphasis on grades by students, faculty members, and graduate admissions committees often reduces the whole educational process to this one standard of measurement. Too great an emphasis on grades teaches students that the process of education is a game of high grades, and the role of experimentation and creativity takes second place to playing back what the professor wants to hear or to what the book says.
- You can be sure that discerning graduate schools will recognize the breadth of your course selection, the variety of your extracurricular activities, and the value of your summer jobs and travel. They will look for signs of originality and creativity. But even if they do not do this, you should recognize the importance of these elements of your education and not succumb to the frantic request for grades.

Several years ago a thoughtful and popular Dartmouth physics professor, Elisha R. Huggins, addressed the problem of grade frenzy at the end of his final exam. He wrote:

> Normally at this time in the course, I pass out a questionnaire to see how students feel about various parts of the course. This time I am going to reverse the process and instead explain my feelings about the Physics 34 students.
>
> Academically this was an outstanding class. In about eight years of teaching these courses I have not seen such consistently good performances on tests and such a high level of quality of projects. And on an individual basis there were a number of students who showed considerable originality and enthusiasm and were extremely enjoyable to work with.
>
> My main comments are reserved for the majority (but not all) of the premedical students in the class who are sacrificing too much of their own personality and life toward the goal of admission to medical school. You know what kind of distortion this has caused in your attitude toward courses and other opportunities here at Dartmouth.
>
> I am aware of the pressures that medical school admissions policies cause—their overemphasis and distorted use of grades and lack of appreciation of human understanding. However, this

is not the first time you will face a screwed-up system, and life is too short to take it as seriously as you have done this year. It is possible to get into a habit of taking everything so seriously that you can never break away and see why it is worth living.

My comment is to let up a bit, look around at the opportunities that you have now and in the next couple of years at Dartmouth, and if you do not break though the med school barricade, to hell with them. I can tell you that there are a lot better things in life than being an overly serious, uptight doctor.

PARTING THOUGHT: USE YOUR FREEDOM WISELY

The diversity, the questioning, the uncertainty, the wasted time, the noise, the energy, the frantic and the relaxed times—all of these describe the freshman year. They are all reasonable elements of your education, and they result from exercising your own freedom, your freedom to speak and act openly and to grow in understanding and confidence. This new freedom is partly defined by the new ideas you have encountered in books, in the lab, in the studio, at the lunch table, over coffee, discussing a paper, or just talking. Your new freedom is also defined by your increasing self-awareness and self-confidence. That may show up in more definite career plans or in using your influence on your roommates to abide by the agreed-upon "rules of the room." Your freedom is also to say "no" to drugs or alcohol or sex when they are not right for you and the freedom to say "yes" to an invitation to go to a friend's house in Mexico for a vacation.

Your new freedom also flows from understanding that you now are in a position to govern your own destiny, to set the questions you will ask of a text, or a person, or of a situation—and to listen and analyze the answers that come back—and then to take an action. This, then, is the joy of your college experience—to understand the implications of that freedom—to learn to be independent and free as well as responsible to yourself and those around you.

INDEX

A

Academic achievement, 101-2
   in senior year, 76
Academic advisers, 241, 276
Academic departments
   assessing strength of, 25-26
   fact sheets for, 25
Academic majors, self-assessment of, 7-9
Academic preparation, 142
Academic programs
   assessing, 23, 25-26
   college choice and, 20, 23, 25-26
Academic skills, self-assessment of, 11-14
Acceptance to college
   decision making after, 235-45
   rates, 222
ACT Assessment
   admission difficulty and, 32-33
   as college performance predictor, 98
   described, 85-86
   Internet resources for, 86
   interpreting scores on, 97-98
   registration for, 86-87
   repeating, 74
   timing of, 75, 77, 78
ACT Math Flash, 81
ACT Success, 81
ACT Word Flash, 81
Activities. *See* Extracurricular activities
Admission categories, 101-8
   all-around candidate, 107-8
   family, 104-5
   scholar, 101-2
   special groups, 105-7
   special talent, 102-4
Admission plans, 38-39
Admissions, 219-33. *See also* Applications
   acceptance, 235-45
   acceptance, rejection, and waiting lists, 235-57
   acceptance rates, 222
   application folder readers, 223-25
   difficulty of, 32-33
   first-choice letters, 40, 78, 159
   history of process, 219-22
   lobbying for, 40, 158-60
   need-blind, 174-75
   need-sensitive, 174-75
   parent letters, 251-52
   parents' role, 104-5, 195-217
   preferential packaging, 176
   profile, 35
   research used in, 225-26
   scoring system used in, 226-28
   tips for process, 232-33
   yield rates, 222
Admissions Committee, 228-30
Admissions officers
   academic major selection and, 8-9
   duties of, 222-23
   first-choice letters to, 40, 78, 159
   on applications, 99-100
   review of essays, 122
Advanced Placement tests, 75-76, 239
   college choice and, 24
   shortening college experience via, 166
Advice, seeking, 19-20
Advisers, college

academic, 241, 276
residential (RAs), 271
African-American students, 105-7, 281. *See also* Minority students
Alumni, as admissions factor, 104-5, 209-11
Anxiety, 201-3
Applications, 99-134. *See also* Admissions
admissions officers' comments upon, 99-100
anxiety about, 201-3
assistance on, 157-58
Common Application, 115
data sheets, 148-51
electronic submission of, 114-16
essays, 109-28
extracurricular activities on, 117-19, 146-47
filling out, 116-17
financial aid forms, 130
focusing of, 108-14
folders, 223-25
high school recommendation, 152-55
honesty on, 109-10, 136
Internet resources for, 131-32
leadership expressed on, 119-20
lobbying for admission, 158-60
midyear school report, 130
parents' role in process, 207-9
private services for, 115
review of, 223-25, 228-30
scoring system used for, 226-28
secondary school report (SSR) form, 129
selective applications strategy, 33-39
special instructors' assistance on, 157-58
strategy for, 41
supplemental material to, 143-51
talents shown on, 110-11, 147-51

teacher recommendations, 130, 155-57
timing of, 78
tracking system for, 130-33
transcript, high school, 137-42
visiting colleges and, 44
work experience on, 117
Armed Services Vocational Aptitude Battery (ASVAB), 6

B

Books/pamphlets
about testing, 13, 74, 75, 81-83, 84, 95
for career planning, 4-5, 6, 21
for choosing colleges, 8, 21, 22
for financial aid, 21, 168
Boyer, Ernest, 17
Bulletin boards on campus, 51, 205-6

C

California Psychological Inventory, 2
Campus visits. *See* Visiting colleges
Career Options, 71
Careers
books for planning, 4-5, 6, 21
exploring in high school, 71-72
planning, 242, 283-84
self-assessment and, 6-7
speaking with parents about, 198-99
Catalogs, college, 22-23, 30
Choosing colleges, 19-42
academic programs assessment, 20, 23, 25-26
access issues and, 24
admission difficulty and, 32-33
admissions videos for, 22
after acceptance, 236-45
catalogs as tool for, 22-24

INDEX

cost considerations, 20, 30-31, 171-72, 244
criteria for, 20
curriculum and, 238
demographics and, 28-29
differences among, 42
directories for, 21, 73
extracurricular activities and, 27-28
facilities assessment, 26-28, 242
faculty, 239-40
guides to colleges, 22
Internet resources for, 21, 22, 26
location, 20, 202
mission/culture of colleges and, 21
parents' role in, 197-200, 204-7
rating system for, 34-37
size of school and, 31-32
social life factors, 28-30, 240-41
software for, 21
College admissions. *See* Admissions
The College Handbook, 21, 75
College Money Handbook, 168
College Scholarship Service (CSS), 31, 172
Communication
with child in college by parents, 198-99, 277-79
with college students, 25, 47-48, 70
with counselors, 71
with parents, 70-71, 73
with people in career fields, 6
Computer programs. *See* Software
Computer skills, 13-14
Computers on campus, 26-27
Costs of college. *See also* Financial aid
and choosing, 20, 30-31, 171-72, 244
comparing, 185-86, 244
hidden costs, 30-31
historic changes in, 221
parents, discussion with, 15, 71

planning ahead for, 161-65
projected, 1998 to 2011, 164
reducing expenses, 166-67, 192-93
visiting colleges and, 44
Counseling services, college, 243, 271-72
Counselors
advice of, 20
assistance after acceptance, 237
duties of, 151-55
hiring private, 213-14
lobbying for applicant, 158
parents' speaking with, 14, 211-12
waiting list help, 247
working with, 71, 152
Courses, college, 238, 259-62, 263-65, 267-68
Curriculum. *See* Courses, college
Custodial accounts, in college savings plan, 165

D

Data sheets, 148-51
Decision making. *See* Choosing colleges
Demographics of colleges, 28-29
Development students, 230
Diary-keeping exercise, 1-3
Dictionary of Occupational Titles, 6
Directories, for choosing colleges, 21, 73
Distancing, 202
Diversity, 224-25, 279-83
Dormitories, 53, 206

E

Early Action, 38-39
Early Decision, 38
Ecclesiastes, advice from, 236

Education, college, myths about, 195–97
Employment. See Careers
Essays, application
　analysis of, 127–28
　common mistakes in, 128–29
　community membership shown in, 111–12
　details to remember, 114
　examples of, 122–27
　honesty in, 109–10, 121–22
　on Common Application, 122–24
　parents' role in, 208
　readers' review of, 223–24
　talents highlighted in, 110–11
　topic examples, 120–21
　uniqueness highlighted in, 112–14
Estimated Family Contribution (EFC), 167, 174, 186–87
Extracurricular activities
　choosing colleges and, 27–28
　in senior year (high school), 76–77
　on applications, 117–19, 146–47
　readers' review of, 223–24
Extracurricular interests, self-assessment of, 10

F

Facilities, college, 242
Fact sheets, 25
Faculty, college, 239–40
Families. See also Parents
　maintaining ties with, 277–79
　support of, 14
Federal Work-Study (FWS) Program, 173, 186
Financial aid. See also Costs of college; Financial planning
　alternative financing program examples, 182–84
　asking colleges about, 31, 79
　award letter, 180–81
　awards, comparing, 185–86, 190–91, 244
　College Scholarship Service (CSS), 31, 172
　components of, 185–86
　continuing in college, 187
　Estimated Family Contribution (EFC), 174, 186–87
　Federal Work-Study (FWS) Program, 173
　forms, 130, 177–82
　Free Application for Federal Student Aid (FAFSA), 77, 173–74
　grant aid, 174
　history of process, 220–21
　Internet resources for, 77, 172, 193–94
　leveraging, 231
　merit scholarships, 174
　myths about, 167–68
　need-blind admissions, 174–75
　need-sensitive admissions, 174–75
　parents' investigating, 51
　Pell Grants, 174
　preferential packaging, 176
　PROFILE form, 77, 78, 172
　questions about, 188–89
　scholarships, 188
　terms and abbreviations, 172–76
　waiting lists and, 232
Financial aid officers, talking with, 175
Financial planning, 161–65, 168–69. See also Costs of college; Financial aid
　benefits of, 162
　income taxes, 162–63
　Internet resources for, 193–94
　investments, 162–64
　tips for, 168–69
First-choice letters, 40, 78, 159

INDEX

Free Application for Federal Student Aid (FAFSA), 77, 173-74
Freedom, in college, 272, 286
Freshman year (college)
   choosing courses, 259-62, 263-65, 267-68
   diversity experiences during, 279-83
   housing, 268-71
   plan of study, 263, 264
   tips for, 274-77
   transition to college life, 272-77
Freshman year (high school), college preparation in, 69-71
Friends, advice of, 20, 237-38

G

Gender issues. *See* Minority students
Grades, college, 283-86
Graduate schools, counseling for, 243
Grants, 170-71, 174, 185-86
Group approach (test anxiety), 89-90
Guidance counselors. *See* Counselors
Guides, to colleges, 22

H

Health, in college, 277
High school
   college preparation in, 69-79, 142
   freshman year, 69-71
   junior year, 73-76
   presenting record, 137-60
   recommendation from, 152-55
   senior year, 76-79
   sophomore year, 71-73
Holland Self-Directed Search Test, 6
Housing, college, 29, 268-71

I

Independent Educational Consultants Association, 214
Index to Majors, 8
Individual Retirement Accounts, 163
Influence, parents', 209-11
International Baccalaureate (I.B.), 166
International students, 105-7, 230
Internet resources
   academic majors, 8, 75
   ACT Assessment, 86
   admissions profiles, 33
   application process, 131-32
   choosing colleges, 21, 22, 26
   choosing courses, 259-60
   colleges' Web sites, 10, 45-46
   costs of colleges, 21
   educational consultants, 214
   electronic applications, 114-16
   financial aid, 77, 172, 193-94
   financial aid forms, 130
   financial planning, 193-94
   loans, 193-94
   scholarship programs, 168
   self-assessment, 2
   social life considerations, 29
   study abroad, 257
   tests, 72-73, 74, 81-82
Internships, 262-63
Interviews
   dress for, 52
   example of admissions, 58-66
   in general, 67-68
   guidelines for, 53-56
   tips for successful, 56-58
   with alumni, 66-67
   with college faculty, 48-50

J

Jackson Interest Inventory Test, 6
Jobs. *See* Careers

Junior year (college), 266-67
Junior year (high school), college planning in, 73-76

L

Leadership, expressed on application, 119-20
Legacies, 104-5, 209-11
Letters of recommendation/support, 78
    example of, 251-52
    readers' review of, 223-24
    supplementary, 151, 155-58, 247-48
    teacher recommendations, 130
Liberal arts education, value of, 200
Libraries, 27
Life insurance, 164
Loans, 186, 191-92
    grants vs., 170-71
    guaranteed student loans, 167-68
    Internet resources for, 193-94
    programs, 176-77
Lobbying, for admission, 40, 78, 158-60
Location of colleges, 20

M

Math Flash, 81
Merit scholarships, 174, 231
Midyear school report, 130
Minnesota Multiphasic Personality Inventory, 2
Minority students, 105-7, 224-25, 230, 279-83
Mission/culture of colleges, and choosing, 21
Moll, Richard, 101
Myers-Briggs test, 2

N

National Achievement Scholarships, 174
National Merit Scholarship Qualifying Test (NMSQT), 72
National Merit Scholarships, 174
Need-blind admissions, 174-75
Need-sensitive admissions, 174-75
Note-taking skills, 11

O

Occupational Outlook Handbook, 6
Oral skills, 11-12

P

Pamphlets/Books
    about testing, 13, 74, 75, 81-83, 84, 95
Pamphlets/books
    for career planning, 4-5, 6, 21
    for choosing colleges, 8, 21, 22
    for financial aid, 21, 168
Panic Plan for the SAT, 81, 95
Parent Loan for Undergraduate Students (PLUS) Loans, 177
Parents. *See also* Families
    admissions process, role in, 104-5, 195-217, 209-11, 214-15, 251-52
    advice from, 216-17
    advice to, 215-17
    application process, role in, 207-9
    career choice and, 198-99
    college choice, role in, 197-200
    communication between child and, 70-71, 73, 198-99, 277-79
    counselors, speaking with, 14, 211-12
    expectations of, 14

INDEX

financial aid, 51, 78, 177
influence, 104-5, 209-11
letters, 251-52
private counselors, hiring, 213-14
separation from children, 203
visiting colleges, 50-51, 204-7
waiting lists, role in, 250-52
Pell Grants, 174
Perkins Loans, 176
Personal interests. *See* Extracurricular activities
Personal inventory tests, 2
Personality types, 4-6
Peterson's Guide to Four-Year Colleges, 8, 21, 32, 73, 75
Plagiarism, 11
PLUS Loans, 177
Portfolios, 78
Preferential packaging, 176
Preliminary ACT (P-ACT+), 72
Preliminary SAT/National Merit Scholarship Qualifying Test (PSAT/NMSQT), 74
Preparing for the ACT Assessment, 75
Princeton Review, 22
PROFILE form, 77, 78, 172

R

Ranking/rating colleges, 34-37, 221-22
Recommendations, 78
   example of, 251-52
   high school's, 152-55
   review of, 223-24
   supplementary, 151, 155-58, 247-48, 251-52
   teacher recommendations, 130
Rejections
   applying to new colleges, 254-55
   by first-choice college, 246
   reapplying to colleges, 255-56

   strategy in response to, 252-54
   year off after, 256-57
Relaxation exercises (test anxiety), 90-91
Research skills, 11
Rewards approach (test anxiety), 91
Rolling admissions, 39
Roommates, college, 269-71

S

SAT. *See* SAT I; SAT II
SAT I
   admission difficulty and scores on, 32-33
   answering questions on, 94
   books on, 81-83
   described, 79-80
   improving performance on, 81-83
   Internet resources for, 81-82
   interpreting scores on, 94-95
   registration for, 86-87
   repeating, 74
   software for, 82-83
   students with disabilities and, 87
   test-preparation courses for, 80-81
   timing of, 74, 77, 80
SAT II
   books on, 84
   described, 83-85
   interpreting scores on, 96-97
   Score Choice option for, 97
   timing of, 72, 74, 76, 78, 84-85
SAT Word Flash, 81
Saving for college, 161-65
Savings Bonds, Series EE, 163-64
The Scholarship Book, 168
Scholarships, 168, 188, 231
   Internet resources for, 168
Scholarships, 168
Score Choice option, 97
Secondary school. *See* High school

Secondary School Report (SSR) form, 129
Selecting colleges. *See* Choosing colleges
Selective applications strategy, 33-39
Self-assessment, 1-17
    of academic majors, 7-9
    of academic skills, 11-14
    of career goals, 6-7
    of college expectations, 15-17
    diary-keeping exercise, 1
    example of, 8
    of extracurricular interests, 10
    of family, 14
    Internet resources for, 6
    of personality types, 4-6
    skills inventory, 2-3
    in sophomore year (high school), 71
    tools for, 2
    values assessment, 3-4
Senior year (college), 266-67
Senior year (high school), 76-79
Series EE Savings Bonds, 163-64
Size of school, 31-32
Skills inventory, 2-3
Social life, choosing colleges and, 28-30, 240-41
Software
    for choosing colleges, 21
    for SAT, 82-83
Sophomore year, of college, 265-66
Sophomore year (high school), 71-73
Spiritual needs, 276
Stafford Loans, 176-77
Strategic paragraphs, 137
Student Aid Report (SAR), 173-74
Student guides, 25
Subject tests. *See* SAT II

T

Taking the SAT I: Reasoning Test, 74, 81

Taking the SAT II: Subject Tests, 13, 74, 84
Teacher recommendations (TRs), 130
Teachers (high school)
    recommendations from, 155-57
    waiting list help from, 247-48
10 Real SATs, 74, 81, 95
Tests. *See also* specific tests
    answering questions on, 94
    anxiety over, 87-91
    Internet resources for, 72-73, 74, 81-82
    interpreting scores on, 94-98
    in junior year, 74
    pamphlets on, 13, 74, 75, 81-83, 84, 95
    preparation for, 87-91, 91-94
    review of scores, 223-24
    in sophomore year, 72
    students with disabilities and, 87
    tips for taking, 91-94
Three-year college degrees, 166-67
Tour of campus. *See* Visiting colleges
Transcripts (high school)
    in application, 137-42
    readers' review of, 223
    supplemental material to, 143-45
Tuition. *See* Costs of college; Financial aid

U

Uniform Gifts to Minors Act (UGMA), 165
Uniform Transfers to Minors Act (UTMA), 165
U.S. News & World Report, 22

V

Values assessment, 3-4
Videos, admissions, 22

INDEX

Viewbooks, 22–23
Visiting colleges, 43–69
   after acceptance, 237
   in junior year, 75, 76
   parents' role in, 50–51, 204–7
   preparing for, 52
   reasons for, 43–44
   in senior year, 79

W

Waiting lists, placement
   action plan for, 247–48
   calling admissions office, 248–49
   college's objectives in using, 245
   and financial aid, 232
   parents' role in, 250–52
   reasons for, 245–47
   responses to, 78
Web sites, of colleges, 50, 73
What Color is Your Parachute?, 4–5
Word Flash, 81
Work. *See* Careers
Work experience, on applications, 117
Writing skills, 11, 12–13

Y

Year off, 256–57
Yield rates, 222

NOTES

NOTES

Peterson's unplugged

graduate programs
distance learning
adult education
executive training
colleges and universities
private secondary schools
internships and careers
study-abroad programs
financial aid/scholarships
summer programs

Peterson's quality on every page!

For more than three decades, we've offered a complete selection of books to guide you in all of your educational endeavors. You can find our vast collection of titles at your local bookstore or online at **petersons.com**.

High school student headed for college?

Busy professional interested in distance learning?

Parent searching for the perfect private school or summer camp?

Human resource manager looking for executive education programs?

AOL Keyword: Petersons
Phone: 800-338-3282

P Peterson's
Thomson Learning

Virtually anything is possible @ petersons.com

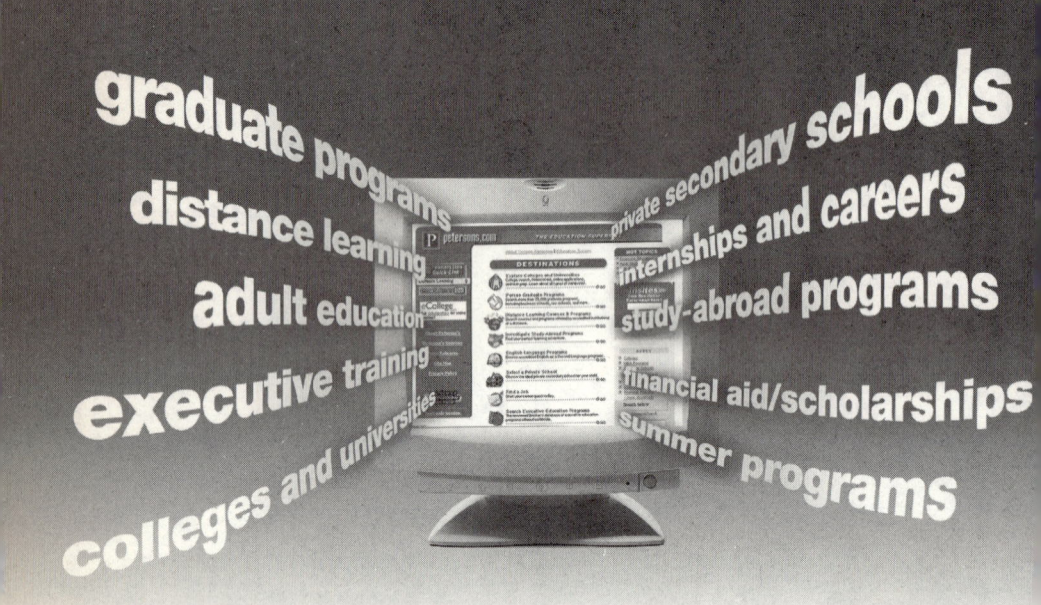

graduate programs
distance learning
adult education
executive training
colleges and universities
private secondary schools
internships and careers
study-abroad programs
financial aid/scholarships
summer programs

Peterson's quality with every click

Whether you're a high school student headed for college or a busy professional interested in distance learning, you'll find all of the tools you need, literally at your fingertips!

Petersons.com is your ultimate online adviser, connecting you with "virtually any" educational or career need.

Count on us to show you how to
Apply to more than 1,200 colleges online
Finance the education of your dreams
Find a summer camp for your child
Make important career choices
Earn a degree online
Search executive education programs

Visit us today at **petersons.com**
AOL Keyword: Petersons

Peterson's
Thomson Learning™